Fashion Illustration Techniques
By Zeshu Takamura

First designed and published in 2007 by Graphic-sha Publishing Co., Ltd.
First English edition was produced in 2009 by Graphic-sha Publishing Co., Ltd.
1-14-17 Kudankita, Chiyoda-ku, Tokyo 102-0073, Japan

First published in the United States of America by
Rockport Publishers, a member of
Quayside Publishing Group
100 Cummings Center
Suite 406-L
Beverly, Massachusetts 01915-6101
Telephone: (978) 282-9590
Fax: (978) 282-2742
www.rockpub.com

ISBN: 978-1-59253-795-2

10 9 8 7 6 5 4 3 2 1

Author: Zeshu Takamura
Production assistance: Joe Ueda (chief assistant/CG operator),
Shigure (photographer), Ayaka Sugino (CG operator)
Model: Thang Ah
Wardrobe coordinator: Yuma Koga, Jun Sato
Special thanks to: Imai (photographer)
English edition layout: Shinichi Ishioka
English translation: Hedges Design Plus
Production and management: Kumiko Sakamoto (Graphic-sha Publishing Co., Ltd.)
Printed and bound in China

a super reference book

for beginners

# Fashion Design Techniques

Zeshu Takamura

PAGE ONE

# Table of Contents

Supplement: Grid for eight-head proprtion

# The 1st week

Let's Master Body
Drawing

# Orientation

## What is fashion design drawing?

The fashion design drawing i.e. a blueprint for clothing used by apparel makers, can be broadly divided into two types. One, known as design drawing (or fashion drawing) renders the overall coordination and sense of dressing, in addition to the design of a garment. Another, known as technical drawing (or product drawing, 'hanger drawing' and 'hira-e flat drawing') simply renders the form and details of clothing.

Fashion designers, based on the design concept conveyed by the merchandiser (MD), think of ideas for a design in accordance with elements which change by season such as textiles or materials, colors, forms and detail. During this process, the design drawing is used as a medium to express and convey their ideas to others. Patterners use such drawings to make patterns and prepare sewing specifications, based on which the garments are sewn and finished as a product. In retail stores, fashion design drawings are sometimes used as a product catalog to show to customers. Thus fashion design drawings play an essential role in indicating the direction of the apparel makers.

As fashion design drawings come in a wide ranging variety, from carefully detailed to distorted, deciding how to create the right drawing for the right purpose may often be confusing. In this phase, an explanation is given along with various design drawings.

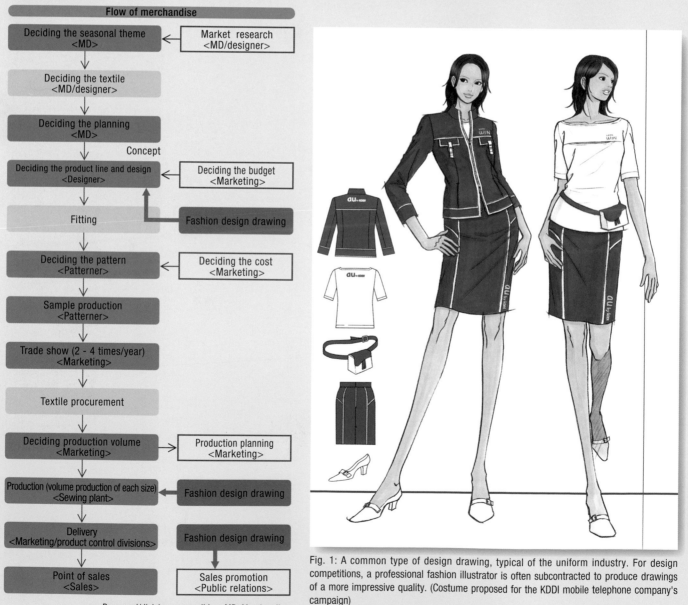

**Flow of merchandise**

Deciding the seasonal theme <MD> ← Market research <MD/designer>

Deciding the textile <MD/designer>

Deciding the planning <MD>

Concept

Deciding the product line and design <Designer> ← Deciding the budget <Marketing>

Fitting ← Fashion design drawing

Deciding the pattern <Patterner> ← Deciding the cost <Marketing>

Sample production <Patterner>

Trade show (2 - 4 times/year) <Marketing>

Textile procurement

Deciding production volume <Marketing> ← Production planning <Marketing>

Production (volume production of each size) <Sewing plant> ← Fashion design drawing

Delivery <Marketing/product control divisions> — Fashion design drawing

Point of sales <Sales> → Sales promotion <Public relations>

< >: Personnel/division responsible     MD: Merchandiser

Fig. 1: A common type of design drawing, typical of the uniform industry. For design competitions, a professional fashion illustrator is often subcontracted to produce drawings of a more impressive quality. (Costume proposed for the KDDI mobile telephone company's campaign)

Figs. 1 and 2 show the most common fashion design drawings, in which the main designs are placed in the center, while the invisible parts are shown beside them in the form of technical drawings or small illustrations.

Apparel makers apply the division of labor system, and when their work flow is implemented by several parties such as MD, designer, patterner, sewing plant and retail store, it is evident how important it is for a single drawing to fully communicate in detail.

In the case of a designer collection where the illustrator is in charge of the entire direction, a design drawing focused on image (see Fig. 3) is more effective in conveying the feeling created by the garment. The design drawings used for competitions are also made using individual artistic rendition.

Fig. 2: In some cases, the dressing of items not fully shown e.g. innerwear is presented separately (uniform proposed for Chanel Parfum).

Fig. 3: An image-oriented drawing method like this is commonly applied to drawings for collections and competitions (hand painted and processed by computer).

Fig. 4: A group of figures; common in comprehensive layouts for presentation purposes. One-point perspective is used for the background. The perspective representation is important in drawings with multiple figures. Here the eye-level is positioned at the eyes of the female figures, which are on the same horizontal line (hand painted and processed by computer).

Eye level

Figure 4 consists of more than one figure. Using multiple figures in one drawing creates a design with visual rhythm, in other words, this method of repeatedly and effectively conveying the designer's idea appeals to the deep psyche of consumers, by having a subliminal effect. With the visual composition being as sophisticated as this, it may be classified as fashion illustration rather than simple design drawing, however, the method used here is very effective in differentiating the design work from that of competitors and seeks superiority in cases such as design competitions in order to win the right for planning and production.

Figure 5 shows a sewing specification which serves as a mediator linking an apparel maker and a sewing plant, containing information regarding sizes, textile and sewing method. It is prepared by the patterner, with technical drawings made by the designer.

Figure 6 shows the apparel makers' answers, including some technical drawings, to the questionnaire sent by a magazine. The apparel maker, through its PR division communicates to various media, seasonal theme and design features using drawings and comments. If the personnel of the PR division has some experience in making technical drawings, he or she can understand correctly the drawings made by the designer. In fact some can make supplemental drawings themselves when necessary. Regardless of profession, PR or marketing, once you are involved in the garment business, having drawing skill makes a big difference in giving depth to your career.

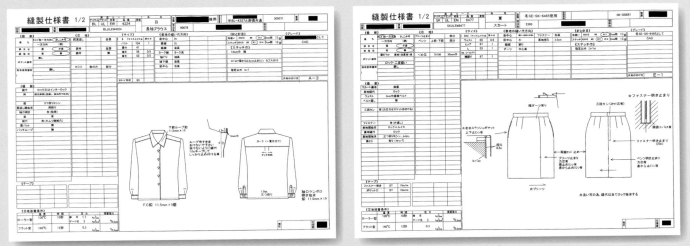

Fig. 5: Sewing specifications containing not only the garment structure but also precise instructions including sewing method.

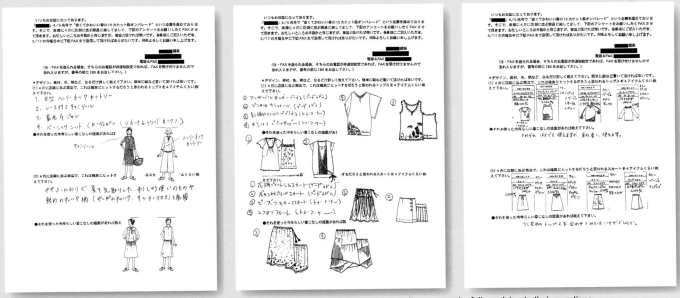

Fig. 6: Information provided to the media; the PR division of the apparel maker makes sure to promote its company by fully replying to their questions.

As explained, there is a broad range of methods of representation according to each purpose, however the common vital objective in making a fashion design drawing is "to correctly represent and communicate ideas and images".

To achieve this;
• Study what is the most well-balanced body proportion when dressed.
• Study the garment structure, well-balanced dressing and proper coloring.

While focusing on these two points, let us try to make a fashion design drawing.

## Freehand drawing of a line

First, start by drawing a smooth line. Straight and curved lines are the basic elements for design drawing. Practice to draw these two lines for 10 minutes every day, and you will be able to draw them well in one month.

### Draw a straight line as if cutting with a knife

**Correct**

Maintain stability by keeping the side of the hand (small finger) on the paper, and slide as you draw a line.

Use a pencil with a B or softer lead. Pencils with a hard lead such as F and H produce scars, i.e. an uneven surface on the paper. Draw a line softly, without too much pressure.

**Incorrect**

The hand is unstable when supported by the pencil lead only.

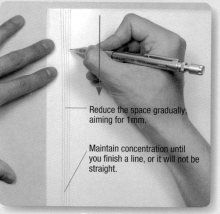

Reduce the space gradually, aiming for 1mm.

Maintain concentration until you finish a line, or it will not be straight.

Draw a line as if cutting paper with a knife. Move the arm, while keeping the wrist fixed. If the elbow makes contact with your body, move the paper sideways in the direction of the drawing hand.

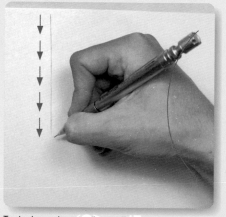

Try to draw a long continuous line without stopping. Do not move the wrist, or you will make short curved lines.

Cut off the ends of the thumb and index finger for better control.

If the hand becomes sticky due to perspiration from tension, use a glove. A silk one is recommended for its smoothness and breathability.

The glove slips well and you can draw a smooth line.

### Look at a point half a step ahead

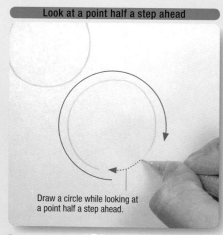

Draw a circle while looking at a point half a step ahead.

Draw a circle from the bottom upward.

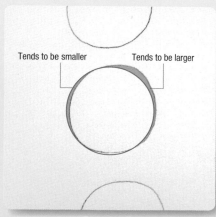

Tends to be smaller      Tends to be larger

When the dominant hand is the right one, the right half of the circle tends to become larger. Be aware of this and try to make the other side larger.

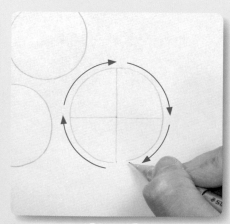

If you fail to draw a good circle, draw a cross as a guide.

## Prepare the following for the exercises in Phases 1 to 12

- B4-size sketchpad or layout pad, or any other paper transparent enough to see the draft sketch through.
- Pencil with B or softer lead or mechanical pencil.
- 30cm and 50cm rulers. A section scale is useful for checking parallel lines.

### Draw a straight/curved line in steps

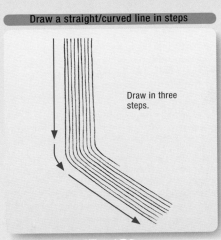

Draw in three steps.

When a line consists of straight and curved parts, draw in steps by stopping at a point just before sharply curving. **10**

Draw the straight part. **11**

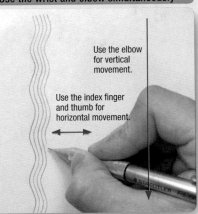

Track of straight line; tapered by gradually reducing the pressure.

Track of a curved line; gradually increasing the pressure to join the straight line.

End of straight line; tapered by reducing the pressure.

Draw the curved part. **12**

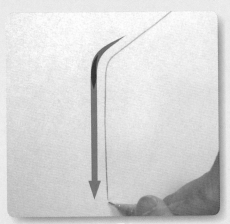

To join the straight line with the curved line, increase the pressure little by little. **13**

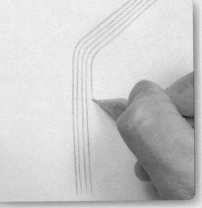

Draw many parallel lines at even intervals. **14**

### Use the wrist and elbow simultaneously

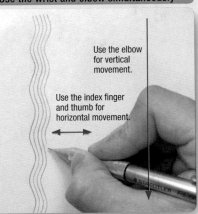

Use the elbow for vertical movement.

Use the index finger and thumb for horizontal movement.

Draw in the same way as the straight line while adding wrist movement, to create a wavy line. **15**

---

## Phase 1 review

For this first phase, concentrate on line drawing, while keeping the following points in mind:

- Keep and slide the side of the hand and small finger on the paper for smooth movement.
- Move the arm to draw a straight line.
- Draw straight and curved lines in steps.
- Draw wavy lines by combining vertical and horizontal movements.

---

**Next, we will draw the grid lines as a guide to the body proportion!**

# The Eight-Head Proportion

In order to make well-proportioned design drawings, be aware of the body underneath the garment. Plan well before you start, to avoid not having enough space on the paper and failing to fit all of the subject in good balance, or making it too small to be appreciated, or overly focusing on details before establishing good overall balance.

It is essential to take steps to complete a drawing by enhancing the 'resolution', while paying attention to the overall balance. Acquiring the skill to draw a standard well-balanced body will also allow you to properly highlight the key points of the fashion items, which are constantly changing according to fashion trends. The first step is to become capable of freely drawing a body with the same proportions from all angles.

### Use the grid as an underlay to maintain a constant balance

As shown in the human bone structure illustration on page 19, the joints act as fulcrums for the body's movements, and the body parts are between these joints. Thus, by preparing a grid based on the positions of the joints, and using it as an underlay guide, you can make as many body drawings with a constant proportion as you like without problems.

### The human body proportions are constant regardless of race

Considering the long history of earth, human existence is still relatively recent compared with other animals, and there is little difference between the races in terms of evolution. For example, if we compare avian species, such as the penguin, ostrich and hawk, their skeletal structures have entirely different proportions. In contrast, although the skin and hair color of Caucasians, Africans, Asians and people of mixed blood differ, their skeletal structures have approximately the same relative proportions. Such a species, i.e. the human being with few individual structural differences, can be drawn by studying certain fixed principles. Let's look more closely at those principles.

### Refer to the fashion model's proportion

Any type of garment looks great on the models cat-walking the runway at fashion shows. What are the features of the fashion model?
They are:
1. A small face relative to the body.
2. A slimmer body than that of ordinary people.
3. Long limbs.

These features are intentionally applied to the figures for fashion design drawings by designers. For example, the small face (1.) contributes to making the garments appear relatively larger and highlights their design. The slim body (2.) is due to the medium used to provide fashion information, such as TV monitors and magazines. As they are flat (two-dimensional), figures seen in these media appear fatter due to a lack of clear perspective and depth, unless the drawing is made one-size slimmer by eliminating the shadings of the body outline. The reason why celebrities look fatter on TV than in life is because the monitor screen is flat and has no depth. The long limbs (3.) help produce drawings with a vivid impression as their dynamic movements are more effectively expressed.

Based on the above points, let us prepare a grid containing the principles of body proportion.

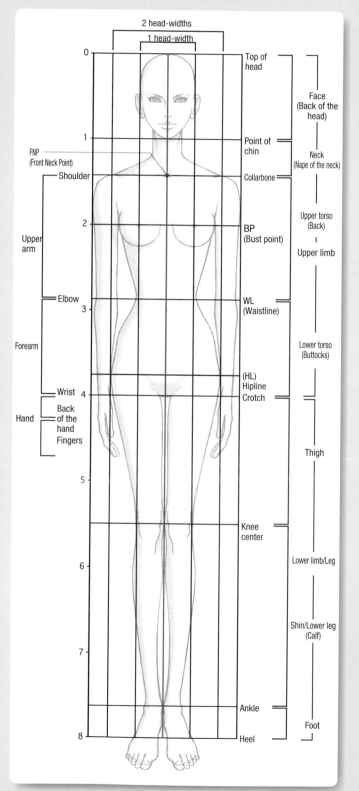

The grid for eight-head proportion and names of body parts. Names in brackets are of the back of the body.

**\*All sizes shown in this book are based on the paper size B4 (9.84in. x 13.90in. or 250mm x 353mm).**

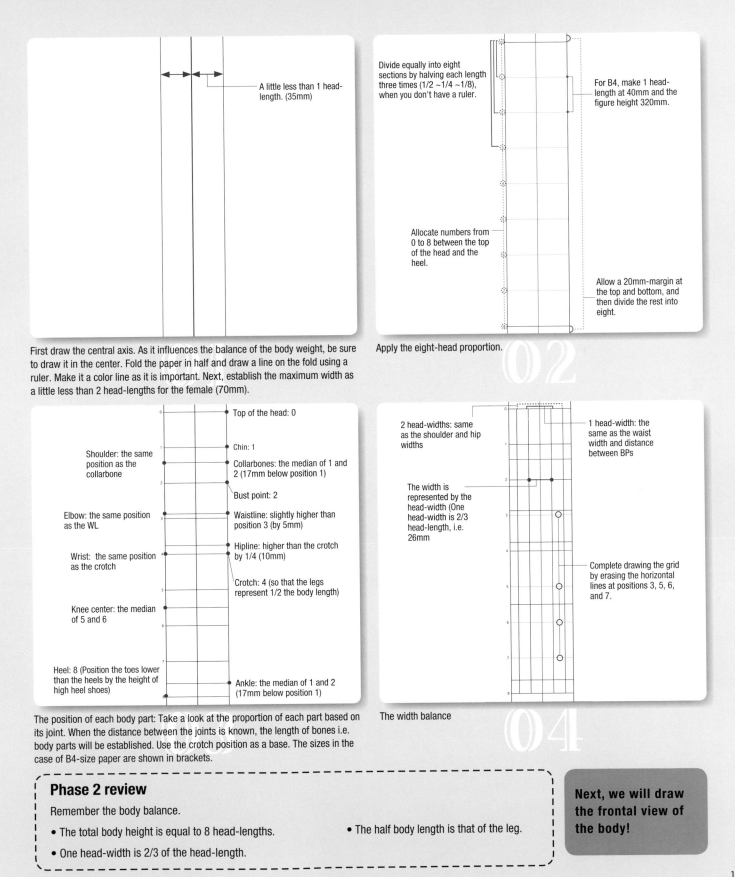

A little less than 1 head-length. (35mm)

First draw the central axis. As it influences the balance of the body weight, be sure to draw it in the center. Fold the paper in half and draw a line on the fold using a ruler. Make it a color line as it is important. Next, establish the maximum width as a little less than 2 head-lengths for the female (70mm).

Divide equally into eight sections by halving each length three times (1/2 ~1/4 ~1/8), when you don't have a ruler.

For B4, make 1 head-length at 40mm and the figure height 320mm.

Allocate numbers from 0 to 8 between the top of the head and the heel.

Allow a 20mm-margin at the top and bottom, and then divide the rest into eight.

Apply the eight-head proportion.

Top of the head: 0

Chin: 1

Shoulder: the same position as the collarbone

Collarbones: the median of 1 and 2 (17mm below position 1)

Bust point: 2

Elbow: the same position as the WL

Waistline: slightly higher than position 3 (by 5mm)

Wrist: the same position as the crotch

Hipline: higher than the crotch by 1/4 (10mm)

Crotch: 4 (so that the legs represent 1/2 the body length)

Knee center: the median of 5 and 6

Heel: 8 (Position the toes lower than the heels by the height of high heel shoes)

Ankle: the median of 1 and 2 (17mm below position 1)

The position of each body part: Take a look at the proportion of each part based on its joint. When the distance between the joints is known, the length of bones i.e. body parts will be established. Use the crotch position as a base. The sizes in the case of B4-size paper are shown in brackets.

2 head-widths: same as the shoulder and hip widths

1 head-width: the same as the waist width and distance between BPs

The width is represented by the head-width (One head-width is 2/3 head-length, i.e. 26mm

Complete drawing the grid by erasing the horizontal lines at positions 3, 5, 6, and 7.

The width balance

## Phase 2 review

Remember the body balance.

• The total body height is equal to 8 head-lengths.

• One head-width is 2/3 of the head-length.

• The half body length is that of the leg.

**Next, we will draw the frontal view of the body!**

# 03
*phase*

# Erect Frontal Pose (Female)

Now you will begin a body drawing. Start with a body part divided by the joint, so that you acquire a better knowledge of its movements. Aim to maintain a constant body proportion for every drawing you make. We will start with the most basic pose; the erect frontal.

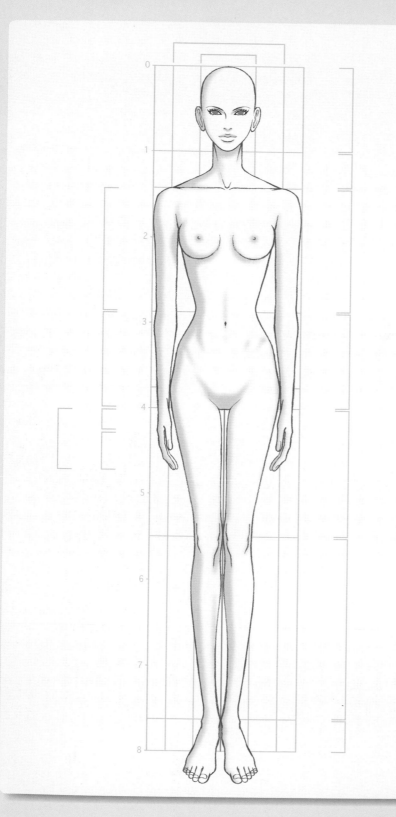

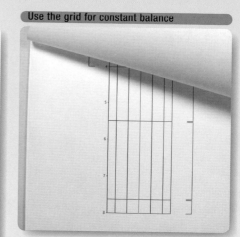

**Use the grid for constant balance**

Use the grid you prepared, or the one attached here as an underlay of the layout pad or sketchpad.

*01*

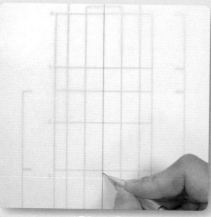

Trace the central axis and positions of all parts. Draw the central axis straight down.

*02*

**Draw the face as an egg shape**

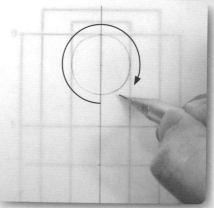

Divide 1 head-length into three and draw a circle to fill the top 2/3.

*03*

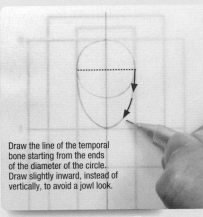

Extend the outline smoothly towards the chin to create an egg-like form. Be sure to draw symmetrically.

Draw the line of the temporal bone starting from the ends of the diameter of the circle. Draw slightly inward, instead of vertically, to avoid a jowl look.

**04**

## Draw the neck as a forward tilted cylinder

Draw two straight lines, 1/2 head-width apart.

Be sure both sides are the same width.

**05**

Draw the bottom line of the neck as a half oval.

Draw the upper torso as one part

Make the bottom line rounded so that the cylinder appears tilted like the neck.

**06**

## Draw the upper torso as one part

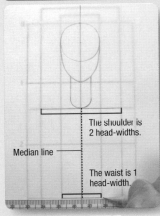

As a bent-over position is not used for the design drawing, consider the chest and abdomen as one area.

The shoulder is 2 head-widths.

Median line

The waist is 1 head-width.

**07**

Join the ends of the shoulder and waist grid lines with straight lines.

**08**

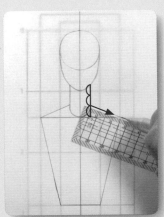

Draw the shoulder, by starting from a point 1/3 above the bottom of the neck (8mm above the collarbone) diagonally.

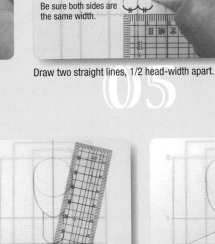

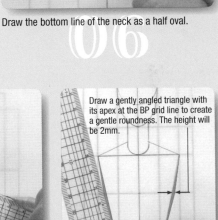

Draw a gently angled triangle with its apex at the BP grid line to create a gentle roundness. The height will be 2mm.

As most body parts are basically spindle-shaped, add some volume. In other words, the joints come at the narrowest points.

## Draw the lower torso as if wearing large underwear

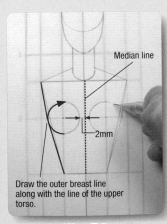

Establish the BPs 1 head-width apart.

1 head-width

**11**

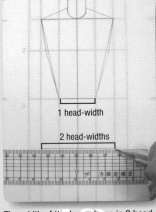

Median line

2mm

Draw the outer breast line along with the line of the upper torso.

Draw the breasts as circles with a 20mm diameter, imagining them in a foundation undergarment.

**12**

1 head-width

2 head-widths

The width of the lower torso is 2 head-widths

**13**

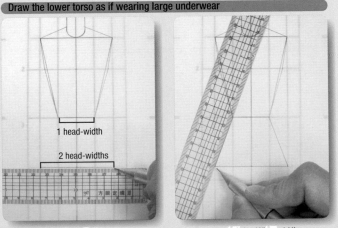

Join the ends of the WL and HL.

**14**

13

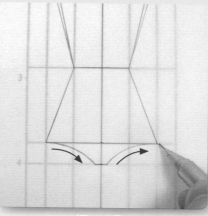

Allow a small space each side of the center (2mm each).

Draw the legs with a small space between them.

**15**

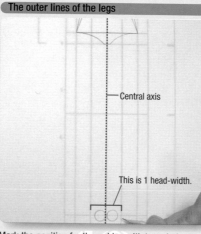

Draw the lower torso as if wearing large underwear.

**16**

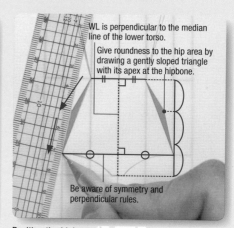

WL is perpendicular to the median line of the lower torso.

Give roundness to the hip area by drawing a gently sloped triangle with its apex at the hipbone.

Be aware of symmetry and perpendicular rules.

Position the hipbone about 1/3 above the bottom of the lower torso.

**17**

## The legs form a letter 'V'

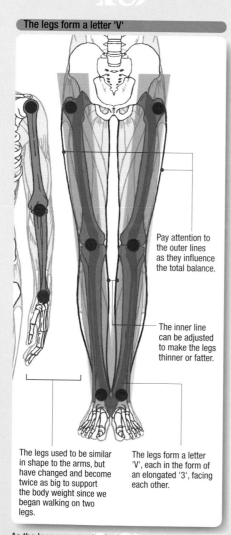

Pay attention to the outer lines as they influence the total balance.

The inner line can be adjusted to make the legs thinner or fatter.

The legs used to be similar in shape to the arms, but have changed and become twice as big to support the body weight since we began walking on two legs.

The legs form a letter 'V', each in the form of an elongated '3', facing each other.

As the legs are complex in their form and highly exposed, pay attention to them. Humans successfully eased the load of gravity on the legs using their subtle curved forms, when they began walking on two legs.

## The outer lines of the legs

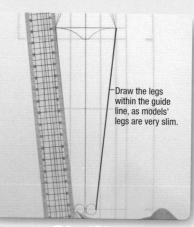

Central axis

This is 1 head-width.

Mark the position for the ankles with two circles (each with a diameter of approx. 2/3 head-width). As the figure stands erect, make them symmetrical based on the central axis.

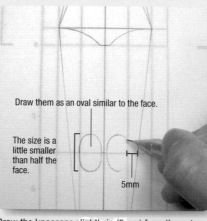

Draw them as an oval similar to the face.

The size is a little smaller than half the face.

5mm

Draw the kneecaps slightly in (5mm) from the outer leg line.

**21**

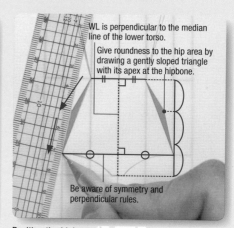

Draw the legs within the guide line, as models' legs are very slim.

Join the hip joints (the greater trochanter to be precise, or groin) to the ankle with one straight line.

**20**

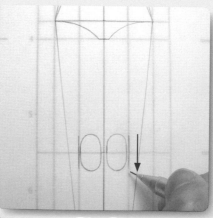

Draw the outer lines of the kneecaps as a straight line.

**22**

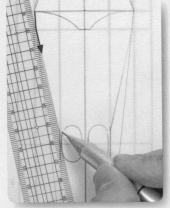

Draw the outer thigh line by following the guide line until point 4, and from there extend the line straight toward the knee.

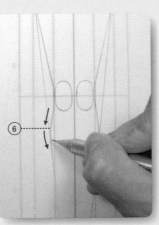

Draw the outer calf line by making a curve at point 6, joining the guide line thereafter.

**The inner leg lines**

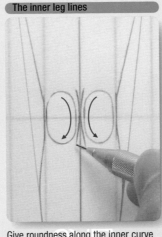

Give roundness along the inner curve of the knee, to imply that the thighbone extends from the hip joint to the inner knee.

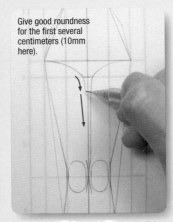

Give good roundness for the first several centimeters (10mm here).

Draw the inner thigh line by smoothly joining the knee and crotch.

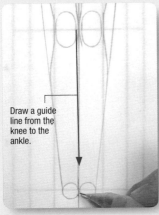

Draw a guide line from the knee to the ankle.

As the shin is often exposed, pay special attention when drawing the legs. Due to the great influence of gravity, they are bent and form a letter 'V' when closed.

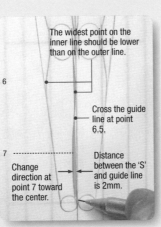

The widest point on the inner line should be lower than on the outer line.

6

Cross the guide line at point 6.5.

7

Change direction at point 7 toward the center.

Distance between the 'S' and guide line is 2mm.

Draw an elongated 'S' using the guide line as a base.

**The foot is shaped like a necktie**

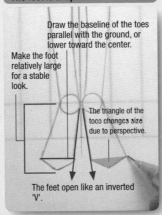

Draw the baseline of the toes parallel with the ground, or lower toward the center.

Make the foot relatively large for a stable look.

The triangle of the toes changes size due to perspective.

The feet open like an inverted 'V'.

The foot has the shape of a necktie. Represent the toe part as a triangle, which is flat and small when seen from the front.

**Focus on the shoulder's roundness**

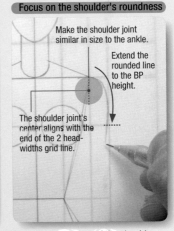

Make the shoulder joint similar in size to the ankle.

Extend the rounded line to the BP height.

The shoulder joint's center aligns with the end of the 2 head-widths grid line.

Draw the roundness of the shoulder.

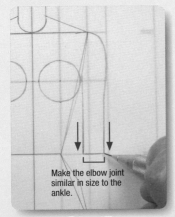

Make the elbow joint similar in size to the ankle.

Draw the upper arm downward vertically from the shoulder. Draw the inner line starting from the BP height, while making the arm width one size smaller than the neck.

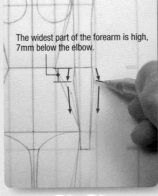

2mm

Draw the forearm slightly tapered, 2mm each side at the bottom.

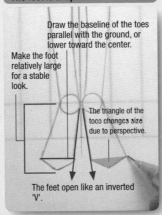

The widest part of the forearm is high, 7mm below the elbow.

Give a little roundness to the forearm.

**Hand consisting of the back and fingers**

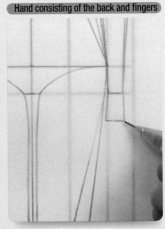

Make the hand as long as the head. Divide it into the back and fingers. Draw the side of the back of the hand as a square, a little shorter than half the head-length.

15

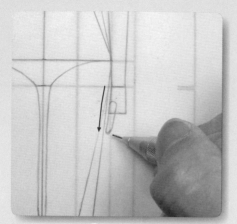

Draw the thumb separately from the other fingers, imagining it starting from the wrist.

*35*

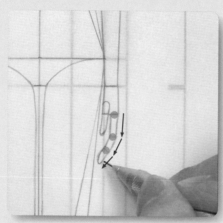

Draw the other fingers as long as the back of the hand or a little longer, a maximum 1.5 times longer. Bend it a little for a natural look. Note that there are three joints.

*36*

**See p. 76-98 for more details in drawing the face**

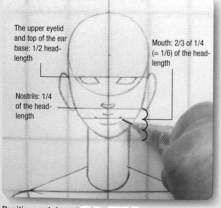

The upper eyelid and top of the ear base: 1/2 head-length

Mouth: 2/3 of 1/4 (= 1/6) of the head-length

Nostrils: 1/4 of the head-length

Position and draw the face parts in good balance.

*37*

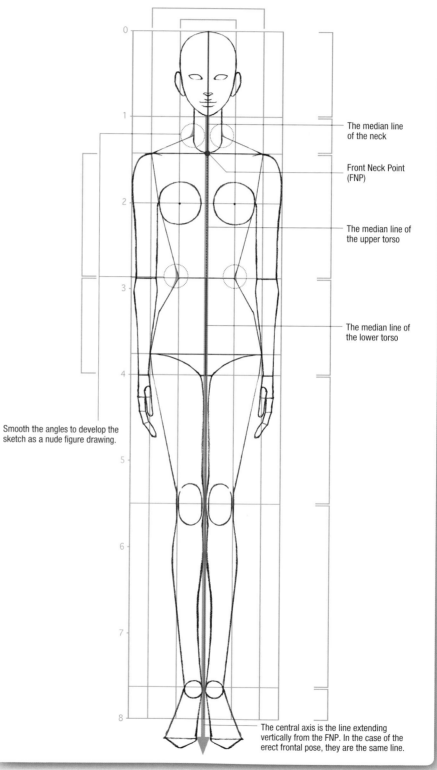

The median line of the neck

Front Neck Point (FNP)

The median line of the upper torso

The median line of the lower torso

Smooth the angles to develop the sketch as a nude figure drawing.

The central axis is the line extending vertically from the FNP. In the case of the erect frontal pose, they are the same line.

Erase the guide lines for the face and legs to complete the body sketch. The line representing the center of the body or spine is called the 'median line' which links the neck, and upper/lower torsos. The line extending vertically from the FNP is called the 'central axis', which indicates the direction of gravity. The median line and central axis are the same line in the erect frontal pose.

**Clean up**

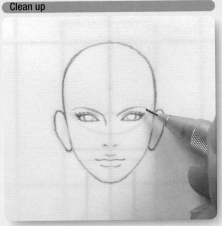

Make a nude figure drawing on a sketchpad or layout pad using the completed body sketch as an underlay. Create the softness of the human body by smoothing out the ragged lines at joints in the neck and waist areas.

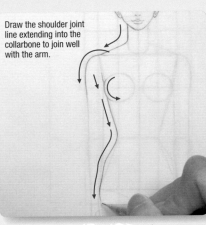

Draw the shoulder joint line extending into the collarbone to join well with the arm.

Draw lines, part by part to give contrast.

**40**

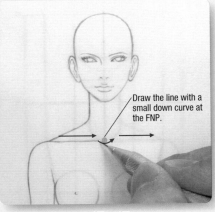

Draw the line with a small down curve at the FNP.

The line representing the shoulder width also represents the collarbone.

**41**

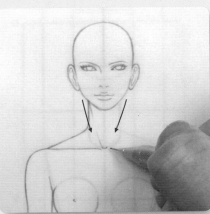

Draw muscle lines of the neck to produce a sharp image.

**42**

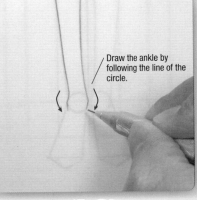

Draw the ankle by following the line of the circle.

Be sure to draw the ankle line.

**43**

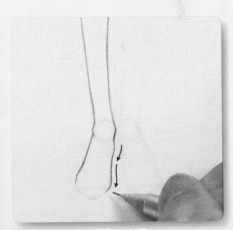

Draw a small inward curve on the inner line to represent the arch of the foot.

**44**

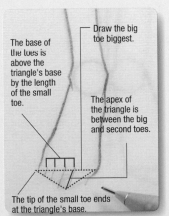

Draw the big toe biggest.

The base of the toes is above the triangle's base by the length of the small toe.

The apex of the triangle is between the big and second toes.

The tip of the small toe ends at the triangle's base.

Draw toes by dividing the front of the foot into five.

**45**

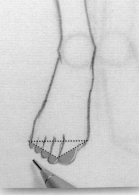

Draw the rounded toe tips extending beyond the front of the triangle.

**46**

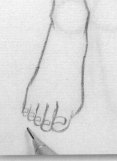

Adding nails helps produce a 3-D effect. Draw them in the shape of roof tiles.

**47**

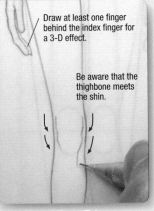

Draw at least one finger behind the index finger for a 3-D effect.

Be aware that the thighbone meets the shin.

Draw the knee as if tracing the kneecap.

**48**

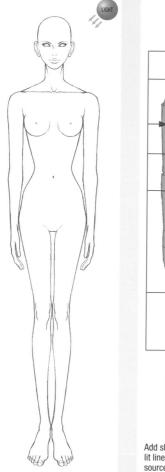

LIGHT

Refer to p. 78 for shading on the face.

A neck muscle line with shading produces a sharp impression.

Add shading as a crescent under the chin.

Add rounded shading under the breasts.

Keep the amount of shading to around 20% of the cylinder width, and avoid overdoing it.

Add shading parallel to the non-lit line, i.e. the left side when light source is on the right hand side facing the drawing.

Add shading to the abdominal muscle line and hipbone to give contrast.

Add shading as an upside-down triangle on the crotch.

Cleaning up of the body outline is completed. Set the light source in order to add shading, most commonly on the upper left or right. In this book, it is set on the upper right facing the drawing.

The form of body parts can be reduced to a cylinder. Add shading to each of these cylinders.

Shading is added to the body by referring to that on the cylinders.

## Phase 3 review

- Express the body balance based on a unit of the head-length. The total body height is equal to eight head-lengths of which half is the leg.
- Extra practice is required for the legs as they are exposed a lot.
- Make the limbs relatively large to gain a stable look.
- Acquire the skill to maintain a constant proportion by making many drawings

**Next, we will give movement to this body!**

Add shading to the uneven areas which could not be represented as cylinders to complete the shading.

# 04 Erect Frontal Pose (Legs apart)

Having studied the body proportion, let us give movement to the limbs little by little. Be sure to do so with the joints as a fulcrum. As the parts given movement tend to become shorter or smaller, draw by placing the body drawing you made in Phase 3 at your side for comparison.

**All you have to keep in mind is two poses**

There are only two poses that are used in the design drawing. One is the 'erect pose' in which the body weight is supported on both legs equally, and the other is the 'pose with weight on one leg'. To create a beautiful pose, it is essential to express how the figure supports its weight.

In this phase, we will try the erect pose with legs apart.

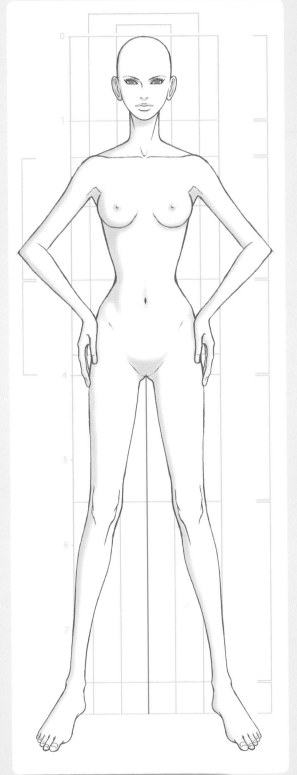

**Human bone structure (Front)**

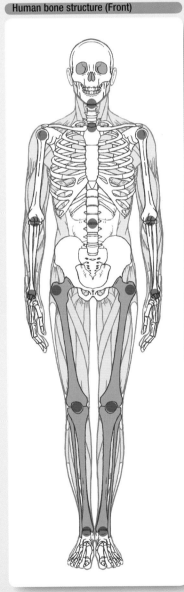

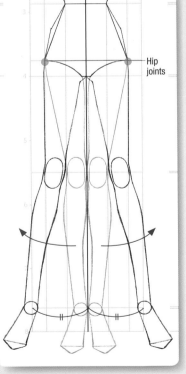

Hip joints

Erect frontal pose with legs apart. Study the movements of the lower half of the body which supports the body weight, to acquire the skill of drawing this pose.

The illustration shows how the body parts move using the joints as a fulcrum.

In the erect pose, the legs can be moved with the hip joints as a fulcrum. Note that the legs are parted by the same distance from the central axis.

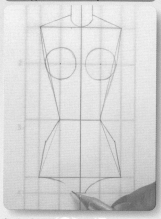

As the face and upper/lower torsos are static, follow the same process in p. 12 - 14. It will be a good review for you.

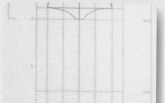

Be sure the distances are the same.

Mark the position for the ankles, making sure that the legs are parted by 'the same distance' from the central axis.

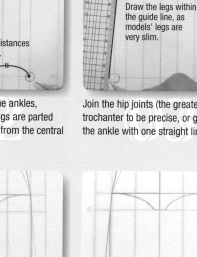

Draw the legs within the guide line, as models' legs are very slim.

Join the hip joints (the greater trochanter to be precise, or groin) to the ankle with one straight line.

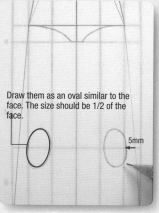

Draw them as an oval similar to the face. The size should be 1/2 of the face.

5mm

Draw the kneecaps slightly in (5mm) from the outer leg line.

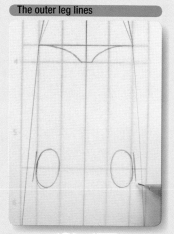

Draw the outer lines of the kneecaps as a straight line.

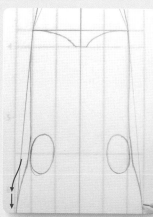

Draw the outer thigh lines by tracing the grid line until point 4, and from there extend the line straight toward the knee.

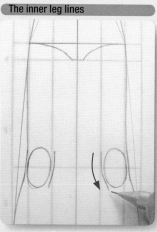

Draw the outer calf line by making a curve at point 6, joining the guide line thereafter.

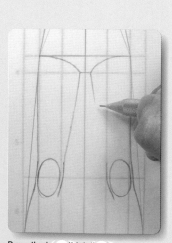

Give roundness along the inner curve of the knee, to imply that the thighbones extend inward toward the inner knees.

Draw the inner thigh line by smoothly joining the knee and crotch.

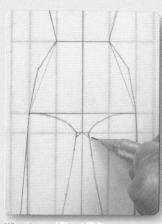

When legs are apart, the buttock can be seen.

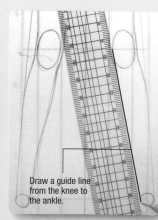

Draw a guide line from the knee to the ankle.

As the shin is difficult to draw, make a guide line first.

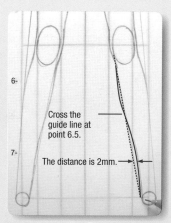

6-

Cross the guide line at point 6.5.

7-

The distance is 2mm.

Draw an elongated 'S' using the guide line as a base. The distance between the 'S' and the guide line is 2mm.

## The heels are revealed when the feet point outward

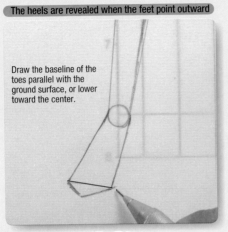

Draw the baseline of the toes parallel with the ground surface, or lower toward the center.

Draw the foot, imagining the shape of a necktie. Draw the top of the foot first. **13**

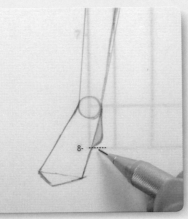

8-

Draw the heel as a triangle, and the arch of the foot at point 8. **14**

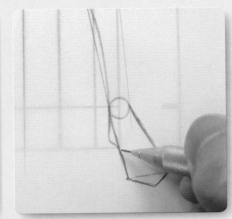

Draw the other foot as a mirror image of the first. Draw the side opposite your dominant hand first, and both feet will match well. **15**

## Raising the arms

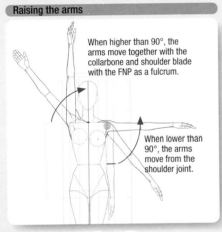

When higher than 90°, the arms move together with the collarbone and shoulder blade with the FNP as a fulcrum.

When lower than 90°, the arms move from the shoulder joint.

Arm movements **16**

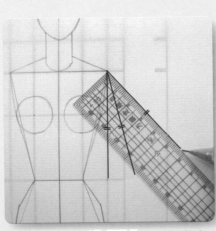

Check the elbow trajectory when the arm is raised. Measure the length of the upper arm and mark three points equal distance from the shoulder point. **17**

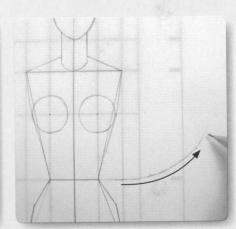

Join the three points and draw an arc. The upper arm rotates around the shoulder joint. **18**

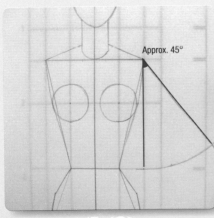

Approx. 45°

Draw the outer line of the upper arm. **19**

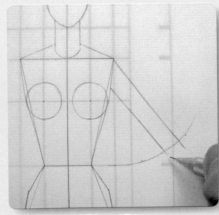

Draw the inner line of the upper arm, making sure that the width is the same as that when pointing straight down. **20**

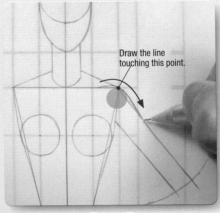

Draw the line touching this point.

Draw the shoulder muscle, making the upper end appear to be buried in the collarbone and extend the line with a curve as if covering the shoulder joint.

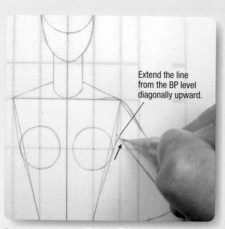

Extend the line from the BP level diagonally upward.

Draw the armpit line revealed when the arm is raised. This helps join smoothly the upper arm and torso.

*22*

Draw the hand on the hip, before the forearm

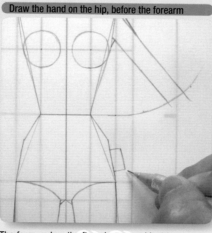

The forearm length often changes subject to perspective. Draw the hand first to secure a good balance. Here, the back of the hand is placed on the hip.

*23*

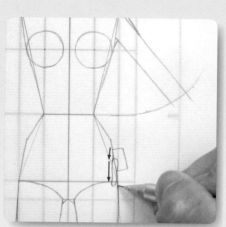

Draw the thumb extending from the wrist.

*24*

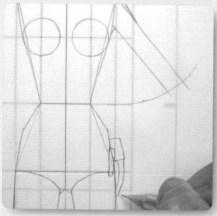

Draw the fingers, paying attention to keeping their sizes the same as those of the erect body pose.

*25*

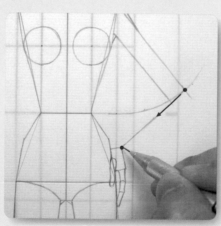

Join the elbow and the wrist.

*26*

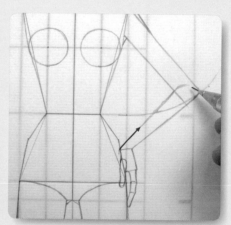

Draw the inner line of the forearm, tapering it toward the wrist in the same width as when pointing straight down.

*27*

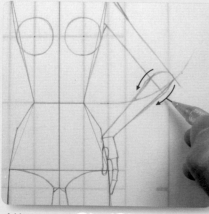

Add some roundness typical of the forearm.

*28*

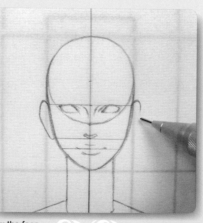

Draw the face.

*29*

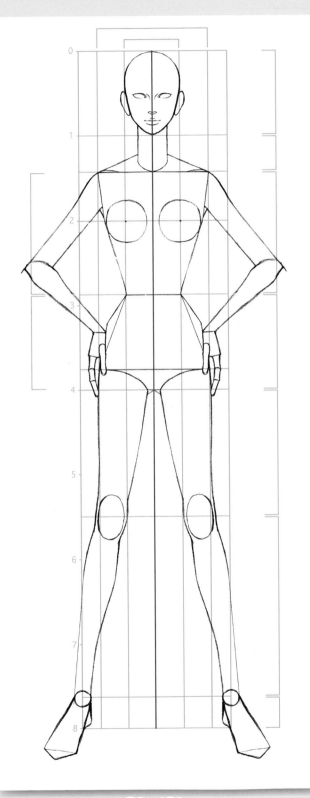

Erase the guide lines to complete the body sketch.
*30*

**Draw a nude figure with smoothly joined line**

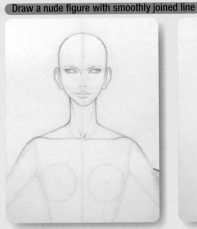

Place a paper over the sketch and clean up by joining the lines smoothly. Imagine covering the body sketch with a thin and supple skin.
*31*

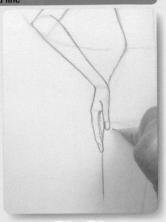

Adding nails is effective for showing the direction of fingers.
*32*

Be sure to draw symmetrically, in a single quick stroke between joints. It is better to produce a strong and non-hesitant line, even running off the underneath sketch a little.
*33*

Draw a line in a single quick stroke from the shin to the ankle.
*34*

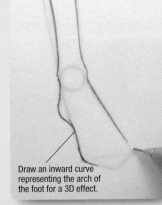

Draw an inward curve representing the arch of the foot for a 3D effect.

Draw the outline of the foot. Draw the weight-bearing heel strongly.
*35*

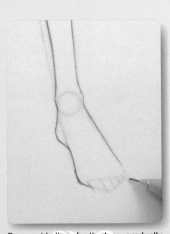

Draw guide lines for the toes, gradually shorter toward the smallest toe.
*36*

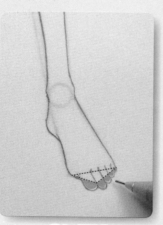

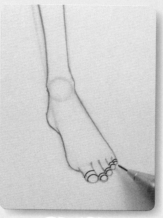

Add the rounded toe tips to the front of the triangle. **37**

Adding nails helps produce a 3-D effect. Draw them in the shape of rounded roof tiles. **38**

## Phase 4 review

- Try drawing the erect pose with various distances between the feet.
- When you add movement to parts of the body, you may draw it smaller due to lack of confidence. Draw such parts while confirming that their size is the same as those of the erect pose in phases 3 and 4.
- The apparent arm length (especially the forearm) often changes subject to perspective. Draw the upper arm and hand first, and then the forearm by filling the space between.
- When the feet are pointed diagonally, the heels are revealed. Give them extra attention as they support the body weight.
- Acquire the skill to maintain a constant proportion by making many drawings

**Next, we will try the standing model pose!**

## Add shading

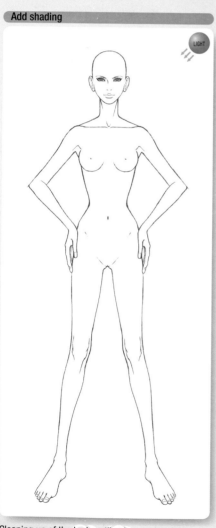

LIGHT

Cleaning up of the body outline is completed. Now add shading by setting the light source on the upper right facing the drawing. **39**

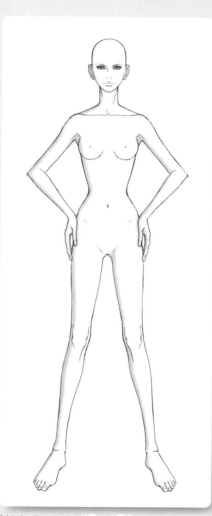

Add shading along the non-lit side outline of each part. **40**

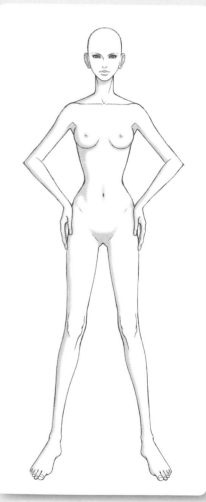

Add shading to the face and breasts while considering their volume to complete the shading. **41**

# Fashion Model's Standing and Walking Poses

**Frontal pose with weight on one leg**

The reason why the so-called standing pose of fashion models looks so elegant lies in their way of standing. Instead of assuming a stable 'erect pose' in which the body weight is supported equally by both legs, their way of standing expresses a dynamic sense of rhythm generated through the bone structure, while the body curves as its entire weight is on one leg. The pose with weight on one leg is most important for design drawings.

### Names of legs

Following the exercise of drawing the pose with both legs equally bearing the weight, but because in this phase the legs have different roles depending on whether they are left or right, we name them as follows:
- Weight bearing leg: supporting leg or pivotal leg
- Non-weight bearing leg: idle leg or bracing leg

### Movement in the pose with weight on one leg

When shifting from the erect pose to one with the weight on one leg, not only the legs but also the lower torso rotates. How to successfully draw this 'rotated and angled torso' is the key task in this phase.

### Two main characteristics

- The ankle of the pivotal leg is near the point where the central axis descends vertically from the FNP.
- The lower torso rotates on the waist point (WP). When the supporting leg side is higher, the waistline (WL) becomes tilted.

When these two points are expressed, you can obtain a pose with the weight on one leg.

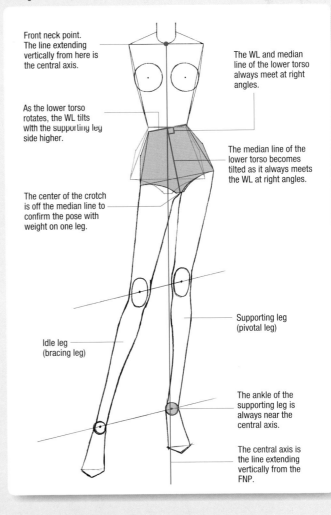

Front neck point. The line extending vertically from here is the central axis.

The WL and median line of the lower torso always meet at right angles.

As the lower torso rotates, the WL tilts with the supporting leg side higher.

The median line of the lower torso becomes tilted as it always meets the WL at right angles.

The center of the crotch is off the median line to confirm the pose with weight on one leg.

Supporting leg (pivotal leg)

Idle leg (bracing leg)

The ankle of the supporting leg is always near the central axis.

The central axis is the line extending vertically from the FNP.

Frontal pose with weight on one leg

**No change in the upper half of the body**

**Draw the angled lower torso correctly**

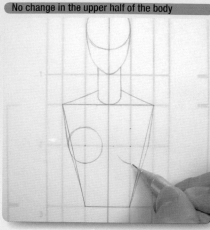

As movement occurs in the lower half of the body, follow the same process for the face, neck and upper torso as before. *01*

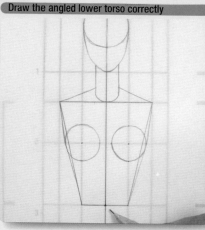

Mark the WP. The lower torso rotates around this point as a fulcrum. *02*

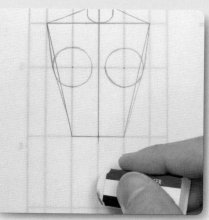

Erase the central axis, as it will be confused with the diagonal median line of the lower torso. *03*

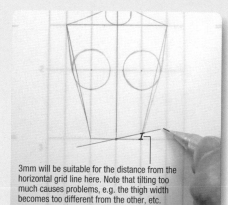

3mm will be suitable for the distance from the horizontal grid line here. Note that tilting too much causes problems, e.g. the thigh width becomes too different from the other, etc.

Draw the waistline diagonally passing over the WP. The higher end represents the supporting leg side, i.e. the left leg (on the right facing the drawing) here. *04*

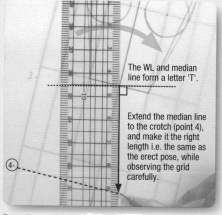

The WL and median line form a letter 'T'.

Extend the median line to the crotch (point 4), and make it the right length i.e. the same as the erect pose, while observing the grid carefully.

Draw the median line of the lower torso at right angles to the WL. Draw by rotating the paper so that the WL becomes horizontal. This assures correct horizontal, right angle and symmetrical lines. *05*

Key point

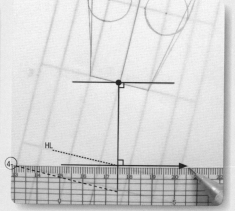

HL

Draw the HL parallel to the WL and at right angles to the median line. *06*

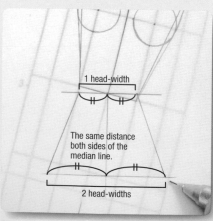

1 head-width

The same distance both sides of the median line

2 head-widths

Draw the outline by joining the WL and HL. Be sure to make it symmetrical. *07*

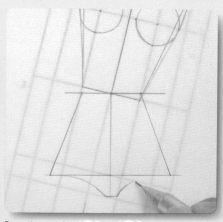

Draw the crotch, as if it is wearing large underwear. *08*

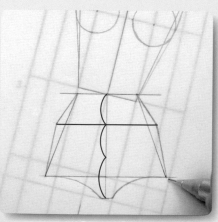

Add some roundness to the hip, setting the highest point at 1/3 lower. *09*

**Draw the supporting legs with a strong line**

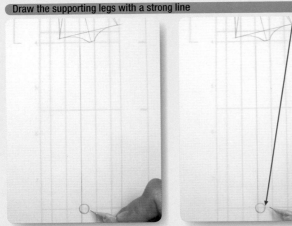

As the ankle of the supporting leg is near the central axis (extending vertically from the FNP), circle its position accordingly.

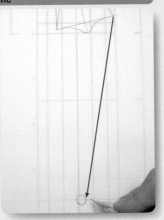

Join the hip joints (the greater trochanter to be precise, or groin) to the ankle with one straight line. As models' legs are very slim, be sure that the leg line does not extend beyond this line.

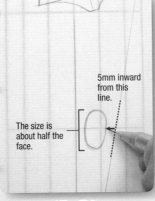

5mm inward from this line.

The size is about half the face.

Draw the kneecaps slightly in (5mm) from the outer leg line, in an oval similar to the face.

Draw the outer lines of the kneecaps as a straight line.

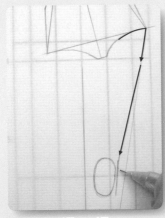

Draw the outer thigh line by following the guide line until point 4, and from there extend the line straight toward the knee.

Draw the outer calf line by making a curve at point 6, joining the guide line thereafter.

Give roundness along the inner curve of the knee, to imply that the thighbone extends from the hip joint to the inner knee.

Draw the inner thigh line overlapping the crotch, to avoid the supporting leg becoming slimmer.

As the inner thigh overlaps the lower torso, draw its line running from the crotch line to express its volume.

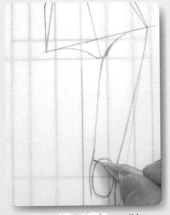

Join the knee and crotch smoothly.

Draw a guide line in a single stroke from the knee to the ankle.

As the shin has a complex form, draw a guide line first.

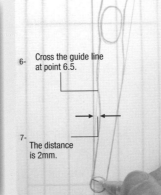

6-
Cross the guide line at point 6.5.

7-
The distance is 2mm.

Draw an elongated 'S' using the guide line as a base. The distance between the 'S' and the guide line is 2mm.

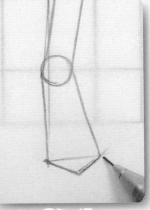

The foot has the shape of a necktie. Represent the toe part as a triangle. Make the foot relatively large for a stable look.

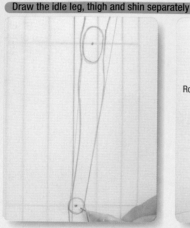

Mark the centers of the knee and ankle with dots.

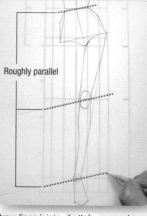

Roughly parallel

Draw lines joining both knees and ankles parallel to the WL, to make both legs the same length.

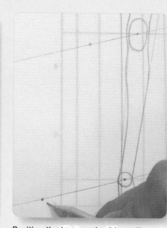

Position the knee and ankle on the lines. The ankle looks natural when placed a little away from the central axis.

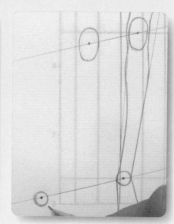

Draw the knee and ankle. Be sure to make them the same size.

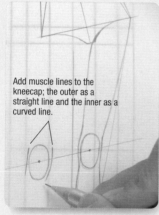

Add muscle lines to the kneecap; the outer as a straight line and the inner as a curved line.

As the idle leg can be freely moved, you can draw its parts, i.e. the thigh and shin separately as in the case of the arm.

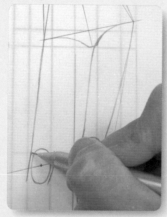

Draw the thigh with the outer line extending more or less straight from the hip joint to the knee.

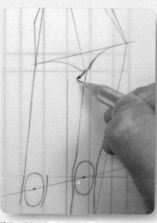

If the thigh becomes too wide, adjust it by adding the buttock line. The idle leg is usually a little wider with less tension as it does not support the body weight.

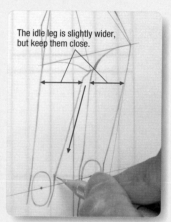

The idle leg is slightly wider, but keep them close.

Having adjusted the width with the buttock line, extend it to the knee as a straight line.

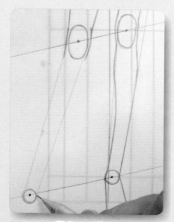

Join the knee to the ankle with a straight line.

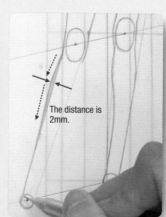

The distance is 2mm.

Draw the outer line of the calf as a gentle elongated triangle.

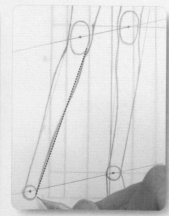

Draw the inner calf line as an elongated 'S'. The first one third is convex and the rest concave.

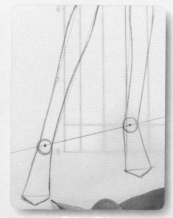

As the idle leg is nearer to you than the supporting leg, draw it a little larger using perspective.

**Draw the hand on the hip first, and the forearm at the end**

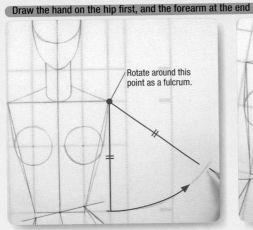

Rotate around this point as a fulcrum.

The arm has a rotary motion around the shoulder joint. Draw the elbow trajectory in an arc. Rotate around this point as a fulcrum.

34

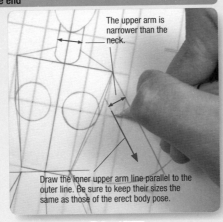

The upper arm is narrower than the neck.

Draw the inner upper arm line parallel to the outer line. Be sure to keep their sizes the same as those of the erect body pose.

The upper arm 35

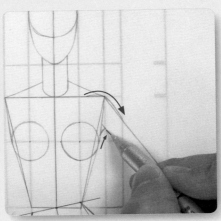

Draw the shoulder muscle and the side to smoothly join the upper arm to the upper torso. 36

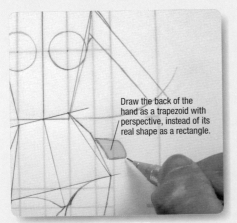

Draw the back of the hand as a trapezoid with perspective, instead of its real shape as a rectangle.

The forearm is difficult as its length often changes subject to perspective. Draw the hand, starting with the back. 37

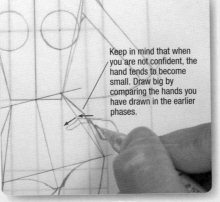

Keep in mind that when you are not confident, the hand tends to become small. Draw big by comparing the hands you have drawn in the earlier phases.

It is easier to draw fingers when they are holding something by dividing them between the thumb, index finger and the other three. Draw the index finger by extending the top line of the back of the hand in the same direction and bending at its joints.

Due to perspective, the finger part appears larger than the back of the hand.

Draw the rest of the three fingers together, imagining a mitten. 39

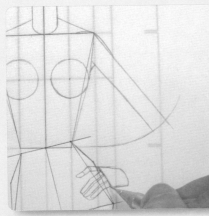

Draw as three fingers. The middle finger is the longest. 40

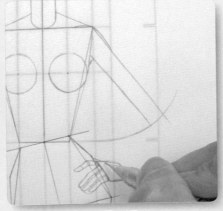

Draw the thumb. 41

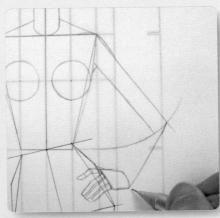

Draw the forearm by joining the wrist and elbow. Start with the outer line. 42

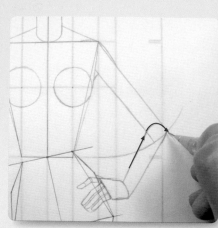

Note that the inner line of the forearm makes the width slightly wider at the elbow. **43**

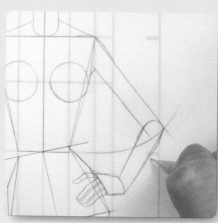

Add some roundness typical of the forearm. **44**

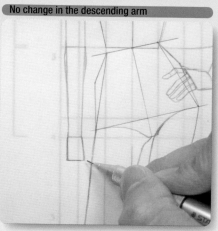

Draw the upper arm, the forearm and the back of the hand. **45**

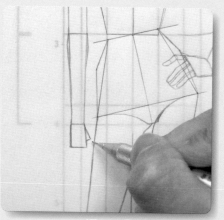

Draw the base of the thumb, as if it is growing out of the wrist. **46**

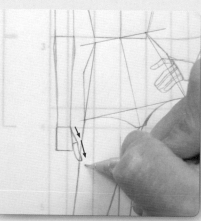

Draw the thumb. **47**

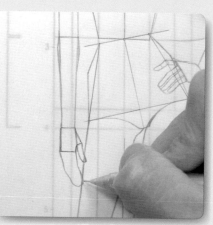

When fingers are hanging naturally, draw the four together. **48**

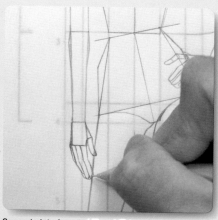

Separate into four. The middle finger is the longest. **49**

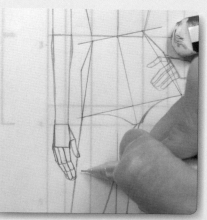

Add the joints, three in each finger. **50**

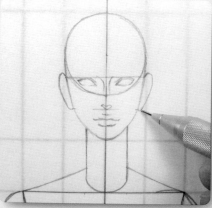

Draw the face parts. **51**

30

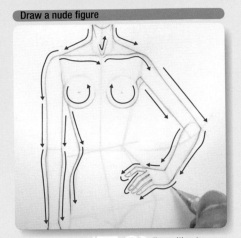

**Draw a nude figure**

Draw each part smoothly with one line without breaking it.
53

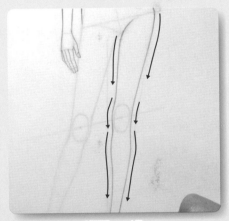

When drawing the legs, always start with the supporting leg. Confirm its stability before adding the idle leg.
54

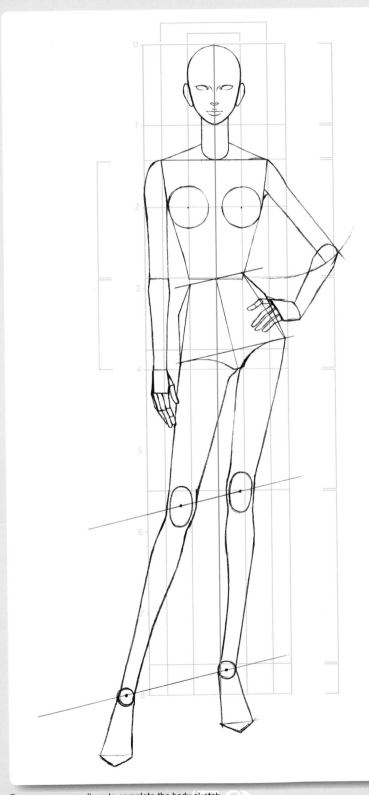

Erase unnecessary lines to complete the body sketch.
52

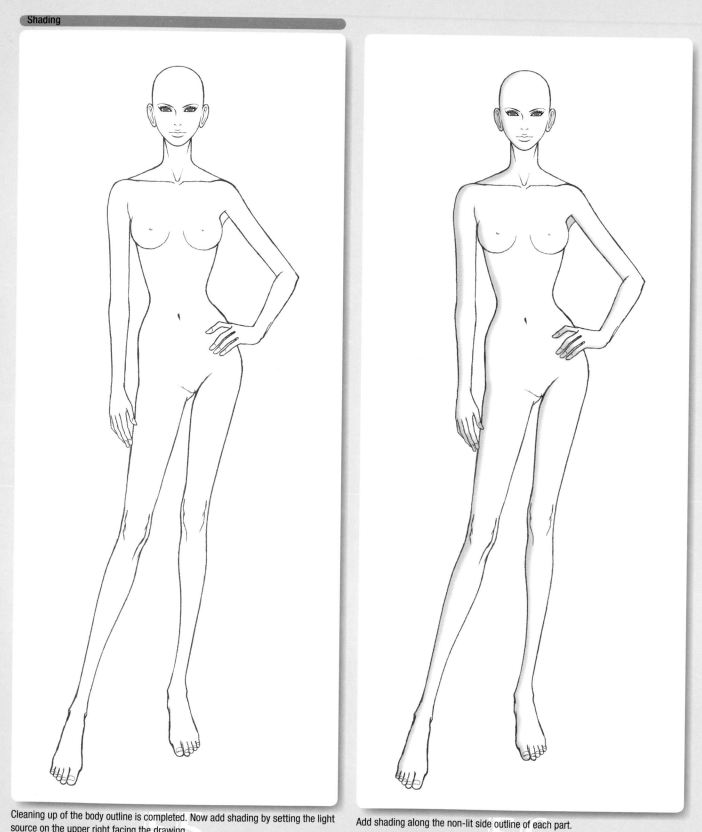

Cleaning up of the body outline is completed. Now add shading by setting the light source on the upper right facing the drawing.

55

Add shading along the non-lit side outline of each part.

56

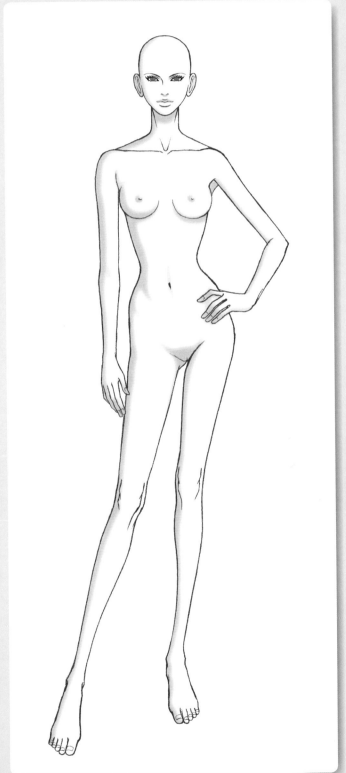

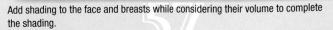

Add shading to the face and breasts while considering their volume to complete the shading.

**Variation of the pose with weight on one leg**

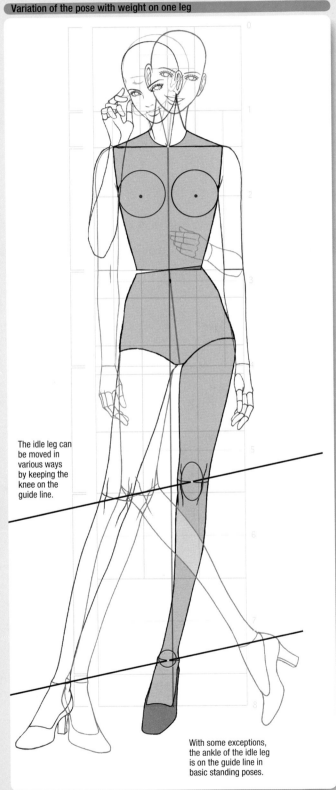

The idle leg can be moved in various ways by keeping the knee on the guide line.

With some exceptions, the ankle of the idle leg is on the guide line in basic standing poses.

When you give movement to each part while maintaining the balance between the angle of the lower torso and the supporting leg, you can create various poses. For example, as long as you keep the knees on the guide line, you can try a number of movements

## Walking pose

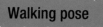

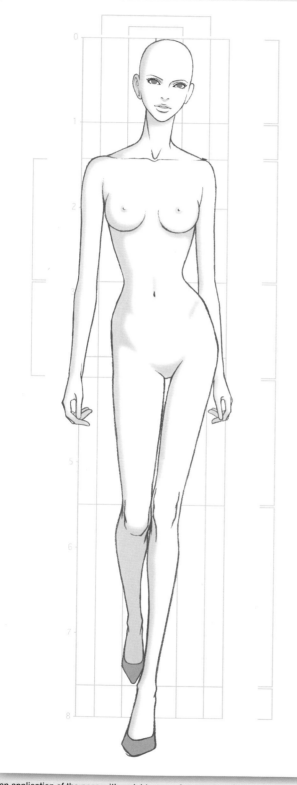

As an application of the pose with weight on one leg, you can draw a walking pose. The key is how to draw the shin of the idle leg extending backward.

**Draw the idle leg extending backward as you drew the arm, using perspective**

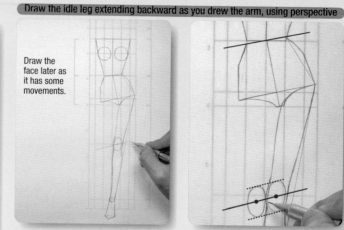

Draw the face later as it has some movements.

From the upper half of the body to the supporting leg, follow the same process as in p. 12 - 14. It will be a good review for you.

Establish the knee position of the idle leg, by drawing a line parallel to the WL passing through the center of the supporting knee.

Draw the thigh of the idle leg. The inner side of the knee is hidden a little behind the supporting leg.

When drawing a part with perspective (i.e. the shin), first establish the position of its end (i.e. the ankle). This is the same approach used when you drew the forearm with the hand on the hip.

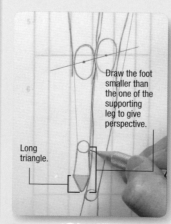

Draw the foot smaller than the one of the supporting leg to give perspective.

Long triangle.

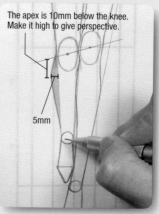

The apex is 10mm below the knee. Make it high to give perspective.

5mm

Draw the foot. The triangle of the toes looks longer when looking down onto the foot.

The outer line of the shin forms a long triangle. Join the knee and ankle with a straight line and use it as a guide line to make drawing easier.

**The face**

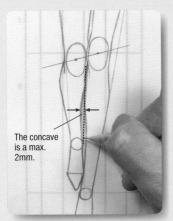

Using an elongated letter 'S', represent the convex and concave form of the inner shin.

**07**

The concave is a max. 2mm.

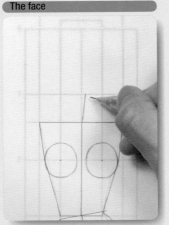

Start with the median line of the neck. Represent movement by tilting toward the right.

**08**

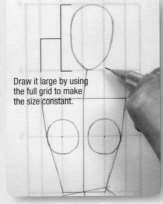

Draw it large by using the full grid to make the size constant.

Draw the face on the median line.

**09**

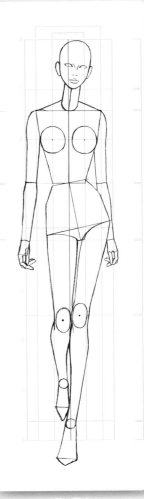

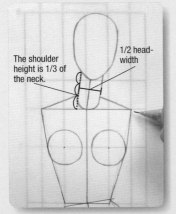

The shoulder height is 1/3 of the neck.

1/2 head-width

Draw the neck and shoulder. Be sure to keep the width and height constant.

**10**

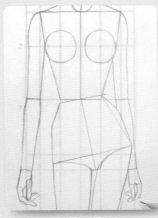

Placing the arm of the supporting leg side behind the body produces the effect of the figure swinging her arms alternately.

**11**

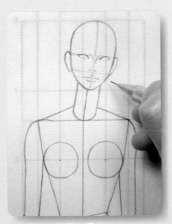

Draw the face slightly tilted. See p. 76-98 for how to draw.

**12**

The body drawing is completed.

**13**

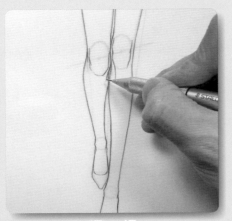

Place a paper over the sketch and make a nude figure drawing. The key point is to join the lines smoothly.

**14**

## Phase 5 review

- The most important point is the tilted lower torso. Practice many times, while paying extra attention to the four elements; right angle, parallel, symmetry and length in relation to the WL, median line and hipline for stability of the moving torso.
- When giving movement to the body parts, you may draw such parts smaller due to lack of confidence. In this phase, pay attention to the lower torso as it is likely to become smaller.
- Be sure not to draw the legs too different in width.
- Try many different poses by moving the arm and face.
- As long as you keep the knees on the guide line passing through the center of the knee of the supporting leg, you can try a number of movements for the idle leg. Try many different poses by moving the arm and face.

**We will call it completed for the time being regarding frontal poses. Next, we will turn the body!**

# 06 Changes When the Body is Turned

### How to draw the erect diagonal pose

You have learned that the standing pose consists of two kinds; the erect pose and the pose with weight on one leg. From now on you will learn how the body changes when it is turned. The body shows different expressions when seen from different angles. For example, the body drawing is symmetrical for the frontal pose, but not for the diagonal pose.

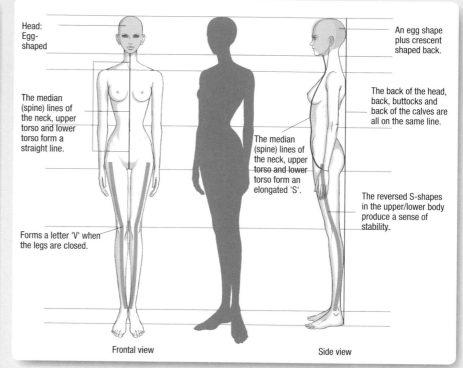

Head: Egg-shaped

The median (spine) lines of the neck, upper torso and lower torso form a straight line.

Forms a letter 'V' when the legs are closed.

An egg shape plus crescent shaped back.

The back of the head, back, buttocks and back of the calves are all on the same line.

The median (spine) lines of the neck, upper torso and lower torso form an elongated 'S'.

The reversed S-shapes in the upper/lower body produce a sense of stability.

Frontal view                Side view

First, look at the features of the frontal and sideways poses.

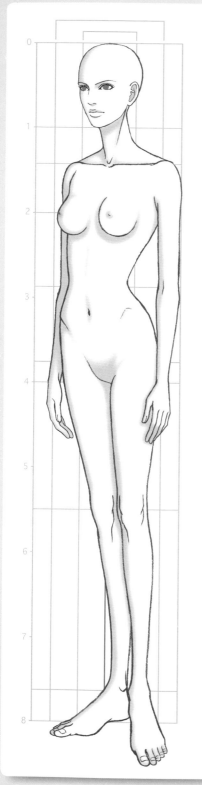

Erect diagonal pose

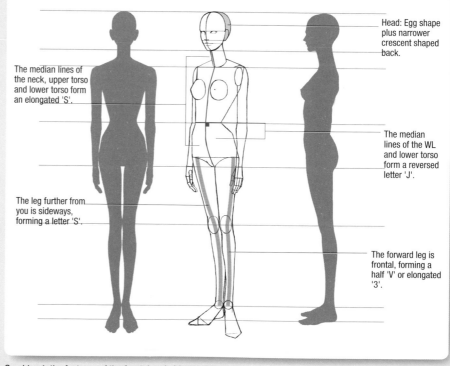

The median lines of the neck, upper torso and lower torso form an elongated 'S'.

The leg further from you is sideways, forming a letter 'S'.

Head: Egg shape plus narrower crescent shaped back.

The median lines of the WL and lower torso form a reversed letter 'J'.

The forward leg is frontal, forming a half 'V' or elongated '3'.

Combined, the features of the frontal and sideways poses create new ones as shown above.

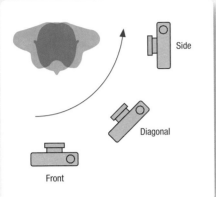

The diagonal pose is viewed in the same way as when a camera is moved from the front to the side. Areas which were not visible from the front e.g. the back of the head, back and buttocks become visible, and you can draw the body more in three-dimension.

Draw a line in the center to make both spaces equal.

When viewed diagonally, the right side appears larger as a result of perspective.

Narrower Wider

With perspective, areas further from you look small and areas closer look larger.

### The median line changes to an 'S' curve

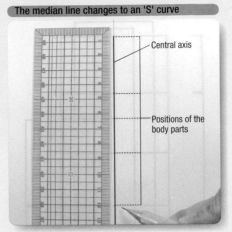

Central axis

Positions of the body parts

Trace the lines of the attached grid sheet onto a sketchpad or layout pad. **01**

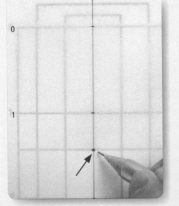

Draw the median line and mark the FNP with a dot. **02**

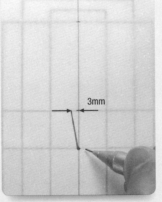

3mm

Neck: Draw a line from the FNP, tilting forward a little. **03**

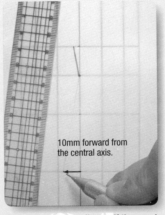

10mm forward from the central axis.

Upper torso: Draw a line as if the navel is protruding. **04**

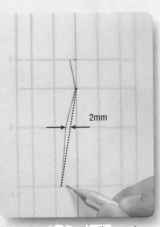

2mm

Draw a line representing the roundness of the ribs. The highest point will be the BP area. **05**

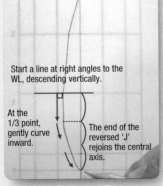

Start a line at right angles to the WL, descending vertically.

At the 1/3 point, gently curve inward.

The end of the reversed 'J' rejoins the central axis.

Lower torso: The median line forms a reverse letter 'J'. **06**

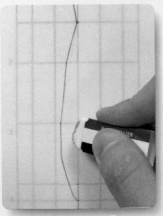

Having completed the median line, erase the central axis to avoid confusion. **07**

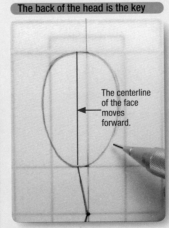

The centerline of the face moves forward.

Draw an egg-shape oval on the neck median line. **08**

### The back of the head is the key

Add a small part of the back of the head as a crescent in the top 2/3. **09**

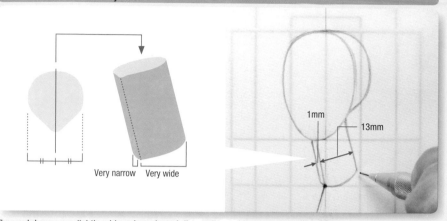

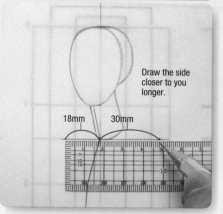

Draw the side closer to you longer.

The neck becomes slightly wider when viewed diagonally, and its cross-sectional view is in the form of an inverted teardrop. This tilted cylinder, when viewed diagonally, has a significant width difference on the left and right sides, as shown above.

The shoulder is 2 head-widths when viewed from the front, but becomes a little shorter when viewed diagonally. It is 48mm here. Note that the left and right widths from the median line are very different as a result of perspective.

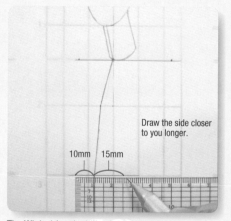

Draw the side closer to you longer.

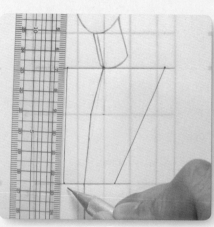

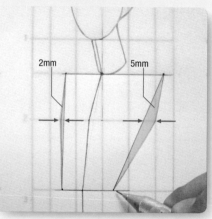

The WL is 1 head-width when viewed from the front, but becomes a little shorter when viewed diagonally. It is 25mm here. Note also that as in the shoulder width, the left/right widths from the median line are very different as a result of perspective.

Join the shoulder and waist with straight lines.

Add roundness to the bust and the back lines with the highest points at the BP level.

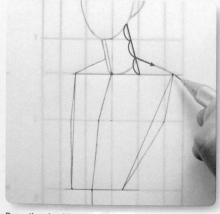

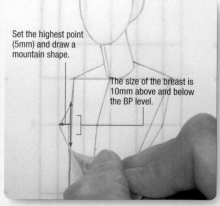

Set the highest point (5mm) and draw a mountain shape.

The size of the breast is 10mm above and below the BP level.

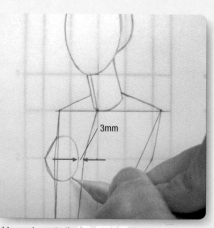

Draw the shoulder, starting from a point 1/3 above the bottom of the neck, 8mm.

Draw a breast.

Add roundness to the breast. Note that the shape which is round when viewed from the front becomes oval when viewed diagonally.

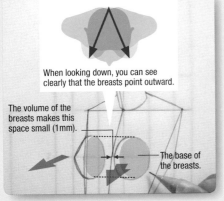

As the breasts protrude from the thoracic spine, when viewed diagonally, the one closer to you appears to point more toward the front, and the further one sideways, instead of as two same forms placed side by side.

When looking down, you can see clearly that the breasts point outward.

The volume of the breasts makes this space small (1mm).

The base of the breasts.

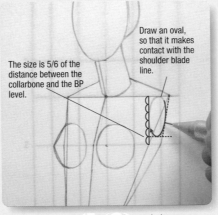

Draw the base of the arm, i.e. the armhole area. **19**

The size is 5/6 of the distance between the collarbone and the BP level.

Draw an oval, so that it makes contact with the shoulder blade line.

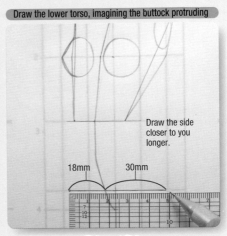

Draw the hip width on the HL. The width is 2 head-widths when viewed from the front, but becomes a little shorter when viewed diagonally. It is 48mm here. Note that, as in the shoulder/waist widths, the left and right widths from the median line are very different as a result of perspective.

Draw the side closer to you longer.

18mm    30mm

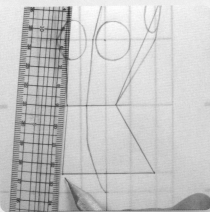

Join the WL and HL with straight lines. **21**

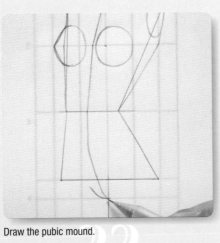

Draw the pubic mound. **22**

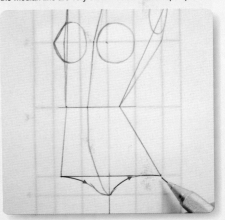

Draw the base of the legs. **23**

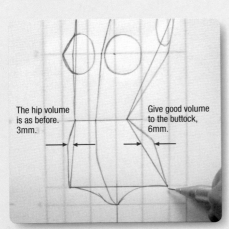

Add roundness to the hip and buttock lines. **24**

The hip volume is as before. 3mm.

Give good volume to the buttock, 6mm.

**Leg**

Establish the ankle position. When viewed diagonally, the ankle further from you touches the central axis. **25**

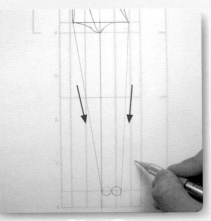

Join the hip joints (the greater trochanter to be precise, or groin) to the ankle with one straight line. **26**

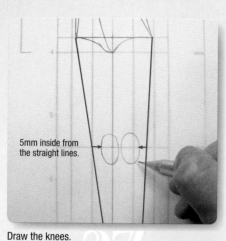

5mm inside from the straight lines.

Draw the knees.

**27**

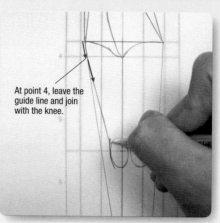

Draw a line along the curving knee.

The leg further from you forms an 'S' as its foot is pointed sideways.

**28**

At point 4, leave the guide line and join with the knee.

Join the hip joints and knee to draw the thigh.

**29**

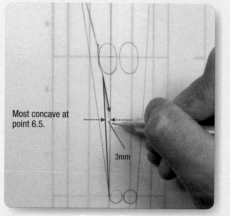

Most concave at point 6.5.

3mm

The shin turned sideways is concave toward the toes.

**30**

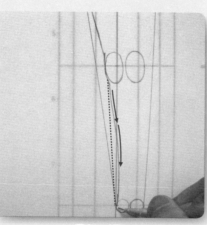

Draw the shin strongly concave toward the ankle.

**31**

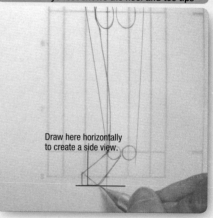

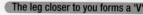

Draw here horizontally to create a side view.

Draw the foot, imagining the shape of a necktie.

**32**

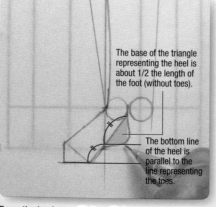

The base of the triangle representing the heel is about 1/2 the length of the foot (without toes).

The bottom line of the heel is parallel to the line representing the toes.

Draw the heel.

**33**

The line of the top of the foot extends to the toes with a little bend.

Draw the tip of the toes.

**34**

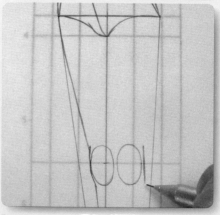

Draw the outer line of the knee.

**35**

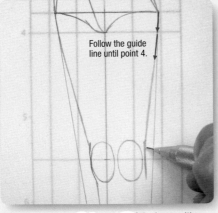

Join the hip joints and outer line of the knee with a straight line.
36

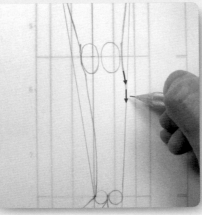

Draw the calf by making a curve at point 6, joining the guide line.
37

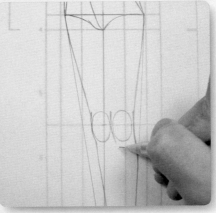

Draw the inner line of the knee.
38

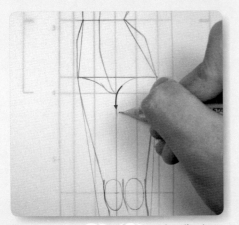

Give good roundness to the first several centimeters (10mm) of the thigh.
39

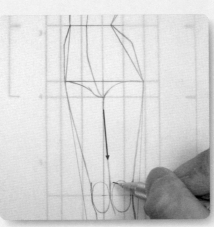

Draw the rest with a more or less straight line.
40

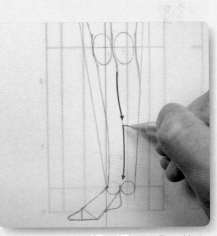

The calf joins the guide line at point 6.5. The widest point on the inner line should be lower than that of the outer line.
41

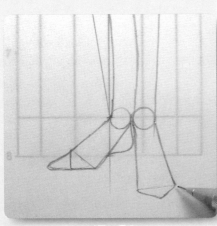

The foot has the shape of a necktie. Represent the toe part as a triangle. Make the foot relatively large for a stable look.
42

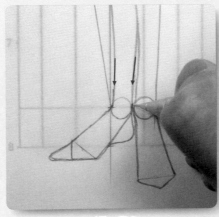

Draw the calf of the leg further from you, making the line near the ankle parallel to the shin line.
43

**Draw the top of the arm as if buried in the shoulder**

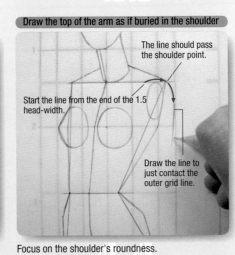

The line should pass the shoulder point.

Start the line from the end of the 1.5 head-width.

Draw the line to just contact the outer grid line.

Focus on the shoulder's roundness.
44

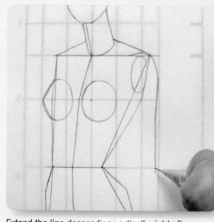

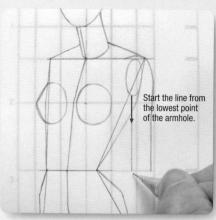

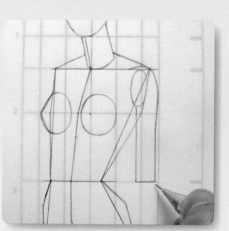

Extend the line descending vertically right after passing point 2.

Draw the inner arm line also vertically. Be sure to make it the same width as the frontal pose.

Start the line from the lowest point of the armhole.

Stop and close at the elbow. Drawing while confirming positions of the joints helps keep a good balance when the body parts are moved. It is tedious but very important.

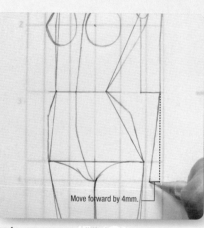

Move forward by 4mm.

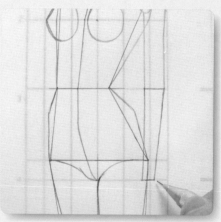

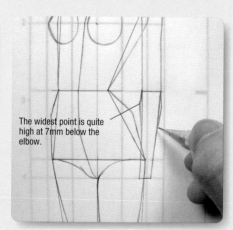

The widest point is quite high at 7mm below the elbow.

The forearm appears a little bent forward when viewed diagonally.

Draw the forearm slightly tapering toward the wrist.

Add a little roundness to the forearm.

**Draw the hand by dividing its back and fingers**

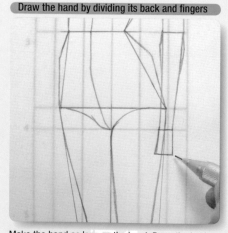

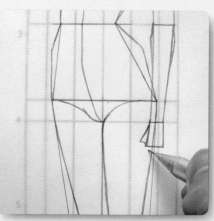

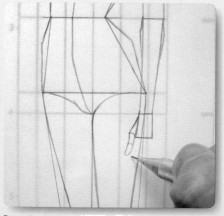

Make the hand as long as the head. Draw the back and fingers separately. The back is rectangular and a little shorter than 1/2 head-length.

Draw the base of the thumb as if it is growing out of the wrist.

Draw the thumb with three joints including the base.

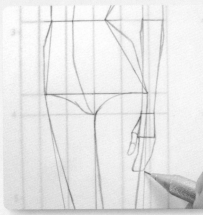

The fingers are the same length or longer than the back of the hand. Bend it a little for a natural look. First draw the outline of four fingers together as if wearing a mitten.

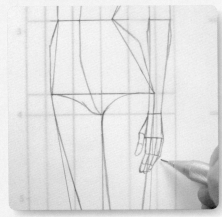

Separate into four. The middle finger is the longest. Note that each has three joints including the base.

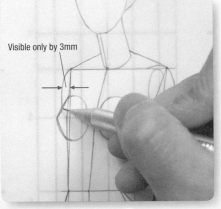

Visible only by 3mm

The arm is mostly hidden. Draw it starting from the round shoulder.

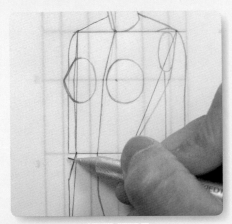

Draw the upper arm vertically.

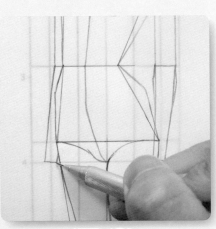

Draw the forearm slightly forward.

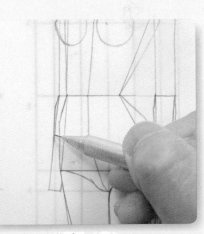

Add roundness to the forearm.

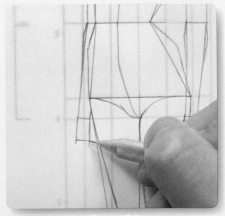

Draw the back of the hand a little smaller (by 1mm) than the one closer to you to give perspective.

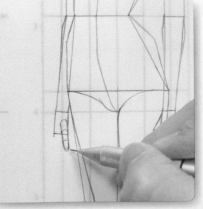

When the hand is viewed from the side, draw the thumb on the back of the hand.

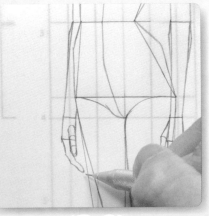

Draw the rest of the fingers.

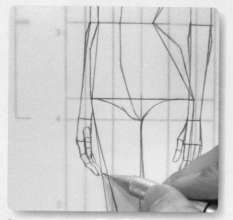

Show a small amount of the middle and ring fingers to give perspective. 63

See p. 81-87 for more details for the angled face

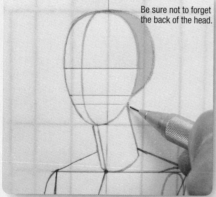

Be sure not to forget the back of the head.

Plan the balance of parts of the face. 64

Draw the eyes, nose and mouth. 65

**Completion of the body sketch**

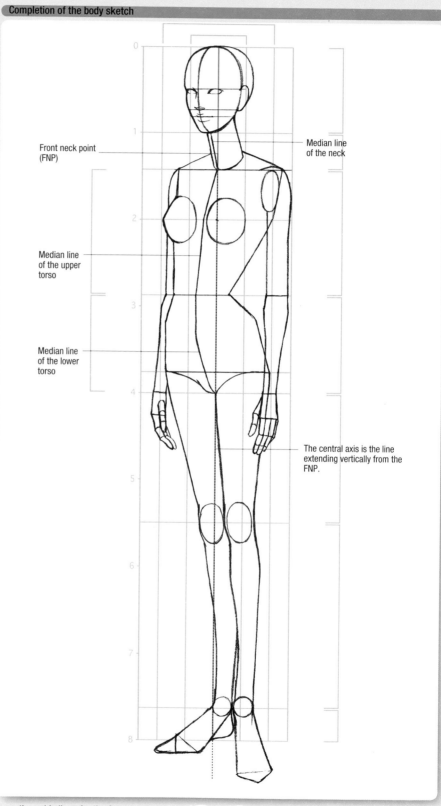

0

Front neck point (FNP)

Median line of the neck

Median line of the upper torso

Median line of the lower torso

The central axis is the line extending vertically from the FNP.

1

2

3

4

5

6

7

8

Erase the guide lines for the face, upper torso and legs to complete the body sketch. 66

44

**Clean up**

Make a nude figure drawing on a sketchpad or layout pad using the completed body sketch as an underlay. Create the softness of the human body by smoothing out the ragged lines at joints in the neck and waist areas.

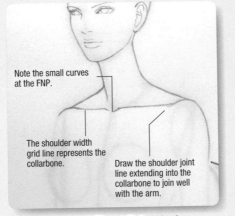

Note the small curves at the FNP.

The shoulder width grid line represents the collarbone.

Draw the shoulder joint line extending into the collarbone to join well with the arm.

Draw the lines, part by part to give contrast.

68

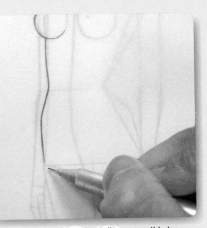

Join the upper and lower torso lines smoothly to create a nice WL.

69

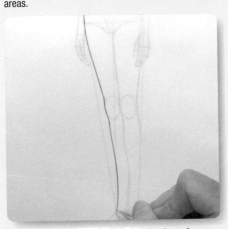

Focus on the concave curve for the leg turned sideways.

70

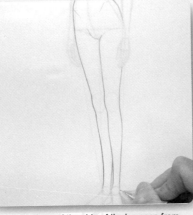

Focus on the form of the shin of the leg seen from the front. Draw it tapered toward the ankle to create a nice line.

71

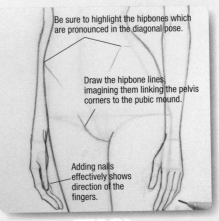

Be sure to highlight the hipbones which are pronounced in the diagonal pose.

Draw the hipbone lines, imagining them linking the pelvis corners to the pubic mound.

Adding nails effectively shows direction of the fingers.

Draw the hand.

72

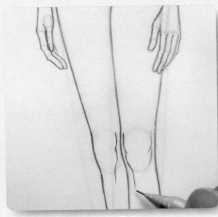

Add lines to the knees.

73

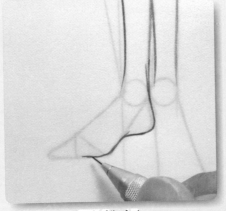

Draw the heel and arch of the foot.

74

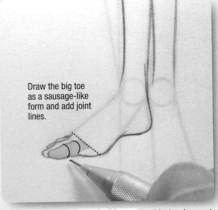

Draw the big toe as a sausage-like form and add joint lines.

When the foot is turned sideways, the big toe is most noticeable.

75

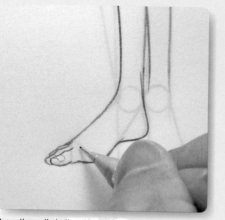

Draw the nails in the shape of rounded roof tiles.

76

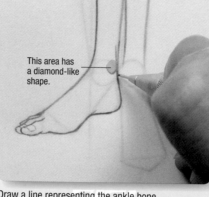

This area has a diamond-like shape.

Draw a line representing the ankle bone.

77

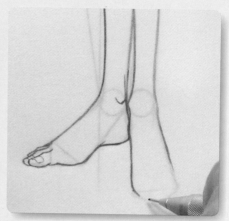

Draw the foot pointing toward you as you have already done. Start with the outline.

78

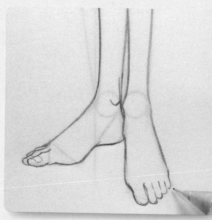

Draw the toes.

79

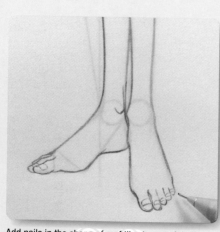

Add nails in the shape of roof tiles to complete the clean up.

80

**Add simple shading, thinking that the body consists of cylinders.**

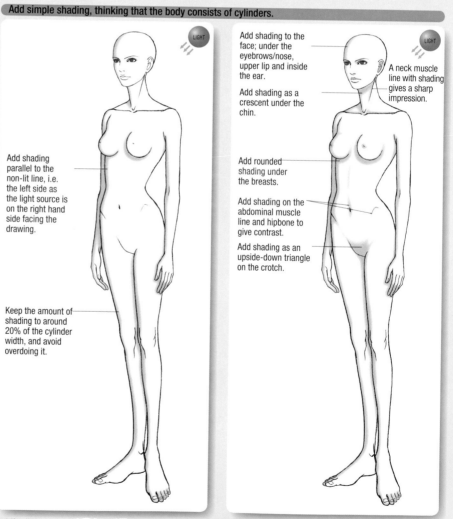

LIGHT

Add shading parallel to the non-lit line, i.e. the left side as the light source is on the right hand side facing the drawing.

Keep the amount of shading to around 20% of the cylinder width, and avoid overdoing it.

Set the light source in order to add shading. In this book, it is set on the upper right facing the drawing. Regarding the body parts as cylinders, add shading to each of them.

81

LIGHT

Add shading to the face; under the eyebrows/nose, upper lip and inside the ear.

Add shading as a crescent under the chin.

A neck muscle line with shading gives a sharp impression.

Add rounded shading under the breasts.

Add shading on the abdominal muscle line and hipbone to give contrast.

Add shading as an upside-down triangle on the crotch.

Add shading to the uneven areas which could not be represented as cylinders to complete the shading.

82

## Erect diagonal pose (legs apart)

Having studied the diagonally turned body proportion, let us now give movement to the limbs with the joints as fulcrums. As the parts given movement tend to become shorter or smaller, practice by placing the body drawing you have just made at your side for comparison. We will now try the diagonal pose with legs apart.

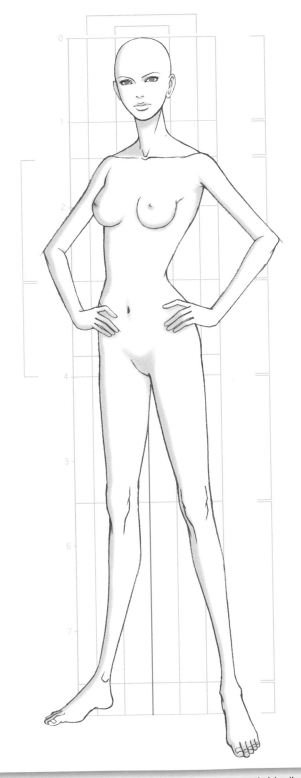

Erect diagonal pose with legs apart. As this is a frontal pose drawing, focus on studying the movements of the lower half of the body which supports the body weight.

Smaller      Larger

In erect pose/legs apart, the distances from the centerline are equal.

Seen diagonally, the distances appear different due to perspective.

Study the perspective when the legs are apart, using an inverted letter 'V' to represent the open legs.

**The upper half of the body remains static**

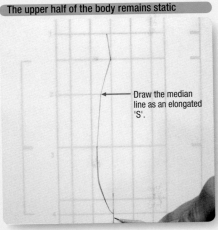

Draw the median line as an elongated 'S'.

Use as an underlay the attached grid here, or the one you prepared in Phase 2. Follow the process in p. 37-39 for the static neck, and upper/lower torsos.

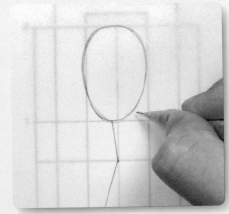

Draw the face on the median line. Be sure to make the width 2/3 head-length.

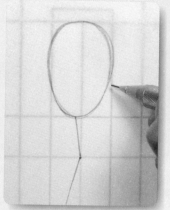

Turn the face slightly toward the front. Of course the back of the head is seen less. *03*

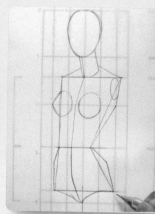

The upper half of the body is completed. *04*

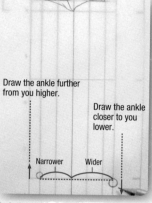

Draw the ankle further from you higher.

Draw the ankle closer to you lower.

Narrower    Wider

Mark the ankle positions with two circles. Unlike the erect pose with legs apart by the same distance from the central axis, here the distance closer to you becomes wider. *05*

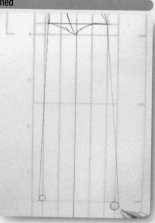

Join the hip joints (the greater trochanter to be precise, or groin) to the ankle with one straight line. *06*

**The leg further from you forms an 'S'**

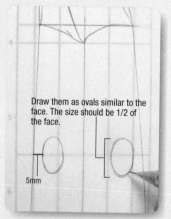

Draw them as ovals similar to the face. The size should be 1/2 of the face.

5mm

Draw the kneecaps slightly in (5mm) from the outer leg line. *07*

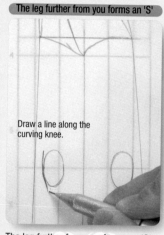

Draw a line along the curving knee.

The leg further from you forms an 'S' as its foot is pointed sideways. *08*

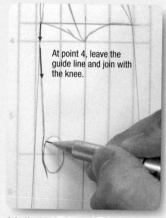

At point 4, leave the guide line and join with the knee.

Join the hip joints and knee to draw the thigh. *09*

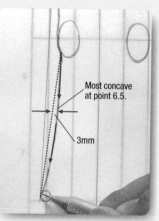

Most concave at point 6.5.

3mm

The shin turned sideways is concave toward the toes. *10*

**The sideways foot shows the heel and toe tips**

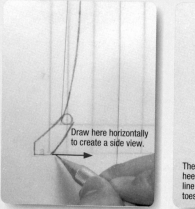

Draw here horizontally to create a side view.

Draw the foot, imagining the shape of a necktie. *11*

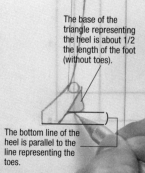

The base of the triangle representing the heel is about 1/2 the length of the foot (without toes).

The bottom line of the heel is parallel to the line representing the toes.

Draw the heel. *12*

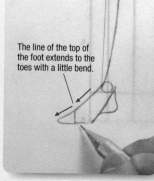

The line of the top of the foot extends to the toes with a little bend.

Draw the tips of the toes. *13*

Draw the inner side of the knee with a straight line. *14*

Make both widths the same, imagining the cross-section of the thighs.

Draw the inner thigh line, making the width equal to the leg closer to you. *15*

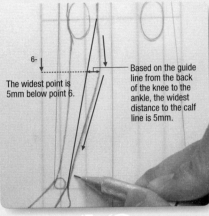

The widest point is 5mm below point 6.

Based on the guide line from the back of the knee to the ankle, the widest distance to the calf line is 5mm.

Draw the calf. *16*

**The leg closer to you forms a 'V'**

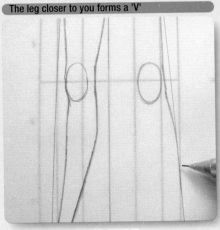

The leg closer to you is frontal, forming an inverted half 'V' or elongated '3'. Draw the outer line of the knee, thigh and shin/calf in this order based on the guide line. *17*

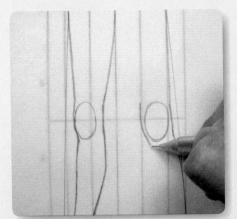

Draw the inner line of the knee. *18*

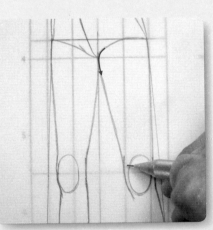

Give good roundness to the first several centimeters (10mm), by extending the curved panty line. *19*

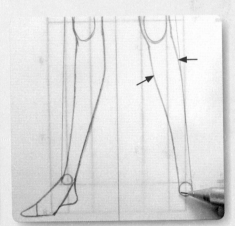

The widest point on the inner line should be lower than that of the outer line. *20*

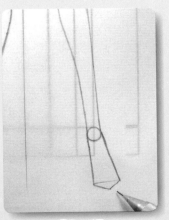

The foot has the shape of a necktie. Represent the toe part as a triangle. Make the foot relatively large for a stable look. *21*

**Raising the arms**

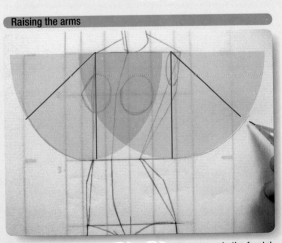

Following the movement of the elbows creates an arc. In the frontal pose, the arc forms half a circle, and in the diagonal half an oval. *22*

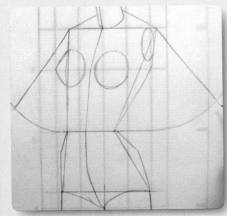

Draw the outer line of the upper arms, raising them to between 30° to 40°. *23*

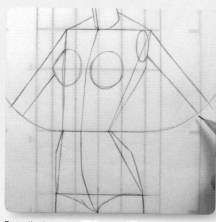

Draw the inner line of the upper arms, making sure that the width is the same as that when pointing straight down.

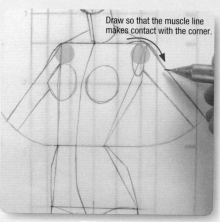

Draw so that the muscle line makes contact with the corner.

Draw the shoulder muscle, making the upper end appear to be buried in the collarbone and extending the line with a curve as if covering the shoulder joint.

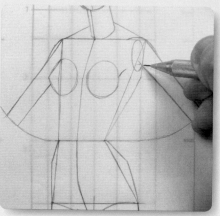

Draw the armpit line revealed when the arm is raised. This helps join smoothly the arm and upper torso.

**Draw the hand on the hip, before the forearm**

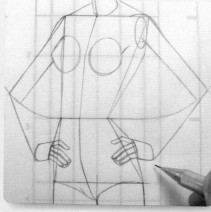

Draw the back of the hand angled as a trapezoid.

The forearm length often changes subject to perspective. Draw the hand first to secure a good balance. Here, the back of the hand is placed on the hip.

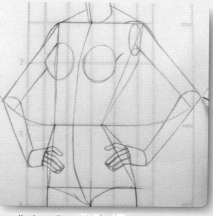

Draw the index finger by extending the top line of the back of the hand in the same direction and bending at its joints.

Draw the finger part with the middle, ring and small fingers as one, as they often move together.

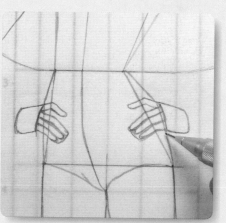

Draw as three fingers, with the middle one the longest and the small one the shortest.

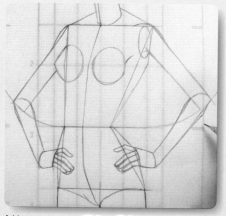

Join the elbow and the wrist.

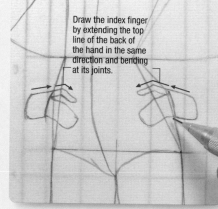

Draw the inner line of the forearm, tapering it toward the wrist in the same width as when pointing straight down.

Add some roundness typical of the forearm.

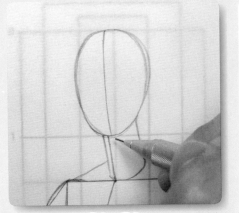

Draw a line in the center of the face, making it slightly curved as the face is turned slightly diagonally.

33

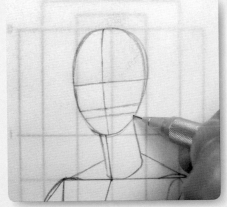

Draw guide lines. See p. 76-98 for more detail.

34

Draw each part of the face.

35

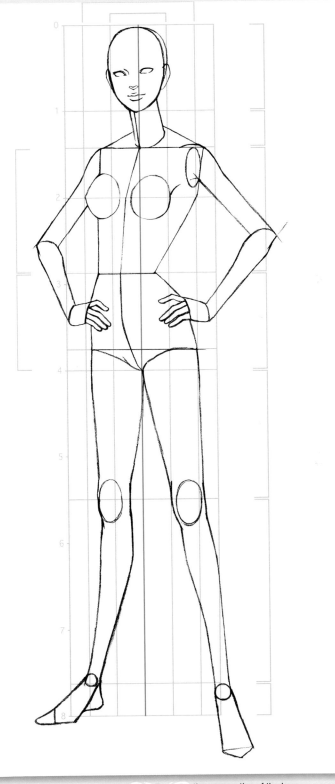

Erase unnecessary lines to complete the body sketch. Focus on the perspective of the legs.

36

**Draw a nude figure with smooth lines.**

Using an underlay, clean up the body outline by joining the lines smoothly. Imagine to cover the body sketch with a thin and supple skin.

**Add shading**

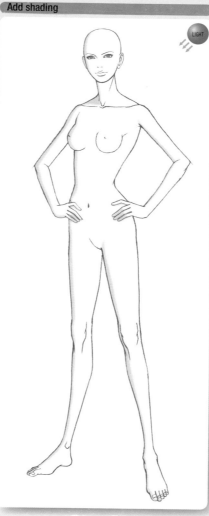

Cleaning up of the body outline is completed. Now add shading along the non-lit side outline of each part; the face, torso, arms and legs, by setting the light source on the upper right facing the drawing.

Add shading to the face and breasts while considering their volume to complete the shading.

## Phase 6 review

- The median lines of the diagonal pose form an elongated 'S'.
- The legs of the side view have a reversed S-shape contrary to the median line.
- Draw the back of the head to give perspective.
- When seen diagonally, the base of the arm appears to be buried in the shoulder.
- Note the difference in sizes due to perspective. Draw the part further from you smaller, and the part closer larger.
- Acquire the skill to maintain constant proportion by making many drawings

**Next, we will try the fashion model's standing pose (diagonal)!**

# Fashion Model's Standing Pose (Diagonal)

**Diagonal pose with weight on one leg (supporting leg behind)**

We draw this pose using the erect diagonal pose. The procedure is exactly the same as that for the erect full frontal pose, except that there are two examples of diagonal pose with weight on one leg; the supporting leg behind and in front. In this phase, we study the pose with the supporting leg behind.

**Two main characteristics are mentioned in phase 5**

- The ankle of the pivotal leg is near the point where the central axis descends vertically from the front neck point (FNP).
- The lower torso rotates at the waist point (WP). The waistline (WL) becomes tilted when the supporting leg side is higher.

When these two points are represented, you can obtain the pose with weight on one leg.

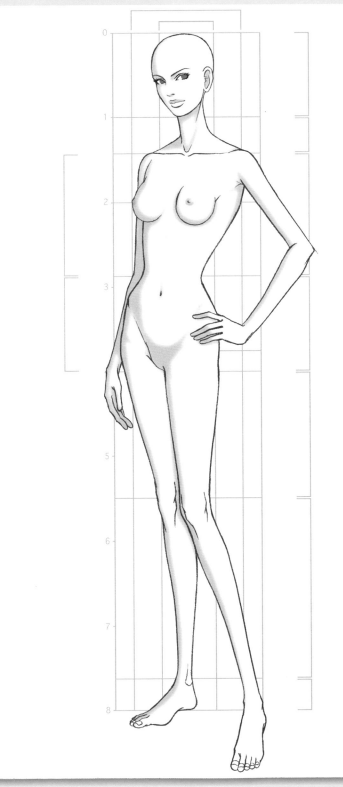

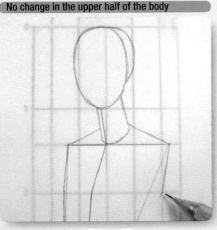

**No change in the upper half of the body**

As movement occurs in the lower half of the body, follow the same process for the face, neck and upper torso as before.

**Key point**

**Draw the angled lower torso correctly**

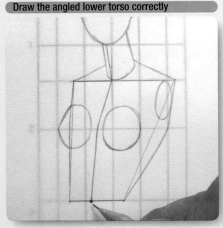

Diagonal pose with weight on one leg (supporting leg behind)

Mark the WP. The lower torso rotates around this point as a fulcrum.

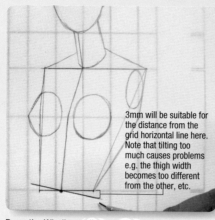

3mm will be suitable for the distance from the grid horizontal line here. Note that tilting too much causes problems e.g. the thigh width becomes too different from the other, etc.

Draw the WL diagonally passing over the WP. The higher end represents the supporting leg side, i.e. the right leg (on the left facing the drawing) here.

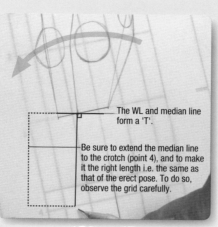

The WL and median line form a 'T'.

Be sure to extend the median line to the crotch (point 4), and to make it the right length i.e. the same as that of the erect pose. To do so, observe the grid carefully.

Draw the median line of the lower torso at right angles to the WL. Draw by rotating the paper so that the WL becomes horizontal. This assures correct horizontal, right angle and symmetrical lines.   **Key point**

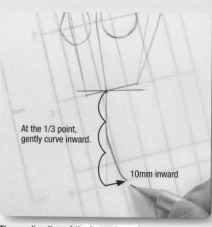

At the 1/3 point, gently curve inward.

10mm inward

The median line of the lower torso forms a reversed 'J'. Start a line at right angles to the WL, descending vertically, and then gently curve inward.

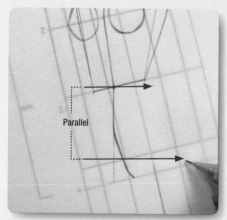

Parallel

Draw the HL parallel to the WL.

**06**

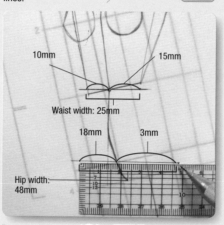

10mm          15mm

Waist width: 25mm

18mm     3mm

Hip width: 48mm

Draw the WL and HL to determine their widths.

**07**

Join the WL and HL with straight lines.

**08**

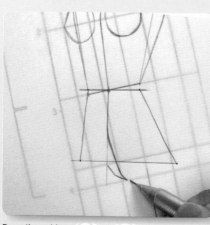

Draw the pubic mound.

**09**

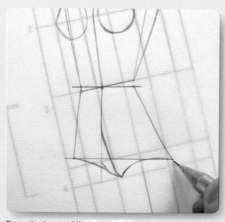

Draw the base of the legs.

**10**

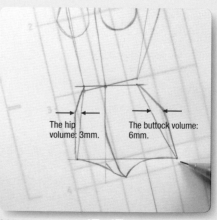

The hip volume: 3mm.     The buttock volume: 6mm.

Add roundness to the hip and buttock lines.

**11**

## Draw the supporting legs with a strong line

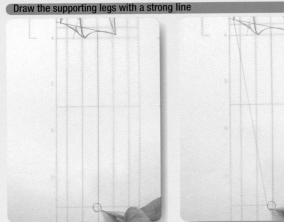

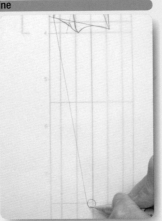

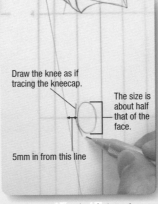

Draw the knee as if tracing the kneecap.

The size is about half that of the face.

5mm in from this line

As the ankle of the supporting leg is near the central axis (extending vertically from the FNP), circle its position accordingly.

Join the hip joints (the greater trochanter to be precise, or groin) to the ankle with one straight line. As models' legs are very slim, be sure that the leg line does not extend beyond this line.

Draw the supporting leg. As turned sideways, it forms an 'S', draw the kneecaps slightly in (5mm) from the outer leg line, and add the outer knee line.

Draw the outer line of the thigh and shin. Focus on the degree of the curve of the shin. See p. 48 for more detail.

## Draw the idle leg, thigh and shin separately

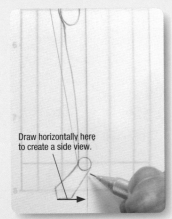

Draw horizontally here to create a side view.

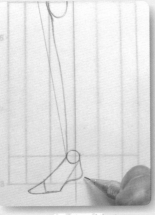

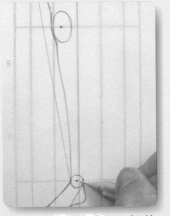

These three lines are roughly parallel.

Draw the foot, imagining the shape of a necktie.

Draw the heel and tips of the toes.

Mark the centers of the knee and ankle with dots.

Draw lines joining both knees and ankles parallel to the WL, to make both legs the same length.

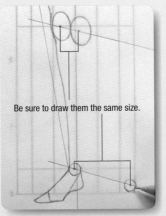

Be sure to draw them the same size.

Add muscle lines by the kneecap; the outer line straight as it is frontal.

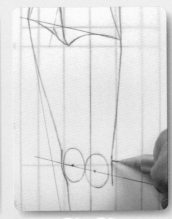

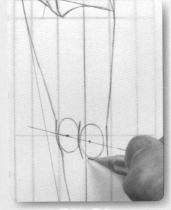

Position the knee and ankle on the lines. The ankle looks natural when placed a little away from the central axis.

As the idle leg can be moved freely, you can draw its parts, i.e. the thigh and shin separately as in the case of the arm.

Draw the thigh with the outer line extending more or less straight from the hip joint to the knee.

Draw the knee as if tracing the kneecap.

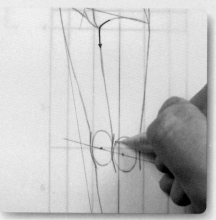

Give good roundness to the first several centimeters (10mm), by extending the line from the crotch.

24

Join the knee to the ankle with a straight line.

25

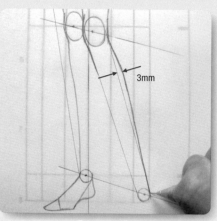

3mm

Draw the outer line of the calf as a gentle elongated triangle.

26

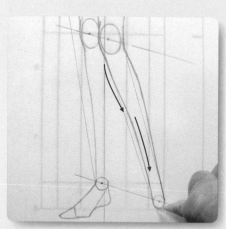

Draw the inner calf line as an elongated 'S'. The first one third is convex and the rest concave.

27

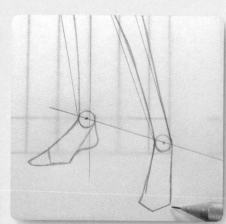

As the idle leg is nearer to you than the supporting leg, draw it a little larger using perspective.

28

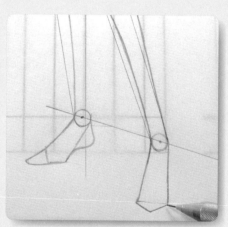

Draw a line representing the base of the toes.

29

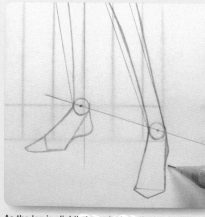

As the leg is slightly turned, show the heel a little.

30

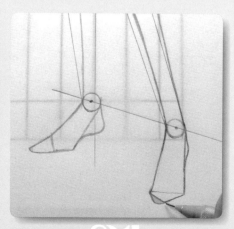

Draw the tips of the toes small.

31

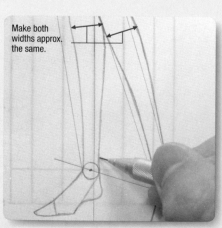

Make both widths approx. the same.

Draw the calf, tapering toward the ankle.

32

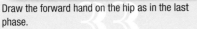
**Draw the hand on the hip first, and the forearm at the end**

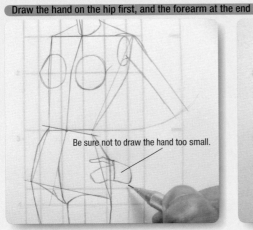

Draw the forward hand on the hip as in the last phase.

*Be sure not to draw the hand too small.*

33

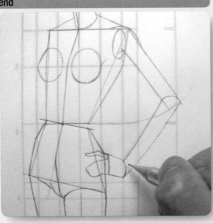

Draw the forearm.

34

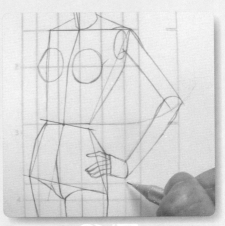

Draw as three fingers.

35

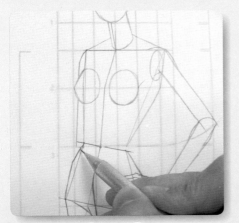

Draw the upper arm straight downward.

36

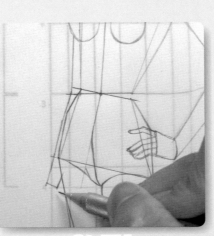

Draw the forearm bent slightly forward. Unless the bending is large, you can draw the upper arm, forearm and hand in this order.

37

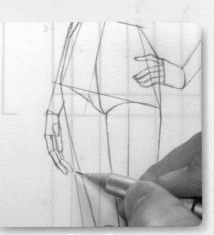

Draw the fingers, paying attention not to make them too small.

38

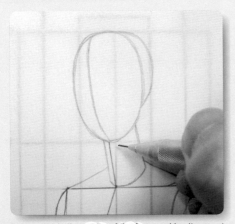

Draw a line in the center of the face, making it curved as the face is slightly turned.

39

Draw guide lines for the balance of the face. See p. 76-98 for more detail.

40

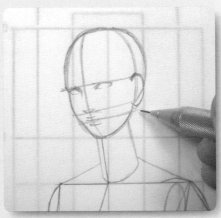

Draw each part of the face based on the guide lines.

41

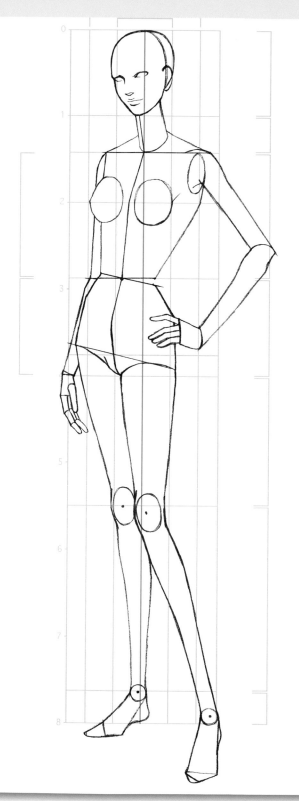

Erase the guide lines to complete the body sketch. 42

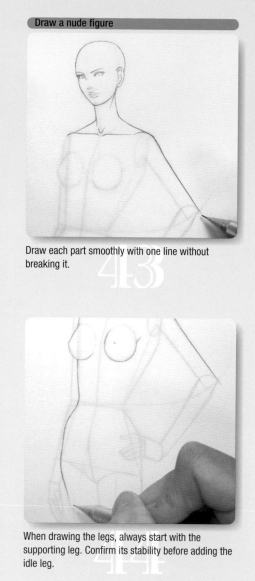

Draw each part smoothly with one line without breaking it. 43

When drawing the legs, always start with the supporting leg. Confirm its stability before adding the idle leg. 44

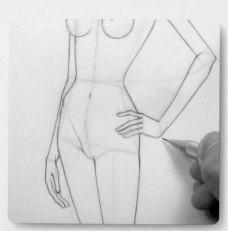

Be sure to draw both hands the same size. 45

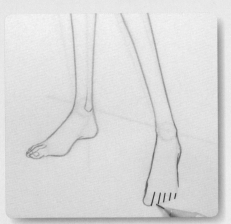

Establish the direction and size of the four toes, based on the big toe.

46

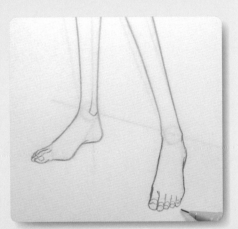

Draw the toes carefully as they play an essential role in determining the direction of the foot.

47

**Shading**

LIGHT

Cleaning up of the body outline is completed. Now add shading by setting the light source on the upper right facing the drawing. Add shading along the non-lit side outline of each part.

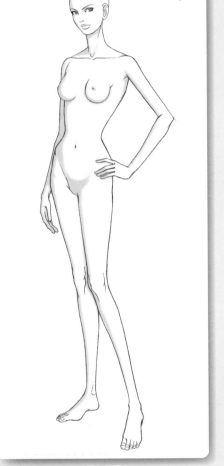

LIGHT

Add shading to the face and breasts while considering their volume to complete the shading.

49

## Diagonal pose with weight on one leg (supporting leg forward)

Now, we will study the pose with the supporting leg forward.

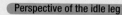

### Perspective of the idle leg

In the case of this pose, as a result of perspective, the arrangement of the ankle position differs from that of the last phases, where the line joining both knees was parallel to the waistline. This was because the idle leg was placed one-step forward, and was therefore drawn lower than the leg behind (Fig.1). However, when the supporting leg is forward the idle leg appears, instead of stepping forward to be sliding sideways (Fig. 2). In other words, the ankles are both on the same horizontal line (Fig. 3).

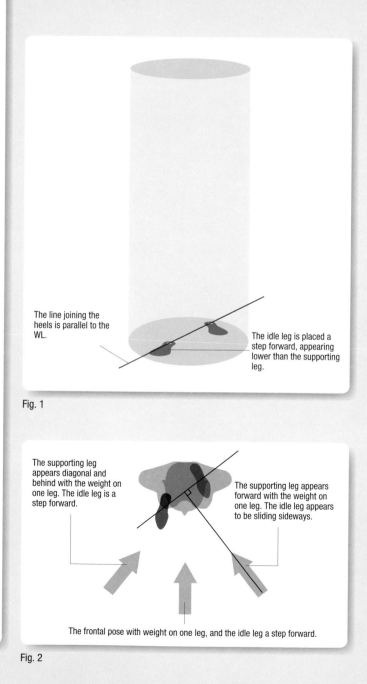

The line joining the heels is parallel to the WL.

The idle leg is placed a step forward, appearing lower than the supporting leg.

Fig. 1

The supporting leg appears diagonal and behind with the weight on one leg. The idle leg is a step forward.

The supporting leg appears forward with the weight on one leg. The idle leg appears to be sliding sideways.

The frontal pose with weight on one leg, and the idle leg a step forward.

Diagonal pose with weight on one leg (supporting leg forward)

Fig. 2

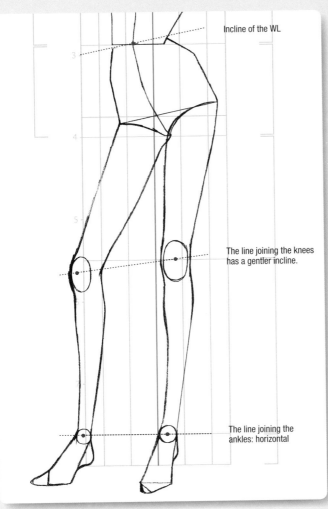

Incline of the WL

The line joining the knees has a gentler incline.

The line joining the ankles: horizontal

Fig. 3

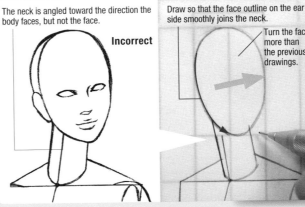

As movement occurs in the lower half of the body, follow the same process for the face, neck and upper torso as before.

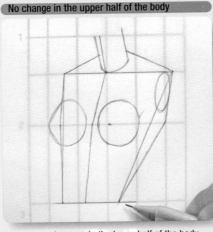

The neck is angled toward the direction the body faces, but not the face.

**Incorrect**

Draw so that the face outline on the ear side smoothly joins the neck.

Turn the face more than the previous drawings.

Draw the face turning, starting with an oval.

**Key point**

**Draw the angled lower torso correctly**

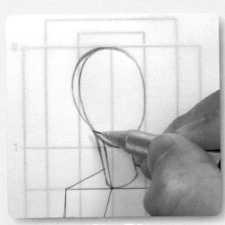

Draw the back of the head as a crescent in the top 2/3.

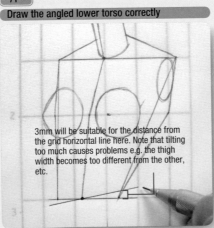

3mm will be suitable for the distance from the grid horizontal line here. Note that tilting too much causes problems e.g. the thigh width becomes too different from the other, etc.

Mark the WP and draw the WL diagonally. The higher end represents the supporting leg side, i.e. the left leg (on the right facing the drawing) here.

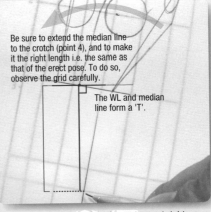

Be sure to extend the median line to the crotch (point 4), and to make it the right length i.e. the same as that of the erect pose. To do so, observe the grid carefully.

The WL and median line form a 'T'.

Draw the median line of the lower torso at right angles to the WL. Draw by rotating the paper so that the WL becomes horizontal. This assures correct horizontal, right angle and symmetrical lines. **Key point**

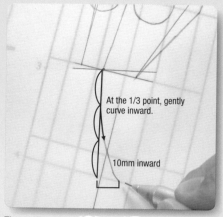

The median line of the lower torso forms a reversed 'J'. Start a line at right angles to the WL, descending vertically, and then gently curve inward.

At the 1/3 point, gently curve inward.

10mm inward

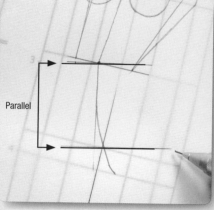

Draw the HL parallel to the WL. **07**

Parallel

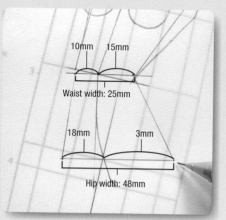

Determine the widths of the WL and HL, and join them with straight lines. **08**

10mm   15mm
Waist width: 25mm
18mm   3mm
Hip width: 48mm

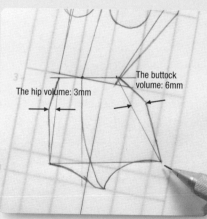

Draw the lower torso in the order of; the pubic mound, base of the legs and roundness to the hip and buttock lines. **09**

The hip volume: 3mm
The buttock volume: 6mm

> **Draw strongly as it supports the body weight.**

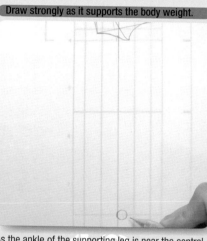

As the ankle of the supporting leg is near the central axis (extending vertically from the FNP), circle its position accordingly. **10**

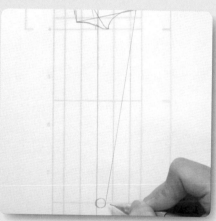

Join the hip joints (the greater trochanter to be precise, or groin) to the ankle with one straight line. As models' legs are very slim, be sure that the leg line does not extend beyond this line.

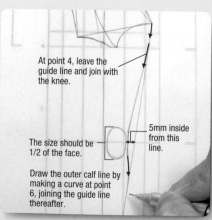

At point 4, leave the guide line and join with the knee.

The size should be 1/2 of the face.

5mm inside from this line.

Draw the outer calf line by making a curve at point 6, joining the guide line thereafter.

Draw the supporting leg. It is frontal, forming a half 'V' or elongated '3'. Draw the kneecaps slightly in (5mm) from the straight guide line, and draw the outer line of the knee, thigh and shin/calf in this order.

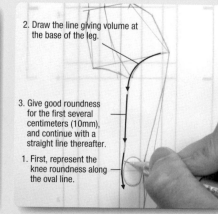

2. Draw the line giving volume at the base of the leg.

3. Give good roundness for the first several centimeters (10mm), and continue with a straight line thereafter.

1. First, represent the knee roundness along the oval line.

Draw the inner line of the thigh. **13**

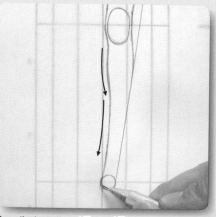

Draw the inner line of the shin as an elongated 'S'. **14**

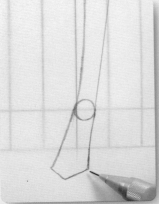

Draw the foot, imagining the shape of a necktie.

**15**

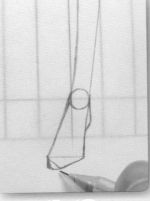

Draw the heel and tips of the toes.

**16**

**Draw the thigh and shin separately**

WL

Less angled than the WL

Horizontal

Draw guide lines passing over the centers of the knee and ankle. As the idle leg is turned sideways, the guide lines should be as above.

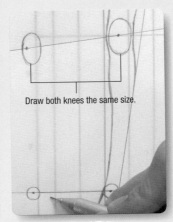

Draw both knees the same size.

Position the knee and ankle on the guide lines. The ankle looks natural when placed a little away from the central axis.

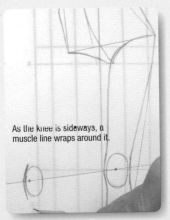

As the knee is sideways, a muscle line wraps around it.

As the idle leg can be moved freely, you can draw its parts, i.e. the thigh and shin separately as in the case of the arm.

**19**

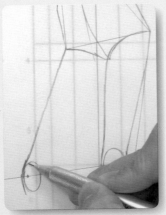

Draw the thigh in a more or less straight sharp line.

**20**

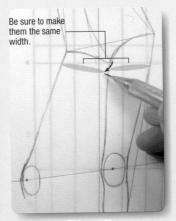

Be sure to make them the same width.

Adjust the width of the thigh by adding the buttock line.

**21**

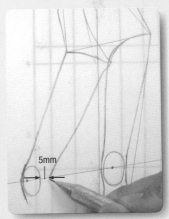

5mm

Extend the inner thigh line toward the back of the knee with a distance of 5mm as above.

**22**

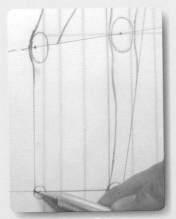

Join the knee to the ankle with a straight line.

**23**

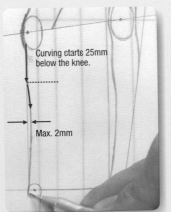

Curving starts 25mm below the knee.

Max. 2mm

Draw the curving line of the shin using the grid line as a guide.

**24**

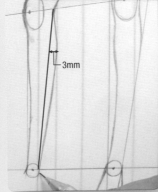

3mm

Draw the calf line as a gentle curve.

**25**

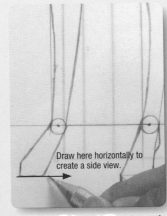

Draw here horizontally to create a side view.

Draw the foot, imagining the shape of a necktie.

**26**

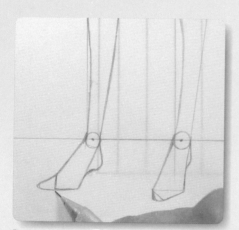

Draw the heels and tips of the toes.

27

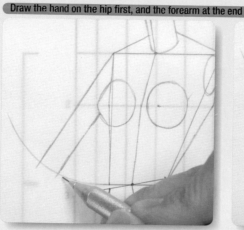

Draw the behind hand on the hip. Draw a line following the elbow movement and then the outer and inner arm lines.

28

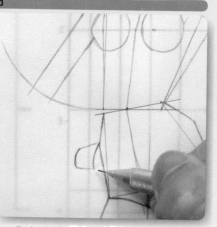

Draw the back of the hand as a trapezoid with perspective.

29

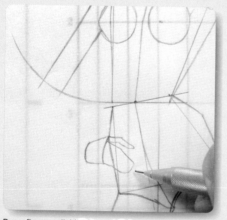

Draw fingers, dividing them into the index and remaining three. Be sure not to make them too small.

30

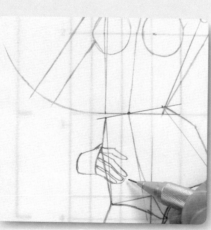

Draw as three fingers.

31

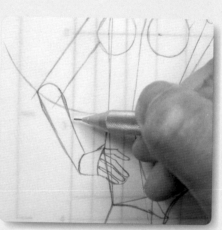

Draw the forearm slightly tapered toward the wrist, adding a little roundness.

32

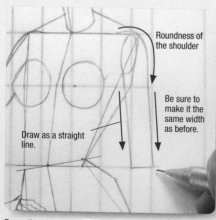

Roundness of the shoulder

Be sure to make it the same width as before.

Draw as a straight line.

Draw the upper arm starting from the armhole.

33

Draw the forearm slightly tapered.

34

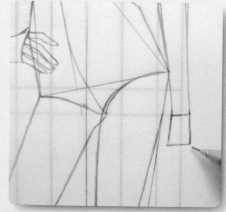

Draw the back of the hand.

35

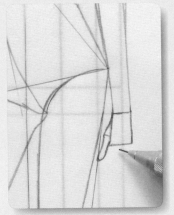

Draw the thumb, as if it is growing out of the wrist. 36

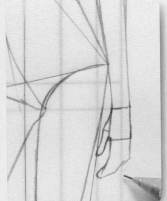

First draw the outline of four fingers together as if wearing a mitten. 37

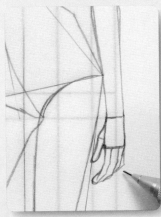

Draw as four fingers. 38

**Turned face**

Draw a line in the center of the face. 39

Draw guide lines for the balance of the face. 40

Draw each part of the face based on the guide lines. 41

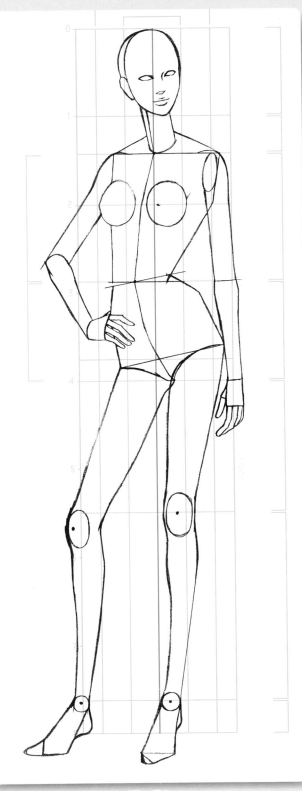

Erase unnecessary lines to complete the body sketch. 42

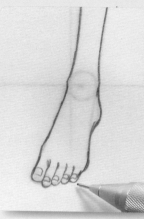

Draw each part smoothly with one line without breaking it.

When drawing the legs, always start with the supporting leg. Confirm its stability before adding the idle leg.

Draw the toes carefully as they play an essential role in determining the direction of the foot.

Drawing the fingers well will perfect the pose.

## Shading

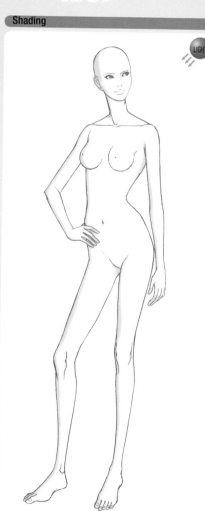

Cleaning up of the body outline is completed. Now add shading by setting the light source on the upper right facing the drawing. Add shading along the non-lit side outline of each part.

Add shading to the face and breasts while considering their volume to complete the shading.

## Phase 7 review

• The most important point is the tilted lower torso. Practice many times, while paying extra attention to the three elements; right angle, parallel and length in relation to the waistline, median line and hipline for stability of the moving torso.

• When giving movement to the body parts, you may draw such parts smaller due to lack of confidence. In this phase, pay attention to the lower torso as it is likely to become smaller.

• Be sure not to draw the legs too different in width.

• Try many different poses by moving the arm and face.

• As long as you keep the knees on the guide line passing through the center of the knee of the supporting leg, you can try a number of movements for the idle leg.

**Next, we will try to give movement to the upper half of the body!**

# The 2nd week

Let's Master Body Parts and
Garment Items Drawing

# Pose Variations

**Movements of the upper body**

In the last phases, we studied the body drawings by moving the lower half of the body, while fixing the upper half. In this phase, we study further to expand a variety of poses by moving the upper body.

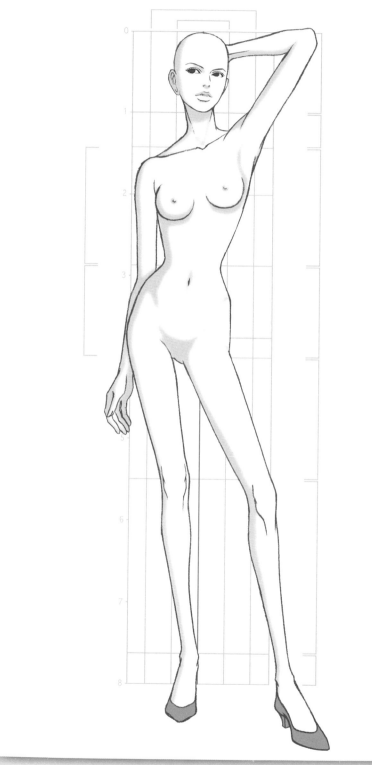

Frontal pose with weight on one leg with upper body movement

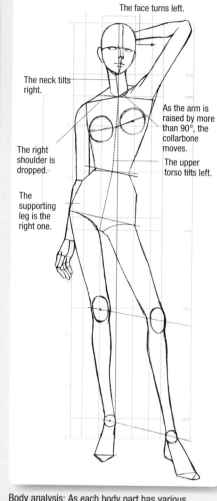

The face turns left.

The neck tilts right.

As the arm is raised by more than 90°, the collarbone moves.

The right shoulder is dropped.

The upper torso tilts left.

The supporting leg is the right one.

Body analysis: As each body part has various movements, confirm where they are.

**The median line is the key**

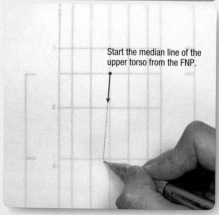

Start the median line of the upper torso from the FNP.

As the standing pose is drawn based on the central axis, draw by focusing on its starting point i.e. the FNP.

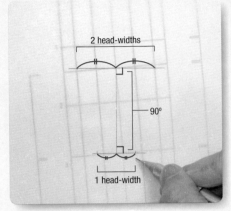

Draw the upper torso based on the median line. As it is frontal, make it symmetrical.

2 head-widths

90°

1 head-width

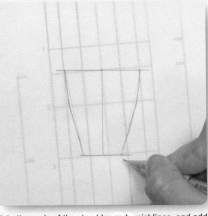

Join the ends of the shoulder and waist lines, and add roundness. It is angled but try to maintain a balanced form.

Draw the WL.

Draw as if it is growing out of the WP.

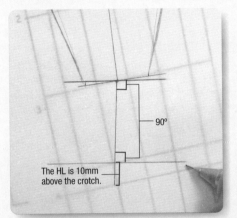

Draw the median line of the lower torso and HL.

90°

The HL is 10mm above the crotch.

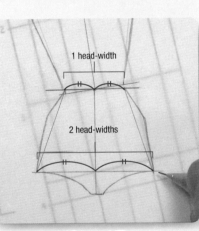

Complete the form of the lower torso. Be sure to make it symmetrical.

1 head-width

2 head-widths

**No change in the supporting/idle legs**

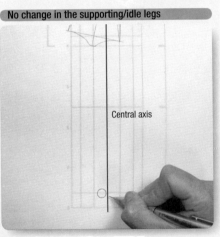

Establish the position of the supporting leg. Remember it is always near the central axis.

Central axis

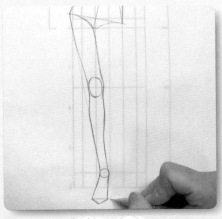

Draw the supporting leg.

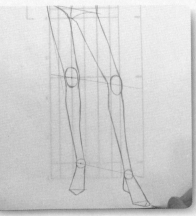

Draw the idle leg by first setting the position of the knee and ankle.

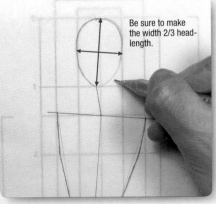

Draw the face on the median line.

Be sure to make the width 2/3 head-length.

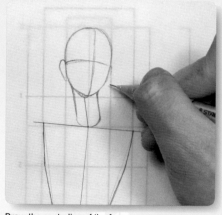

Draw the centerline of the face. **11**

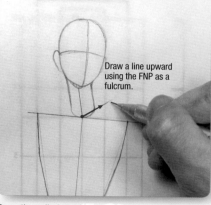

Draw a line upward using the FNP as a fulcrum.

Draw the collarbone in line with the angle of the raised arm. **12**

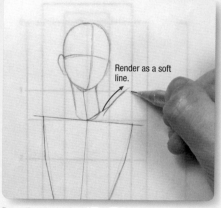

Render as a soft line.

Draw the shoulder muscle. **13**

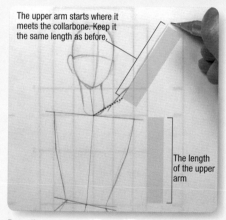

The upper arm starts where it meets the collarbone. Keep it the same length as before.

The length of the upper arm

Draw the upper arm. Be sure to keep the length the same as before. **14**

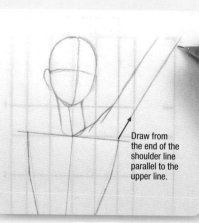

Draw from the end of the shoulder line parallel to the upper line.

Complete the upper arm. **15**

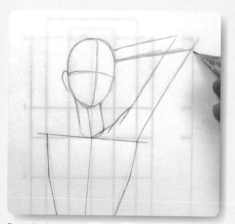

Draw the forearm slightly tapered. **16**

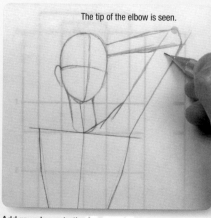

The tip of the elbow is seen.

Add roundness to the forearm. **17**

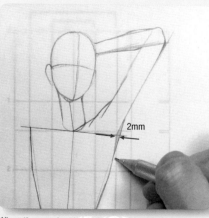

2mm

When the arm is raised, the shoulder blade is revealed. **18**

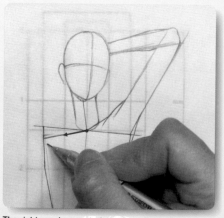

The right arm hangs straight down. Draw the collarbone downward using the FNP as a fulcrum. **19**

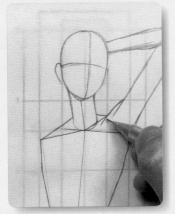

Draw both shoulder lines. **20**

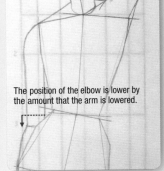

The position of the elbow is lower by the amount that the arm is lowered.

Draw the arm. **21**

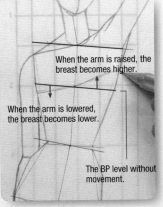

When the arm is raised, the breast becomes higher.

When the arm is lowered, the breast becomes lower.

The BP level without movement.

Each breast moves in line with the movement of the arms. **22**

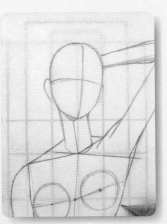

Draw the breasts based on the new guide lines. **23**

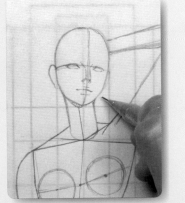

Draw the face. See p. 76-98 for more detail. **24**

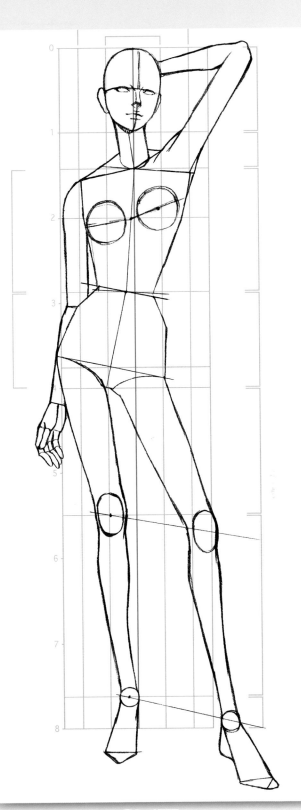

Completion of the body sketch. Clean up and add shading here to complete the nude body drawing. **25**

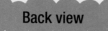

**Back view**

The designs of some garments focus on the back and buttock areas. We study the back view of the body here.

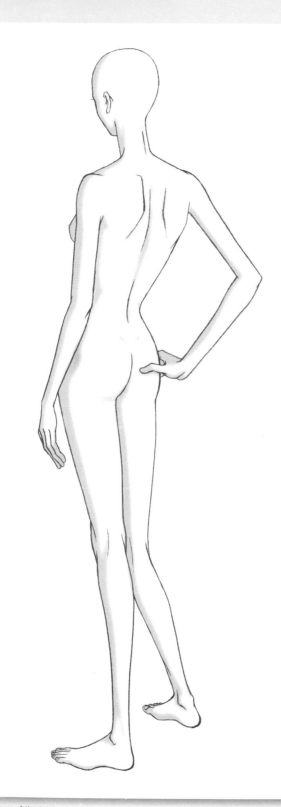

Back view of the body

---

**The silhouette is nearly the same**

Here, we use the diagonal pose with weight on one leg (supporting leg behind). Trace as is, as the front and back silhouettes are nearly the same.

**The back median line is a mirror image of the front**

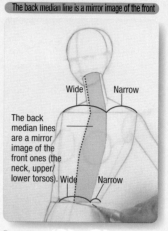

Wide   Narrow

The back median lines are a mirror image of the front ones (the neck, upper/lower torsos). Wide   Narrow

Draw the median lines of the nape of the neck, back and buttocks, which are called the back median lines.

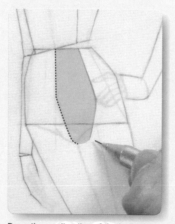

Draw the median line of the buttocks as a mirror image of the front. 03

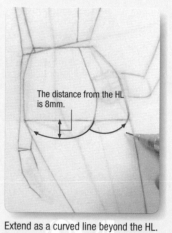

The distance from the HL is 8mm.

Extend as a curved line beyond the HL. 04

**The key is how to draw legs with more movements**

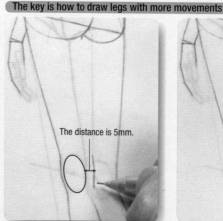

The distance is 5mm.

First establish the thickness of the knee. 05

Represent the thigh as a more or less straight line. 06

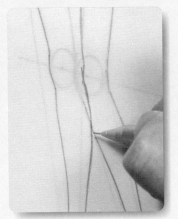

Draw the calf.

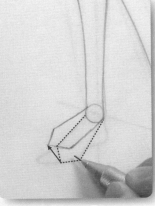

The feet vary significantly from the front view pose. First draw the main part, making it point slightly higher.

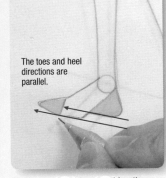

The toes and heel directions are parallel.

Add the heel and toes, making them point diagonally due to perspective.

Smaller and higher than the supporting leg.

As the idle leg is placed further from you, draw it higher and smaller than the supporting leg.

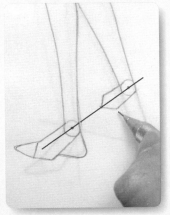

Draw the foot of the idle leg.

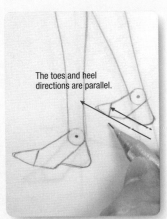

The toes and heel directions are parallel.

Add the heel and toes.

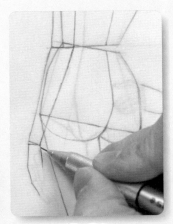

The arm further from you when seen from the front is closer to you here.

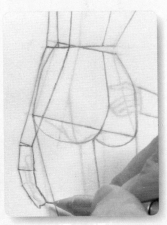

Trace the finger outline.

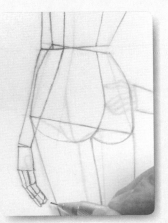

Seen from the back, the small finger is closest to you, while the thumb is hidden.

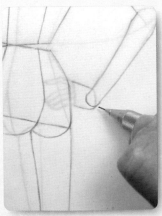

The arm closer to you when seen from the front is now further from you.

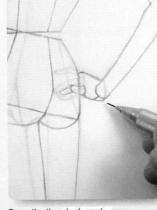

Draw the thumb closer to you.

**The ear and eyelashes complete the head**

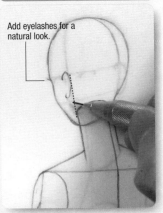

Add eyelashes for a natural look.

Draw the ear as if touching the line extending from the neck.

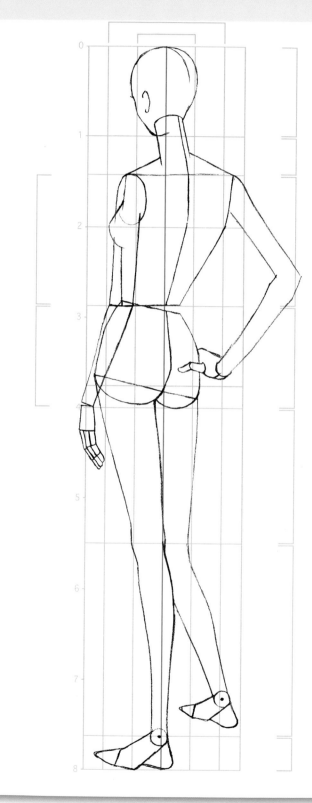

Completion of the body sketch.

19

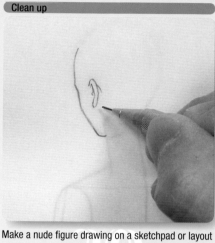

Make a nude figure drawing on a sketchpad or layout pad using the completed body sketch as an underlay. Create the softness of the human body by smoothing out the ragged lines at joints in the neck and waist areas.

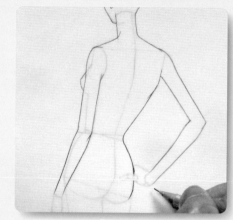

Roundness is the key for the buttock.

21

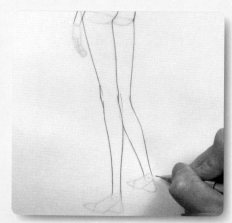

Draw the idle leg slightly thinner, as it is further from you.

22

74

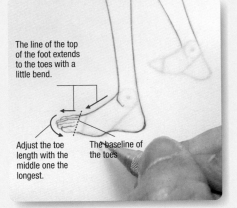

The line of the top of the foot extends to the toes with a little bend.

Adjust the toe length with the middle one the longest.

The baseline of the toes

Draw the feet carefully.

**23**

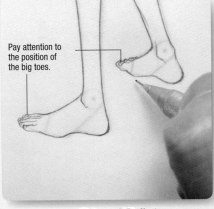

Pay attention to the position of the big toes.

Adding nails helps produce a 3-D effect.

**24**

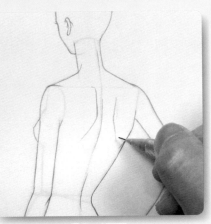

Highlight the shoulder blades as they are the key element for the back view drawing.

**25**

**Shading**

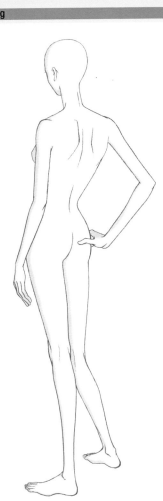

Cleaning up of the body outline is completed. Now add shading along the non-lit side outline of each part, by setting the light source on the upper right facing the drawing.

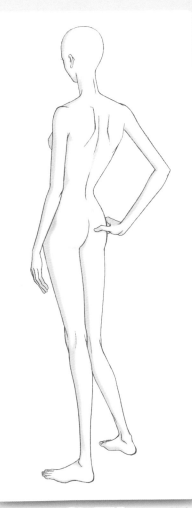

Add shading to the face and breasts while considering their volume to complete the shading.

**27**

### Phase 8 review
• The median line is the key for the upper body movements. Master its movements.
• The arms can be moved independently together with the collarbone using the FNP as a fulcrum.
• The breasts move up and down in line with the movement of the collarbone.
• The body's silhouette is the same for the front/back views. Focus on the direction of the feet only.

**Next, we will draw the face!**

# How to Draw the Face/Head

**Face/head variations based on its direction**

The face/head consists of several parts. Let's master their positional relationship.
*All measurements are based on the 60mm head-length.

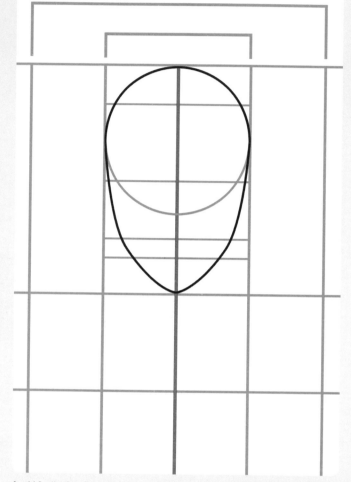

A grid for the face/head drawing exercise, indicating the positions of each part. Copy this to use as an underlay. The size of the face is made 60mm long, a little larger than that of normal fashion drawings, for practicing purposes.

**How to draw the face/head (frontal)**

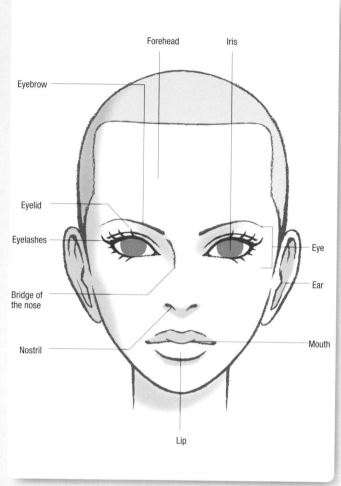

Forehead
Iris
Eyebrow
Eyelid
Eyelashes
Eye
Ear
Bridge of the nose
Nostril
Mouth
Lip

Full frontal face/head

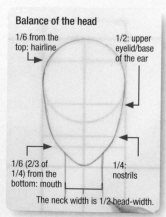

**Balance of the head**

1/6 from the top: hairline

1/2: upper eyelid/base of the ear

1/6 (2/3 of 1/4) from the bottom: mouth

1/4: nostrils

The neck width is 1/2 head-width.

Draw the outline of the head.

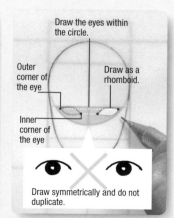

Draw the eyes within the circle.

Outer corner of the eye

Draw as a rhomboid.

Inner corner of the eye

Draw symmetrically and do not duplicate.

Draw the eyes symmetrically, with the upper eyelids touching the horizontal grid line. To achieve consistency, it is recommended to draw the eye on the non-drawing hand side first.

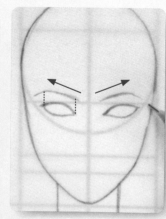

Draw the eyebrows wider than the eyelids.

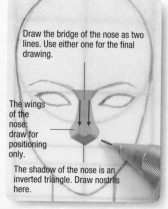

Draw the bridge of the nose as two lines. Use either one for the final drawing.

The wings of the nose: draw for positioning only.

The shadow of the nose is an inverted triangle. Draw nostrils here.

Draw the nose in the center of the face.

Draw the mouth a little wider than the eye.

Draw the lips as if drawing a leaf. Decide their thickness as you like.

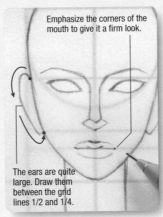

Emphasize the corners of the mouth to give it a firm look.

The ears are quite large. Draw them between the grid lines 1/2 and 1/4.

Add small curves on the top and bottom of the upper lip, and draw the ears.

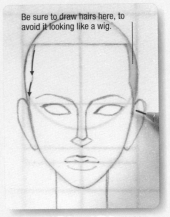

Be sure to draw hairs here, to avoid it looking like a wig.

Draw the hairline, temples and side hair.

The balance of the face/head is established.

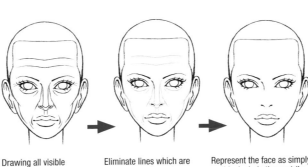

Drawing all visible lines creates an aged appearance.

Eliminate lines which are unnecessary for make-up.

Represent the face as simply as this. Include the nostrils to express the length of the nose and give a 3-D look.

When drawing the face, be sure to add only the lines required for make-up, i.e. those for the eyes/eyebrows, bridge of the nose and mouth. Do not draw the areas to which make-up is not applied or which are covered by make-up; e.g. wrinkles and bags under the eyes.

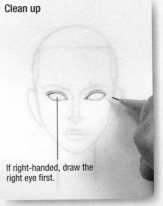

**Clean up**

If right-handed, draw the right eye first.

Draw the double-folded eyelids, starting with the one on the non-drawing hand side first to obtain consistency in size.

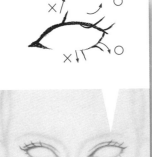

Draw the eyelashes. As they naturally grow downward and are made upward by an eyelash curler, draw the beginning part downward, and then turn them upward to finish.

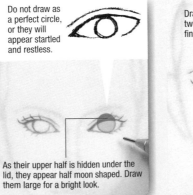

Do not draw as a perfect circle, or they will appear startled and restless.

As their upper half is hidden under the lid, they appear half moon shaped. Draw them large for a bright look.

Draw the irises as a half moon shape.

Draw the bridge of the nose as two lines. Use either one for the final drawing.

Draw the nostrils as a partial letter 'V'.

Draw the mouth. Key points are small curves at the corners and center.

Draw the lips.

Draw the face/head outline.

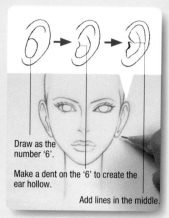

Draw as the number '6'.

Make a dent on the '6' to create the ear hollow.

Add lines in the middle.

Draw the ear in steps to complete the frontal face/head.

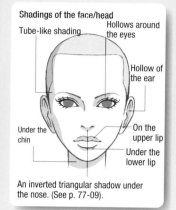

Shadings of the face/head

Tube-like shading | Hollows around the eyes

Hollow of the ear

Under the chin | On the upper lip

Under the lower lip

An inverted triangular shadow under the nose. (See p. 77-09).

Various shadings typical of the face/head are added simply without gradation.

How to draw the face/head (tilted upward)

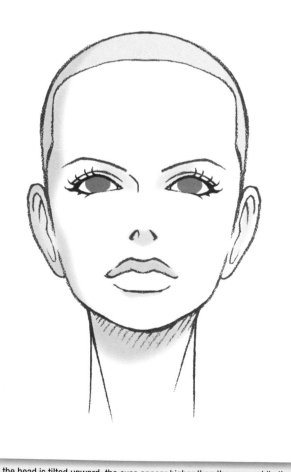

When the head is tilted upward, the eyes appear higher than the ears, while the chin appears shorter.

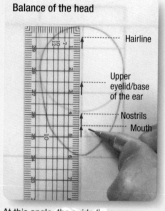

Balance of the head

Hairline

Upper eyelid/base of the ear

Nostrils
Mouth

At this angle, the guide lines are raised. First draw the outline of the head, and raise the original position of each part by 3mm.

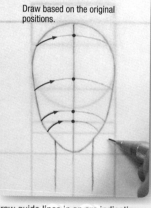

Draw based on the original positions.

Draw guide lines in an arc indicating the position of each part

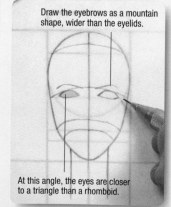

Draw the eyebrows as a mountain shape, wider than the eyelids.

At this angle, the eyes are closer to a triangle than a rhomboid.

Draw the eyes symmetrically with the upper eyelids touching the new grid line. To achieve consistency, draw the eye on the non-drawing hand side first.

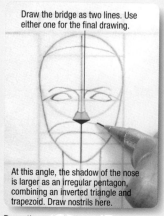

Draw the bridge as two lines. Use either one for the final drawing.

At this angle, the shadow of the nose is larger as an irregular pentagon, combining an inverted triangle and trapezoid. Draw nostrils here.

Draw the nose in the center of the face.

Draw the mouth a little wider than the eye.

**05**

Raise the chin by 3mm.

3mm

**06**

Draw the ears and side hair.

**07**

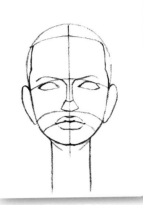

The balance of the head is established.

**08**

**Clean up**

When looking straight ahead.

When looking upward.

Upper half is hidden under the lid.

If right-handed, draw the right eye first.

Add only the lines required for make-up, starting with the eyes. Draw irises as ovals when looking upward to show perspective.

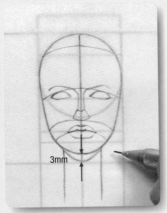

Draw the bridge as two lines. Use either one for the final drawing.

More visible when tilted upward. The triangles are more acute.

When drawing, represent the nostrils by their outline only.

Draw the nostrils as triangles.

**10**

Draw the mouth. Key points are small curves at the corners and center.

**11**

Draw the lips.

**12**

Draw the face/head outline.

**13**

Draw the neck.

**14**

**Shadings of the face/head**

Hollows around the eyes

Tube-like shading

Hollow of the ear

Under the chin

On the upper lip

Under the lower lip

An irregular pentagonal shadow under the nose. (See p. 79-08).

Various shadings typical of the face/head are added simply without gradation.

**15**

## How to draw the face/head (tilted downward)

When the head is tilted downward, the eyes appear lower than the ears while the chin appears shorter.

### Balance of the head

Draw based on the original position.

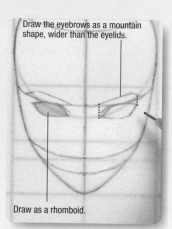

- Hairline
- Upper eyelid/base of ear
- Nostrils
- Mouth

At this angle, the guide lines also are lowered. First draw the outline of the head, and lower the original position of each part by 3mm, and draw guide lines in an arc.

Draw the eyebrows as a mountain shape, wider than the eyelids.

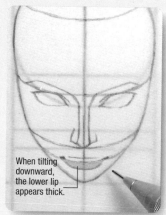

Draw as a rhomboid.

Draw the eyes symmetrically with the upper eyelids touching the new grid line. To achieve consistency, draw the eye on the non-drawing hand side first.

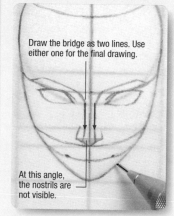

Draw the bridge as two lines. Use either one for the final drawing.

At this angle, the nostrils are not visible.

Draw the nose in the center of the face.

When tilting downward, the lower lip appears thick.

Draw the mouth a little wider than the eye.

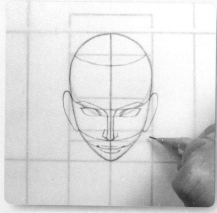

Draw the ears and side hair.

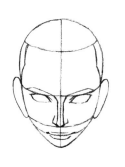

The balance of the face/head is completed.

### Clean up

Add only the lines required for make-up, starting with the eyes.

80

Half the iris is hidden.

Perfect circle

As this is a direct frontal view, draw the irises as perfect circles, showing only half with the other half hidden.

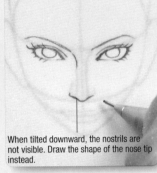

When tilted downward, the nostrils are not visible. Draw the shape of the nose tip instead.

Draw the nose. The bridge can be drawn as two lines. Use either one for the final drawing.

Draw the mouth. Key points are small curves at the corners and center.

Draw the lips.

Draw the face/head outline.

**Shadings of the face/head**

Tube-like shading

Hollows around the eyes

Hollow of the ear

Under the chin

On the upper lip

Under the lower lip

An inverted triangular shadow under the nose.

Various shadings typical of the face/head are added simply without gradation.

## How to draw the face/head (diagonal)

When the head turns diagonally, each part becomes subject to perspective. Some students draw the face at this angle by turning the nose only, while the rest remains frontal. Let us try to give perspective to each part; the eye, nose, mouth and the outline.

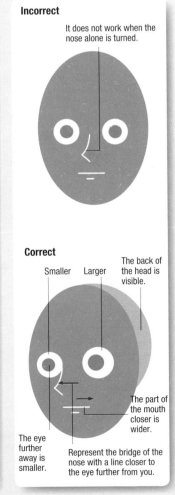

**Incorrect**

It does not work when the nose alone is turned.

**Correct**

Smaller   Larger

The back of the head is visible.

The part of the mouth closer is wider.

The eye further away is smaller.

Represent the bridge of the nose with a line closer to the eye further from you.

Perspective when diagonal

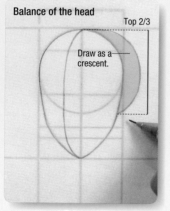

**Balance of the head**

Top 2/3

Draw as a crescent.

Add the outline of the back of the head.

**01**

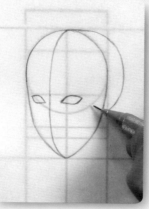

Draw the eyelids, representing the one further from you smaller, and the one closer larger.

**02**

Draw the eyebrows, also making the closer one wider.

**03**

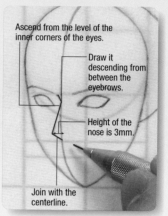

Ascend from the level of the inner corners of the eyes.

Draw it descending from between the eyebrows.

Height of the nose is 3mm.

Join with the centerline.

Draw the centerline of the nose.

**04**

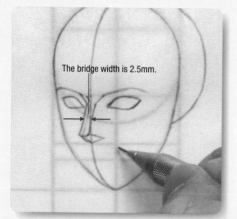

The bridge width is 2.5mm.

Draw the bridge of the nose based on the centerline.

**05**

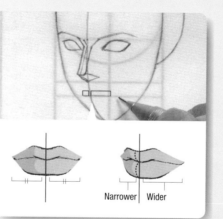

Narrower | Wider

Draw the mouth.

**06**

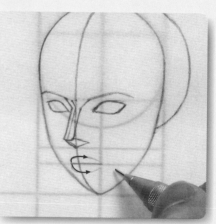

Draw the lips.

**07**

Add small curves on the top and bottom of the upper lip.

**08**

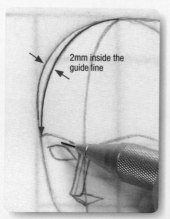

2mm inside the guide line

Draw the forehead.

**09**

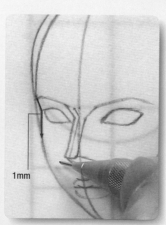

1mm

Draw the line dented at the eye.

**10**

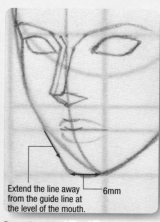

Extend the line away from the guide line at the level of the mouth.

6mm

Draw the chin.

**11**

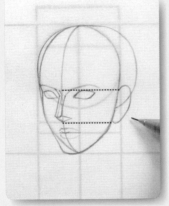

Draw the ears.

*12*

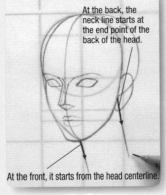

At the back, the neck line starts at the end point of the back of the head.

At the front, it starts from the head centerline.

Draw the neck.

*13*

Draw the hairline

*14*

Draw the side hair.

*15*

The balance of the face/head is established.

*16*

**Clean up**

Add only the lines required for make-up. Draw the double-eyelids first, starting with the one on the non-drawing hand side to achieve consistency.

*17*

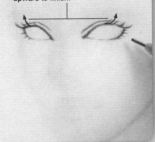

As they naturally grow downward and are made upward by an eyelash curler, draw the beginning part downward, and then turn them upward to finish.

Draw the eyelashes.

*18*

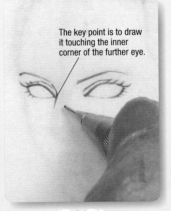

The key point is to draw it touching the inner corner of the further eye.

Draw the bridge of the nose.

*19*

The top half is hidden.

Draw the irises. As they are looking at us, make them perfect circles.

*20*

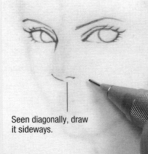

Seen diagonally, draw it sideways.

Draw the nostril.

*21*

With perspective, the part closer to you is wider.

Draw the mouth.

*22*

Draw the lips.

*23*

Draw the outline in a swift stroke from the forehead to chin.

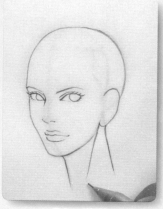

Draw the ear outline and neck.

Draw the inside of the ear and hairline to complete.

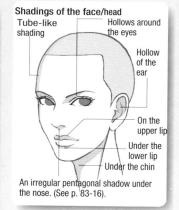

**Shadings of the face/head**
Tube-like shading
Hollows around the eyes
Hollow of the ear
On the upper lip
Under the lower lip
Under the chin
An irregular pentagonal shadow under the nose. (See p. 83-16).

Various shadings typical of the face/head are added simply without gradation.

## How to draw the face/head (tilted diagonally upward)

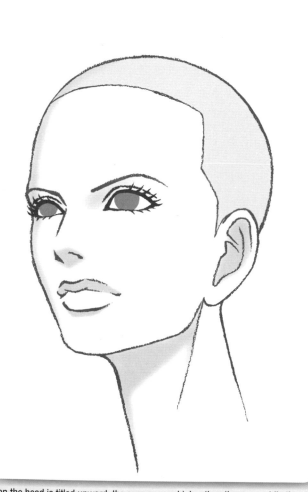

When the head is titled upward, the eyes appear higher than the ears, while the chin appears shorter.

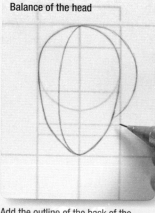

**Balance of the head**

Add the outline of the back of the head.

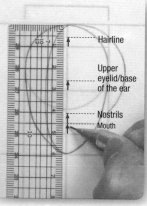

Hairline
Upper eyelid/base of the ear
Nostrils
Mouth

At this angle, the guide lines are raised. First draw the outline of the head, and raise the original position of each part by 3mm.

Draw guide lines. The above cross-section shows that they curve at the outer corner of the eye.

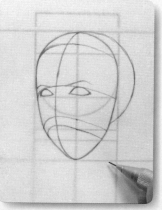

Draw the eyelids and eyebrows, making the one further from you smaller, and the one closer larger.

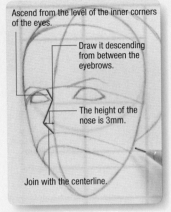

Ascend from the level of the inner corners of the eyes.

Draw it descending from between the eyebrows.

The height of the nose is 3mm.

Join with the centerline.

Draw the centerline of the nose.

*05*

Draw the bridge of the nose based on the centerline, 2.5mm wide.

*06*

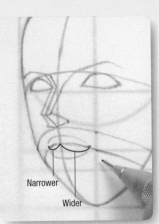

Narrower

Wider

Draw the mouth.

*07*

Add small curves on the top and bottom of the upper lip.

*08*

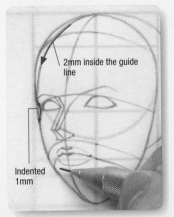

2mm inside the guide line

Indented 1mm

Draw the forehead and dented line at the eye.

*09*

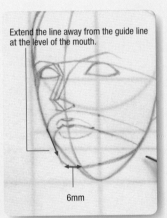

Extend the line away from the guide line at the level of the mouth.

6mm

Draw the chin.

*10*

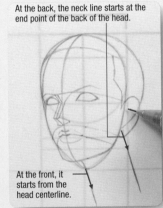

At the back, the neck line starts at the end point of the back of the head.

At the front, it starts from the head centerline.

Draw the side hair, ear and neck.

*11*

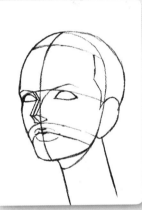

The balance of the head is established.

*12*

Clean up

Add only the lines required for make-up, starting with the eyes. To achieve consistency, draw the eye on the non-drawing hand side first.

Draw the irises as ovals to show perspective.

*14*

The key point is to draw it touching the inner corner of the further eye.

Draw the nostrils as a partially inverted 'V'.

Draw the bridge of the nose.

*15*

Narrower   Wider

Draw the mouth. With perspective, the part closer to you is wider.

*16*

Draw the lips. **17**

Draw the outline in a swift stroke from the forehead to chin. Complete by drawing the ear and hairline. **18**

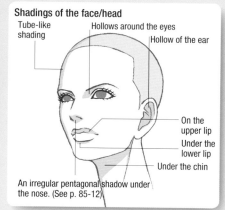

### Shadings of the face/head

Tube-like shading

Hollows around the eyes

Hollow of the ear

On the upper lip

Under the lower lip

Under the chin

An irregular pentagonal shadow under the nose. (See p. 85-12)

Various shadings typical of the face/head are added simply without gradation. **19**

---

**How to draw the face/head (seen diagonally from above)**

When the head is seen diagonally from above, the eyes appear lower than the ears while the chin appears shorter.

### Balance of the head

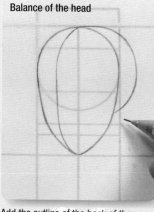

Add the outline of the back of the head. **01**

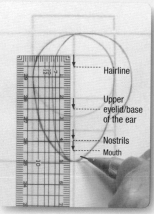

Hairline

Upper eyelid/base of the ear

Nostrils

Mouth

At this angle, the guide lines are lowered. First draw the outline of the head, and lower the original position of each part by 3mm. **02**

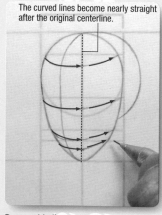

The curved lines become nearly straight after the original centerline.

Draw guide lines. **03**

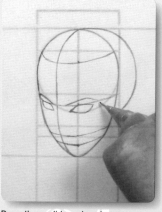

Draw the eyelids and eyebrows, making the ones closer larger. **04**

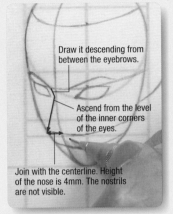

Draw it descending from between the eyebrows.

Ascend from the level of the inner corners of the eyes.

Join with the centerline. Height of the nose is 4mm. The nostrils are not visible.

Draw the centerline of the nose.

**05**

Draw the bridge of the nose based on the centerline, 2.5mm wide.

**06**

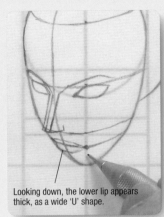

Looking down, the lower lip appears thick, as a wide 'U' shape.

Draw the mouth.

**07**

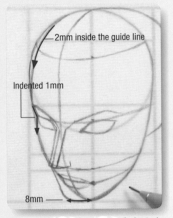

2mm inside the guide line

Indented 1mm

8mm

Draw a line from the forehead, dented at the eye and extending to the chin.

**08**

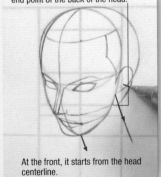

At the back, the neck line starts at the end point of the back of the head.

At the front, it starts from the head centerline.

Draw the side hair, ear and neck.

**09**

The balance of the head is established.

**10**

Clean up

Add only the lines required for make-up, starting with the eyes. To achieve consistency, draw the eye on the non-drawing hand side first.

The key point is to draw it touching the inner corner of the further eye.

The nostrils are not visible.

Draw the bridge of the nose.

**12**

Narrower

Wider

Draw the mouth. With perspective, the part closer to you is wider.

**13**

Draw the outline in a swift stroke from the forehead to chin.

**14**

Complete by drawing the ear, hairline and neck.

**15**

Shadings of the face/head

Tube-like shading

Hollow around the eye

Hollow of the ear

On the upper lip

Under the lower lip

Under the chin

A small shadow under the nose. (See 10 above)

Various shadings typical of the face/head are added simply without gradation.

**16**

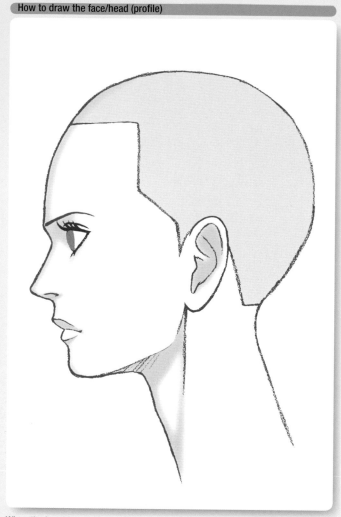

When the head is seen in profile, the chin line becomes prominent, with the ear and back of the head clearly visible, while the eye and mouth are less noticeable as their sizes are reduced to half those seen frontal.

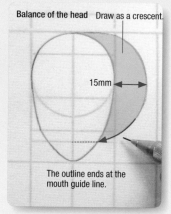

Balance of the head   Draw as a crescent.

15mm

The outline ends at the mouth guide line.

Add the outline of the back of the head. 01

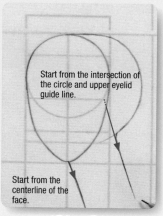

Start from the intersection of the circle and upper eyelid guide line.

Start from the centerline of the face.

Draw the neck a little wider than 1/2 head-width. 02

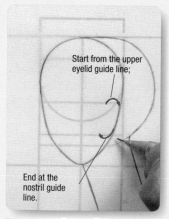

Start from the upper eyelid guide line;

End at the nostril guide line.

Draw the ear so that it will fit inside the oval outline. 03

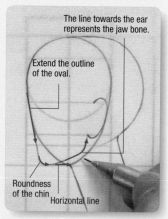

The line towards the ear represents the jaw bone.

Extend the outline of the oval.

Roundness of the chin

Horizontal line

Draw the chin. 04

Draw 3mm inside.

Draw the forehead. 05

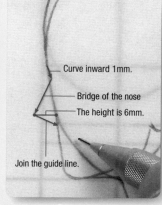

Curve inward 1mm.

Bridge of the nose

The height is 6mm.

Join the guide line.

Draw the nose. 06

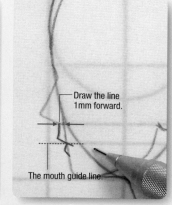

Draw the line 1mm forward.

The mouth guide line.

Draw the mouth. 07

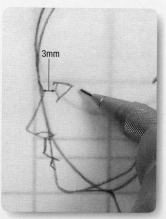

3mm

Draw the eye as a triangle. 08

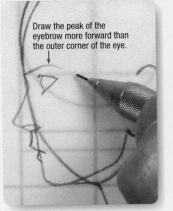

Draw the peak of the eyebrow more forward than the outer corner of the eye.

Draw the eyebrow.

**09**

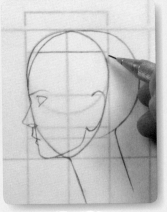

Draw the hairline.

**10**

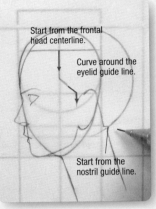

Start from the frontal head centerline.

Curve around the eyelid guide line.

Start from the nostril guide line.

Draw the side hair and nape of the neck.

**11**

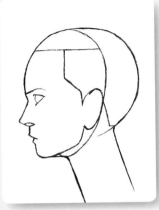

The balance of the head is established.

**12**

**Clean up**

Add only the lines required for make-up. For the profile, start with the face outline.

**13**

Add the head outline in one stroke.

**14**

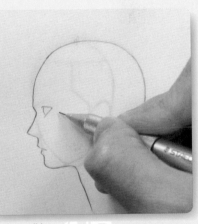

Draw the eyelid.

**15**

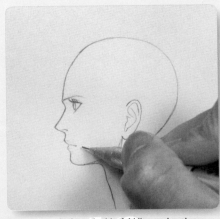

Draw the eyelashes, double-fold line and eyebrow.

**16**

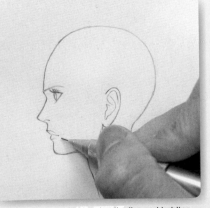

Complete clean-up by drawing the lips and hairline.

**17**

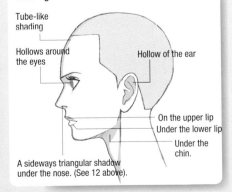

**Shadings of the face/head**

Tube-like shading

Hollows around the eyes

Hollow of the ear

On the upper lip

Under the lower lip

Under the chin.

A sideways triangular shadow under the nose. (See 12 above).

Various shadings typical of the face/head are added simply without gradation.

**18**

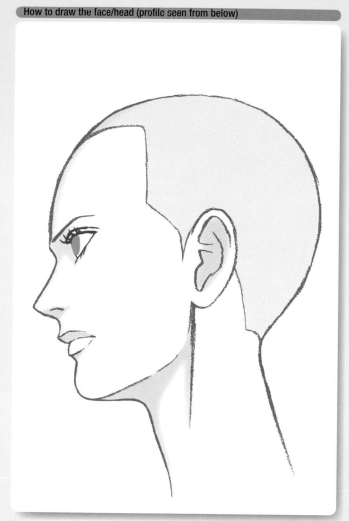

When the profile is seen from below, the eye and ear appear higher, while the root of the nose appears lower than the eye.

## Balance of the head

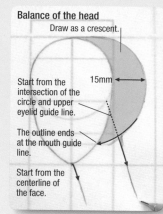

Draw as a crescent.

Start from the intersection of the circle and upper eyelid guide line.

15mm

The outline ends at the mouth guide line.

Start from the centerline of the face.

Add the outline of the back of the head and neck. **01**

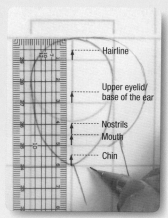

Hairline

Upper eyelid/ base of the ear

Nostrils
Mouth

Chin

At this angle, the guide lines are raised. First draw the outline of the head, and raise the original position of each part by 3mm.

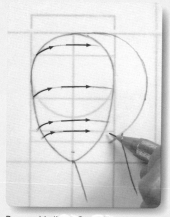

Draw guide lines. Curved lines starting at each guide line become straight near the centerline. **03**

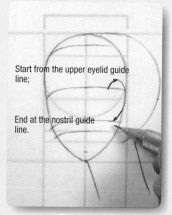

Start from the upper eyelid guide line;

End at the nostril guide line.

Draw the ear so that it will fit inside the oval outline. **04**

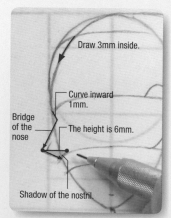

Draw 3mm inside.

Curve inward 1mm.

Bridge of the nose

The height is 6mm.

Shadow of the nostril.

Draw the outline of the forehead towards the nose. **05**

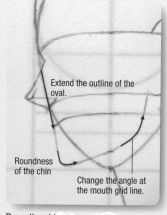

Extend the outline of the oval.

Roundness of the chin

Change the angle at the mouth grid line.

Draw the chin. **06**

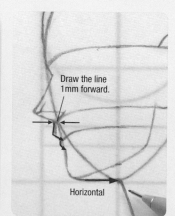

Draw the line 1mm forward.

Horizontal

Join and extend the mouth line to the neck. **07**

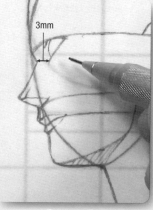

3mm

Draw the eye as a triangle. **08**

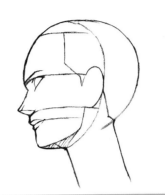

Complete the balance of the head by drawing the hairline, side hair and nape of the neck.

**Clean up**

Add only the lines required for make-up. For the profile, start with the face outline.

Draw the eye and mouth.

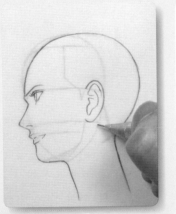

Complete clean-up by drawing the ear and hairline.

**How to draw the face/head (profile seen from above)**

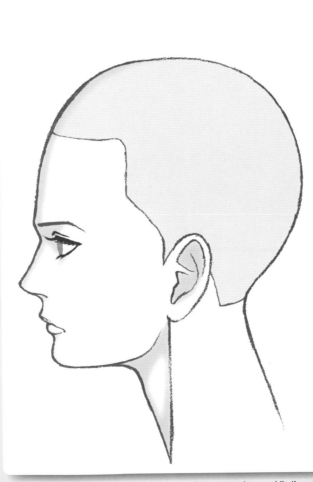

When the profile is seen from above, the eye and ear appear lower while the root of the nose appears higher than the eye.

**Balance of the head**

Draw as a crescent.

Start from the intersection of the circle and upper eyelid guide line.

15mm

The outline ends at the mouth guide line.

Start from the centerline of the face.

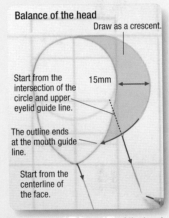

Add the outline of the back of the head and neck.

**Shadings of the face/head**

Tube-like shading

Hollow around the eye

Hollow of the ear

On the upper lip

Under the lower lip

Under the chin

A sideways triangular shadow under the nose. (See 09 above).

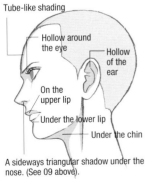

Various shadings typical of the face/head are added simply without gradation.

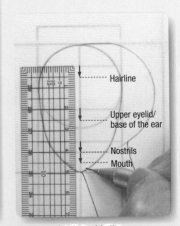

Hairline

Upper eyelid/base of the ear

Nostrils

Mouth

At this angle, the guide lines are lowered. First draw the outline of the head, and lower the original position of each part by 3mm.

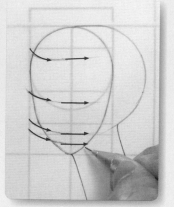

Draw guide lines. Curved lines starting at each guide line become straight near the centerline.

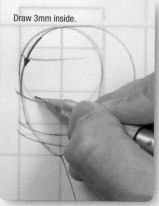

Draw 3mm inside.

Draw the outline of the forehead towards the nose.

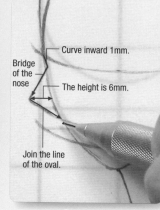

Curve inward 1mm.

Bridge of the nose

The height is 6mm.

Join the line of the oval.

Draw the nose.

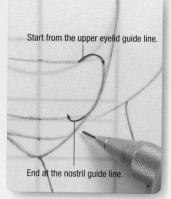

Start from the upper eyelid guide line.

End at the nostril guide line.

Draw the ear so that it will fit inside the oval outline.

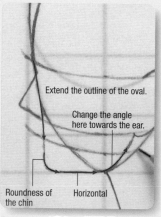

Extend the outline of the oval.

Change the angle here towards the ear.

Roundness of the chin    Horizontal

Draw the chin.

Draw the line 1mm forward.

Draw the mouth.

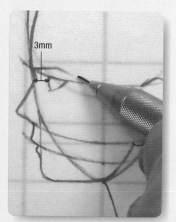

3mm

Draw the eye as a triangle.

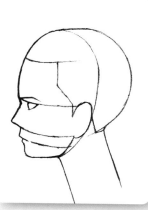

Complete the balance of the head by drawing the hairline, side hair and nape of the neck.

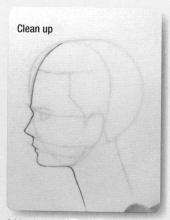

Clean up

Add only the lines required for make-up. For the profile, start with the face outline.

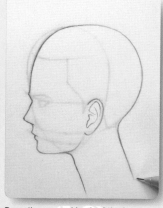

Draw the eye and back of the head.

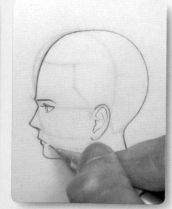

Complete clean-up by drawing the eye, mouth and hairline.

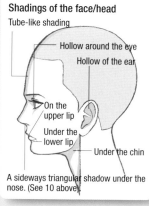

Shadings of the face/head

Tube-like shading

Hollow around the eye

Hollow of the ear

On the upper lip

Under the lower lip

Under the chin

A sideways triangular shadow under the nose. (See 10 above).

Various shadings typical of the face/head are added simply without gradation.

## Hairstyles

Once you have mastered the face/head drawing, the next is various hairstyles. There are three key points.

Hair volume (silhouette): Establish the silhouette by drawing the volume of hair lifted away from the skin, while avoiding the look of wet hair sticking to the head.

Draw the flow of hair with a unit of 100 hairs per band to enable easy coloring Do not try to draw the hairs one by one to fill such bands.

Be sure to taper the tips of the hair.

Key points for drawing hair.

**How to draw straight hair**

With bangs, this hairstyle shows the bands of highlight most effectively.

Bands of highlight (or angel's halo) are seen on beautiful shiny hair. Represent them in an arc on the oval shaped head.

Apply in an arc, with a constant space.

**Outline**

Using 'the balance of the head' as an underlay, draw the face.

**01**

Draw the bangs.

**02**

Allow volume, to avoid a wet and 'just taken a bath' look.

Add some stray hair to give movement.

Draw the outline of the hair.

**03**

Draw so that some hair falls on the chest.

*04*

**Flow of hair** Add some openings to give movement.

First, draw hair flow lines toward the tips.

Taper the tips to give movement.

Draw the hair flow line.

*05*

Complete by drawing the overall hair flow lines.

*06*

The bottom of the bangs is in an upward arc.

An example of the hairstyle with the head tilted upward, drawn the same way.

*07*

The bottom of the bangs is in a downward arc.

An example of the hairstyle with the head tilted downward, drawn the same way.

*08*

**How to draw wavy hair**

The key is to master how to represent the waves. Apply highlights on the high points of the waves.

**Outline**

Using 'the balance of the head' as an underlay, draw the face and bangs. 01

Allow volume, to avoid a wet and 'just taken a bath' look.

Add some stray hair to give movement.

Draw the outline of the hair. 02

Flow of hair

Place hair behind the ear.

Show the ear.

Draw the hair flow line. First on the less wavy front hair. 03

Create the main flow of hair, alternating direction of the waves. 04

Draw hair flow lines in the waves. 05

Complete by adding some small stray hairs. 06

The key is the side hair.

The key is the extremely large hair volume. The light reflects irregularly as the hair curls in all directions. Add wavering bands of highlight all over.

### The outline and hair flow

Taper the tips in an acutely-angled 'V'.

Draw the front and side hair as if they are growing from the hairline.

Complete by drawing the hair flow lines.

Outline

Using 'the balance of the head' as an underlay, draw the face.

*01*

Draw the front hair.

*02*

Establish the volume of the curls.

*03*

Draw by alternating the direction of the curls.

Draw the edge of the hair by linking the small curls.

*04*

Flow of hair

Draw the hair flow line. First on the less curly front hair.

*05*

Create the main flow of curls, while alternating their direction.

*06*

Erase the guide line.

*07*

Complete by filling the overall hair with additional curls by making them double.

*08*

The movement of the eyes, nose and mouth change according to our emotion. Let's study how each facial part changes with different expressions, for example when posing or smiling.

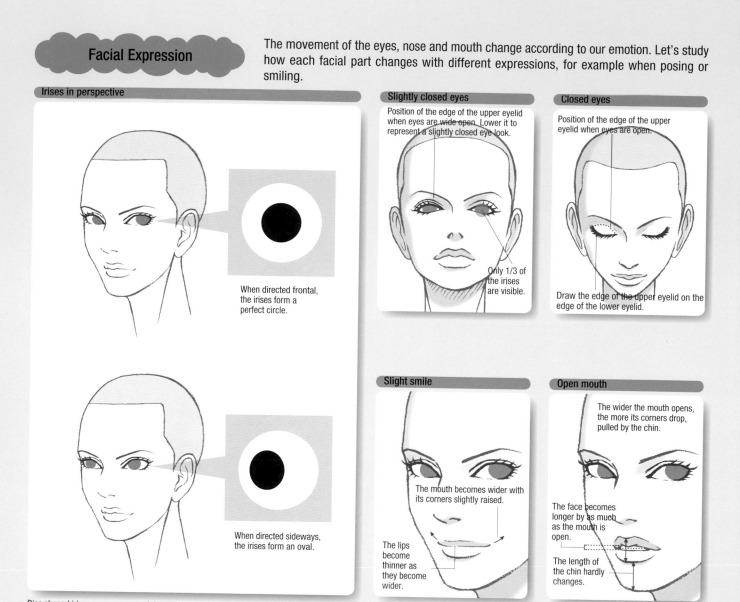

**Irises in perspective**

When directed frontal, the irises form a perfect circle.

When directed sideways, the irises form an oval.

Disc shaped irises may appear oval due to perspective depending on their direction.

**Slightly closed eyes**

Position of the edge of the upper eyelid when eyes are wide open. Lower it to represent a slightly closed eye look.

Only 1/3 of the irises are visible.

**Closed eyes**

Position of the edge of the upper eyelid when eyes are open.

Draw the edge of the upper eyelid on the edge of the lower eyelid.

**Slight smile**

The mouth becomes wider with its corners slightly raised.

The lips become thinner as they become wider.

**Open mouth**

The wider the mouth opens, the more its corners drop, pulled by the chin.

The face becomes longer by as much as the mouth is open.

The length of the chin hardly changes.

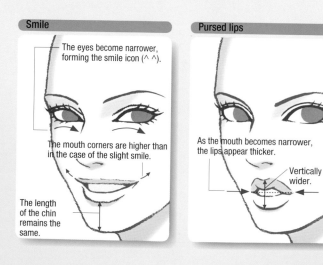

**Smile**

The eyes become narrower, forming the smile icon (^ ^).

The mouth corners are higher than in the case of the slight smile.

The length of the chin remains the same.

**Pursed lips**

As the mouth becomes narrower, the lips appear thicker.

Vertically wider.

## Phase 9 review

- Represent the face as simply as possible, by drawing the parts and lines essential for make-up.
- The basic shape is oval. First, draw the full-frontal view sufficiently to master the balance of the facial parts.
- As the eyes are an especially expressive facial element, make many drawings to master them and find the ones you like.
- Take your time and study little by little regarding the drawing of the facial expression and hairstyles.

**Next, we will make the technical drawing!**
**Observe carefully the garment structure.**

# Technical Drawing 1: Bottoms

A technical drawing is a flat illustration depicting the form and structure of a garment, basically consisting of the front and back. Unlike so-called fashion or design drawings which focus on overall coordination and styling, technical drawings represent the technical details of a garment. Let's master how to draw them precisely, using rulers whenever necessary.

## Four important reminders regarding the technical drawing:

1. Draw garments symmetrically. → Method →First draw the left or right half of the garment and copy it for the other half.

2. Place importance on the garment's length and volume. → Method →Always use the technical drawing guide based on the same body as an underlay.

3. Do not draw creases. → Method →Draw mostly in straight lines using a ruler, ignoring garment creases, except those intended in the design (e.g. gathers, flares and drapes).

4. Clearly represent the composition of garment parts. → Method →Carefully observe the garment details.

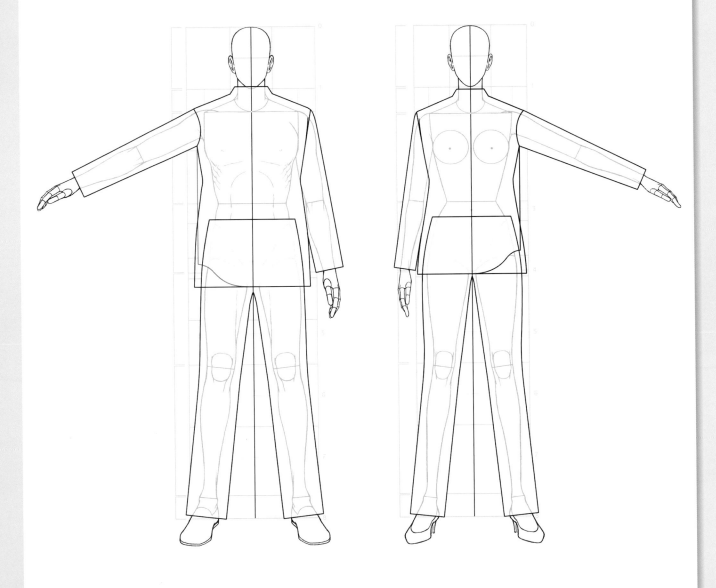

Base drawing for technical drawings:
Enlarge to 150% so that the top is 80mm long and use it as an underlay for technical drawings ('the technical drawing guide').

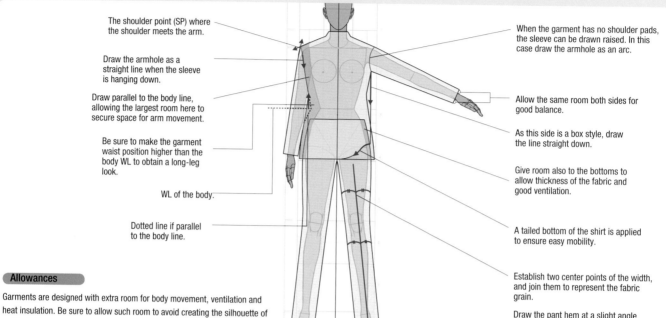

The shoulder point (SP) where the shoulder meets the arm.

Draw the armhole as a straight line when the sleeve is hanging down.

Draw parallel to the body line, allowing the largest room here to secure space for arm movement.

Be sure to make the garment waist position higher than the body WL to obtain a long-leg look.

WL of the body.

Dotted line if parallel to the body line.

When the garment has no shoulder pads, the sleeve can be drawn raised. In this case draw the armhole as an arc.

Allow the same room both sides for good balance.

As this side is a box style, draw the line straight down.

Give room also to the bottoms to allow thickness of the fabric and good ventilation.

A tailed bottom of the shirt is applied to ensure easy mobility.

Establish two center points of the width, and join them to represent the fabric grain.

Draw the pant hem at a slight angle meeting perpendicular to the fabric grain.

### Allowances

Garments are designed with extra room for body movement, ventilation and heat insulation. Be sure to allow such room to avoid creating the silhouette of a skin-tight wetsuit.

## Skirt 1 (Flared)

The name 'flare' is derived from the flare of the sun. The key point is how to render the wavy flares of the skirt hem.

**Preparation**

Prepare a sheet of transparent paper e.g. layout paper, and make a valley fold.

Open the paper.

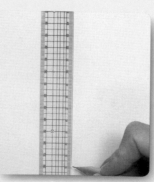

Draw a line on the fold and make it the garment's front center. Be sure to use a pencil with a B or softer lead.

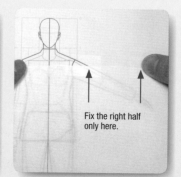

Fix the right half only here.

Place the paper on the technical drawing guide, aligning with the front center, and fix the side to be drawn only with mending tape.

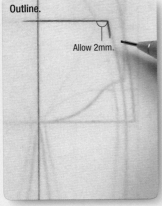

Outline.

Allow 2mm.

Draw the WL.

**05**

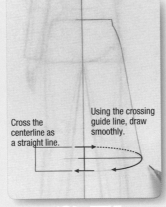

Start with a straight line.

Curve the line gently outward towards the hem.

Draw the flares.

**06**

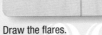

Cross the centerline as a straight line.

Using the crossing guide line, draw smoothly.

Draw the hem, imagining the skirt on a hanger. First draw a half oval.

**07**

Draw the flared hem.

**08**

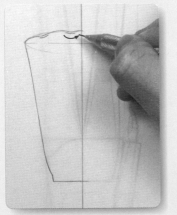

Draw with a few curves for a 3-D effect. Turn the paper upside-down for easy drawing.

**09**

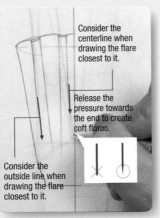

Consider the centerline when drawing the flare closest to it.

Release the pressure towards the end to create soft flares.

Consider the outside line when drawing the flare closest to it.

Draw the flare lines radially.

**10**

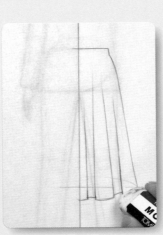

Erase unnecessary lines.

**11**

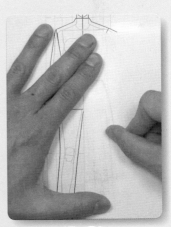

Fold the paper in half and transfer the drawn lines by strongly rubbing the reverse side with a fingernail or the like.

**12**

Open the paper to confirm the transfer. Be sure to use a pencil with a B or softer lead for successful transfer.

**13**

Check both the left and right sides of the overall outline. In this case, as more volume at the hem was preferred, additional flares were drawn.

**14**

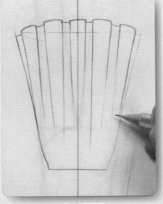

When adjusted, strengthen the transferred thin lines.

**15**

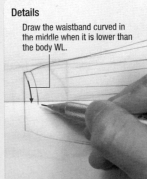

Details

Draw the waistband curved in the middle when it is lower than the body WL.

Draw the waistband.

**16**

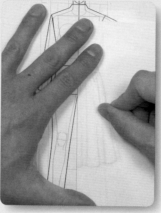

Draw them to go well with the flares.

Alternate check marks and tapered lines.

Do not leave too much space between flares and gather lines. Alternate and mix them for a natural look.

Add gather lines. *17*

Fold the paper in half and transfer the drawn lines by strongly rubbing the reverse side with a fingernail or the like. *18*

Strengthen the transferred thin lines. *19*

Complete by adding nonsymmetrical details. *20*

## Skirt 2 (Pleated)

Pleated skirt

**Outline**

Place the paper on the technical drawing guide, aligning with the front center, and draw the skirt outline. *01*

**Details**

Draw the pleats. Based on the 9 front pleats, establish their position by dividing half of the hem by 4.5. *02*

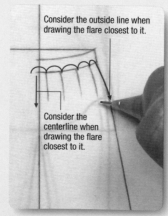

Consider the outside line when drawing the flare closest to it.

Consider the centerline when drawing the flare closest to it.

Draw the pleats at the waist. *03*

Join the top and bottom pleats using a ruler. *04*

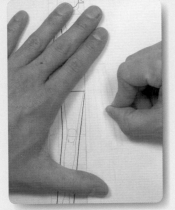

Fold the paper in half and transfer the drawn lines by strongly rubbing the reverse side with a fingernail or the like.

Open the paper to confirm the transfer. Be sure to use a pencil with a B or softer lead for successful transfer.

*05*

*06*

Strengthen the transferred thin lines.

*07*

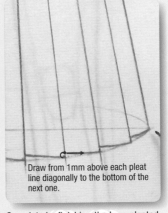

Draw from 1mm above each pleat line diagonally to the bottom of the next one.

Complete by finishing the hem pleated in one direction.

*08*

## Pants

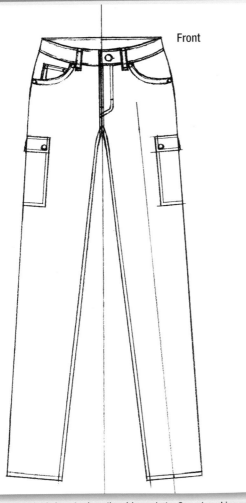

Front

Work pants: The key point is how to draw the side pockets. Casual working pants are drawn with legs wide apart (open stance), while the formal and business types are drawn with legs closer together (closed stance).

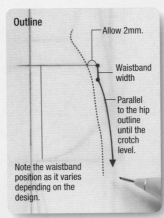

Outline

Allow 2mm.

Waistband width

Parallel to the hip outline until the crotch level.

Note the waistband position as it varies depending on the design.

Place the paper on the technical drawing guide, aligning with the front center, and draw the pants outline.

*01*

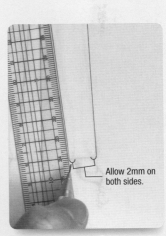

Allow 2mm on both sides.

As these are straight pants, draw the line straight down from the HL.

*02*

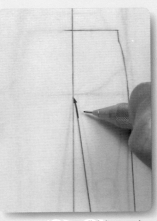

Draw the crotch area slightly curved.

*03*

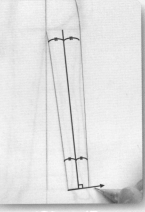

Draw the hem at a slight angle meeting perpendicular to the fabric grain.

*04*

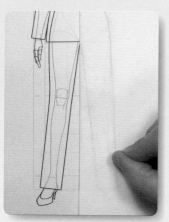

Fold the paper in half and transfer the drawn lines by strongly rubbing the reverse side with a fingernail or the like.

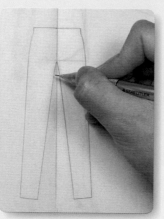

**06** Strengthen the transferred thin lines.

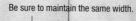
Be sure to maintain the same width.

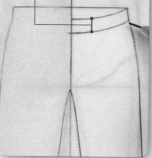

**07** Draw the waistband, curved at the front.

Add the loop perpendicular to the band.

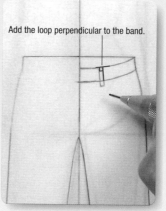

**08** Draw the belt loop.

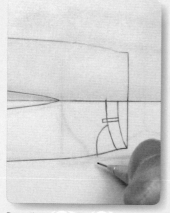

**09** Draw the pocket. The one shown here is an "L-pocket", common for denim and work pants.

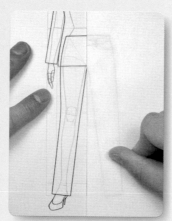

**10** Fold the paper in half and transfer the details by rubbing the reverse side.

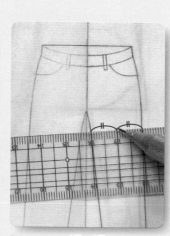

**11** Draw the side pocket. The one shown here is an "L-pocket", common for denim and work pants. First draw the fabric grain, by marking the center point of the width.

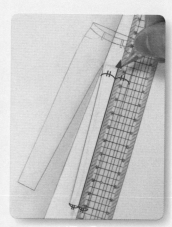

**12** Establish two center points of the width, and join them to represent the fabric grain.

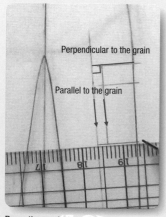

Perpendicular to the grain

Parallel to the grain

**13** Draw the pocket parallel and perpendicular to the fabric grains.

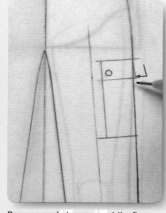

**14** Draw an angle to represent the flap.

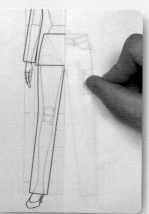

**15** Fold the paper in half and transfer the pocket by rubbing the reverse side.

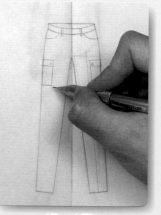

**16** Strengthen the transferred thin lines.

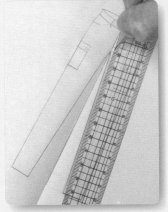

Draw the inseam parallel to the outline.

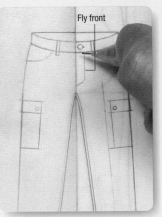

Draw the front button and fly front.

Add the coin pocket.

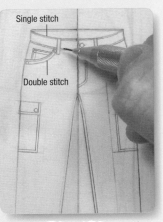

Add stitches with the same intervals. Draw either single or double stitches accordingly.

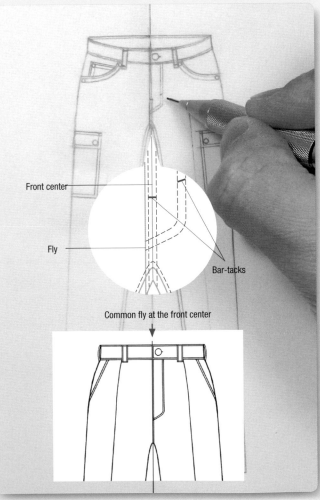

Front center

Fly

Bar-tacks

Common fly at the front center

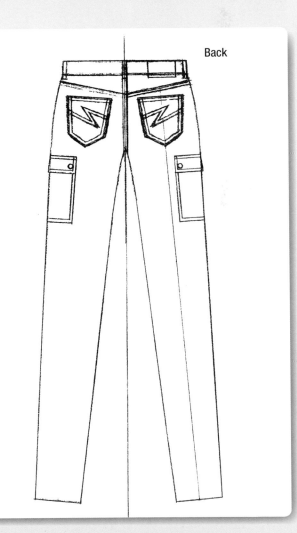

Back

The fly commonly appears at the front center, but in the case of denim pants, both sides of the front fabric often overlap at the center, as the flat fell seam is applied to ensure durability.

As the front and back share the same silhouette, transfer half of the front drawing by rubbing from the reverse side.

Strengthen the transferred thin lines.

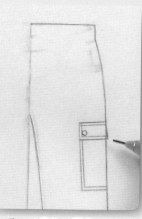

Draw the symmetrical details, starting with the pocket.

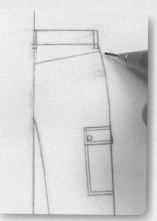

Add the waistband and yoke.

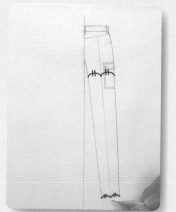

Draw the fabric grain first when drawing the hip pocket.

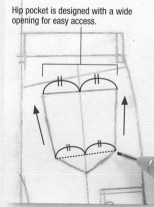

Hip pocket is designed with a wide opening for easy access.

Draw a symmetrical pentagon centering the grain.

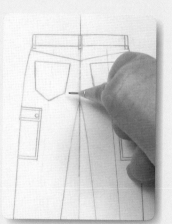

Fold the paper in half and transfer the pocket by rubbing the reverse side.

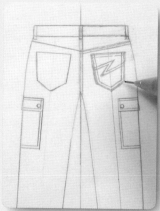

Add the stitches.

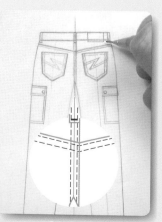

Complete by drawing the leather label.

## Phase 10 review

• Represent the subtle changes of length and volume, using the technical drawing guide as an underlay.

• Focus on the symmetrical elements.

• Confirm their structure, by carefully observing actual garments.

**Next, we will make technical drawings of tops!**

# Technical Drawing 2: Tops

**Shirt**

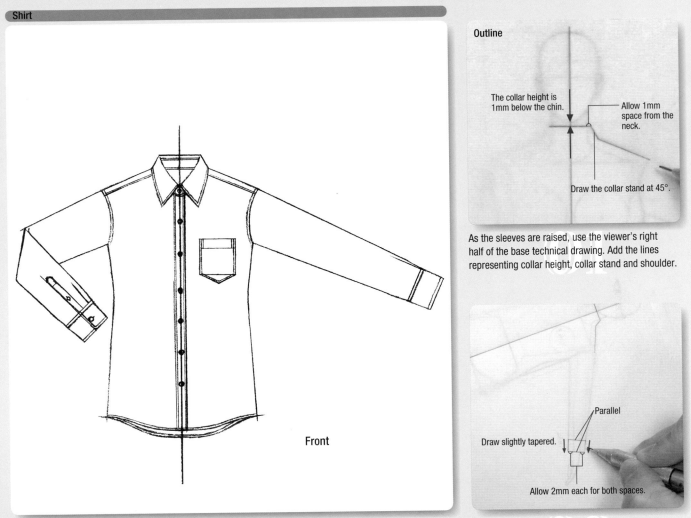

Front

As shirts usually have no shoulder pads, the sleeves are raised when laid flat.

**Outline**

The collar height is 1mm below the chin.

Allow 1mm space from the neck.

Draw the collar stand at 45°.

As the sleeves are raised, use the viewer's right half of the base technical drawing. Add the lines representing collar height, collar stand and shoulder.

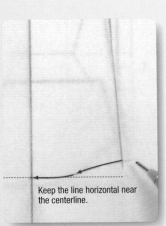

Parallel

Draw slightly tapered.

Allow 2mm each for both spaces.

Draw the cuff. 02

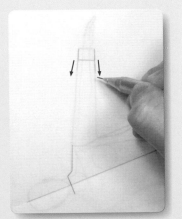

As the sleeve has some tacks, extend the line while gently widening. 03

Complete the sleeve, slightly widening towards the armhole. 04

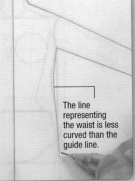

The line representing the waist is less curved than the guide line.

Draw the side of the shirt. As it is an innerwear trace 0.5mm insider the guide line. 05

Keep the line horizontal near the centerline.

Draw the tailed bottom. This long curved standard shirt hem resembles a swallow-tail, also known as a shirt tail. Originally designed to serve as underpants.

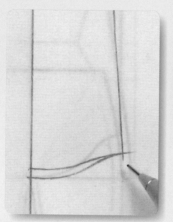

The back hem is usually longer.

**07**

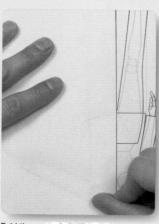

Fold the paper in half and transfer the drawn lines by strongly rubbing the reverse side with a fingernail or the like.

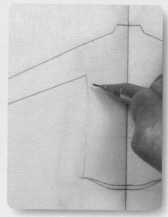

Strengthen the transferred thin lines.

**09**

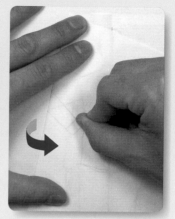

To draw the right sleeve folded, fold the paper so that the end of the sleeve does not touch the body line, rub from the back to transfer.

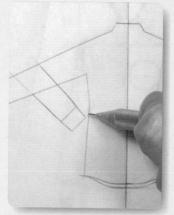

Strengthen the transferred thin lines.

Round the corner a little to represent the thickness of the fabric.

Join and finish the elbow line.

**12**

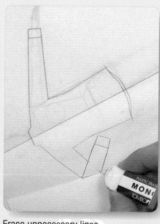

Erase unnecessary lines.

**13**

**Details**

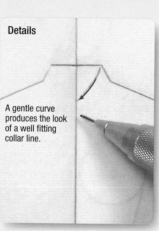

A gentle curve produces the look of a well fitting collar line.

Draw the V opening of the collar.

**14**

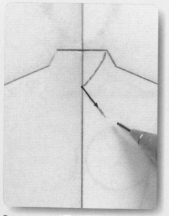

Draw as a straight line toward the collar point.

**15**

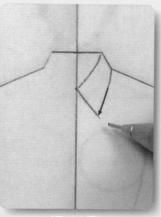

Draw the outer collar line as a gentle curve.

**16**

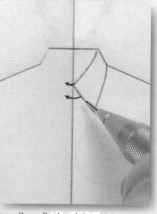

Draw the collar band, to which the collar is sewn. Many women's blouses have no collar band.

**17**

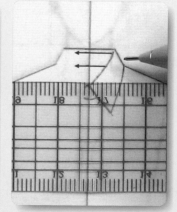

Draw the collar stand, which is the back part of the collar band, and usually higher.

**18**

Draw the shoulder yoke.

19

Draw the top and bottom buttons.

20

Mark the positions for the rest.

21

Complete all buttons.

22

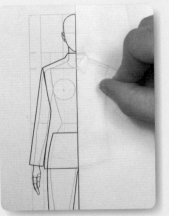

Fold the paper in half and transfer the drawn lines by strongly rubbing the reverse side with a fingernail or the like.

23

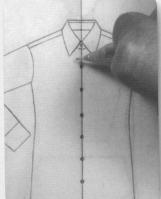

Strengthen the transferred thin lines.

24

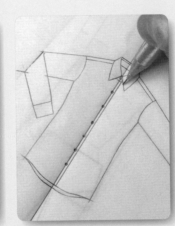

Draw the nonsymmetrical parts, starting with the placket front parallel to the front center.

25

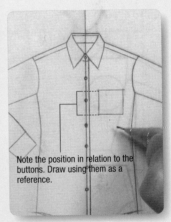

Note the position in relation to the buttons. Draw using them as a reference.

Draw the pocket. It is important to be aware of the relation with other detail elements.

26

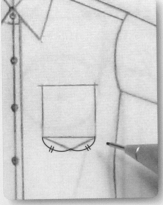

Add an inverted triangle to make the pocket an irregular pentagon.

27

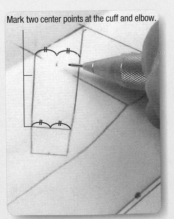

Mark two center points at the cuff and elbow.

Draw the sleeve placket. First, check the fabric grain.

28

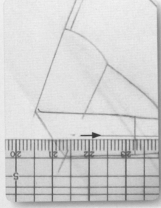

Join the two points to establish the warp grain.

29

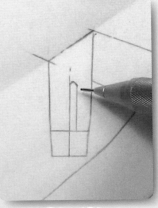

Complete the sleeve placket.

30

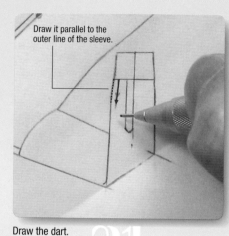

Draw it parallel to the outer line of the sleeve.

Draw the dart.

**31**

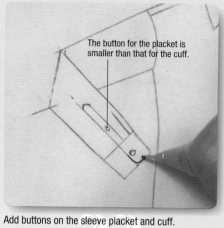

The button for the placket is smaller than that for the cuff.

Add buttons on the sleeve placket and cuff.

**32**

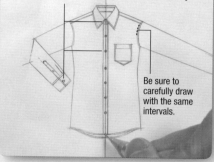

Vertical buttonholes are used for innerwear (shirts, blouses), while horizontal holes are used for outerwear (jackets, coats). For the collar stand and cuffs, horizontal holes are used as the vertical grain runs horizontally.

Be sure to carefully draw with the same intervals.

Complete by adding stitches.

**33**

Back

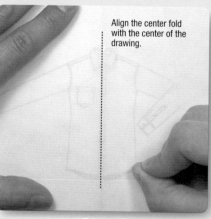

Align the center fold with the center of the drawing.

As the front and back share the same silhouette, transfer half of the front drawing by rubbing from the reverse side.

**01**

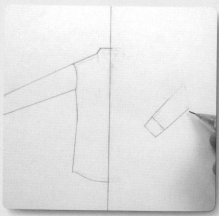

Strengthen the transferred thin lines.

**02**

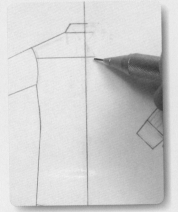

Draw the symmetrical details, starting with the yoke. 03

Draw a box-pleat in the center of the back. 04

Fold the paper in half and transfer. 05

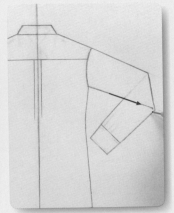

As the sleeve is folded forward, change the elbow line accordingly. 06

Draw the sleeve placket. 07

Complete by adding stitches. 08

**Jacket (Single-breasted)**

Front

The single-breasted jacket has a single row of buttons. When a jacket has a double row, it is called double-breasted. As jackets usually have shoulder pads, making them bulky, draw as if they are on a hanger, instead of laid flat. Raise the sleeves slightly to fully show the body design.

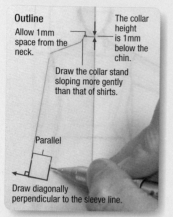

**Outline**

Allow 1mm space from the neck.

The collar height is 1mm below the chin.

Draw the collar stand sloping more gently than that of shirts.

Parallel

Draw diagonally perpendicular to the sleeve line.

As the sleeves are lowered, use the viewer's left half of the technical drawing guide. Add the lines representing collar height, collar stand and shoulder.

Draw the straight lines e.g. the upper side and hem.

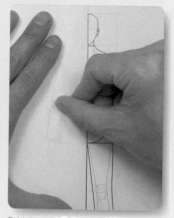

Draw slightly inward.

Draw gradually outward.

With their weight, jackets fall straight down.

Draw the hip line freehand as a gentle curve.

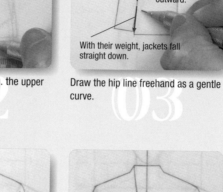

Fold the paper in half and transfer the drawn lines by strongly rubbing the reverse side with a fingernail or the like.

Open the paper and strengthen the transferred thin lines.

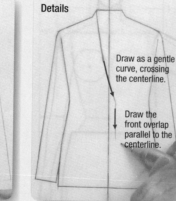

**Details**

Draw as a gentle curve, crossing the centerline.

Draw the front overlap parallel to the centerline.

Draw the V opening of the collar.

Change the direction of the line, and join with the hem at the corner.

As it is single-breasted, the standard front cut is applied.

Draw the collar stand.

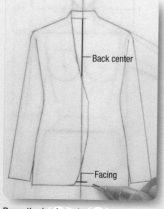

Back center

Facing

Draw the back center and facing.

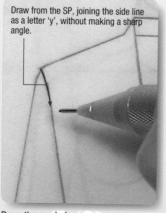

Draw from the SP, joining the side line as a letter 'y', without making a sharp angle.

Draw the armhole.

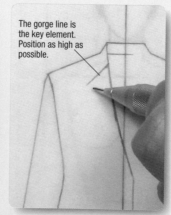

The gorge line is the key element. Position as high as possible.

Draw the lapel, a key detail for jacket design, starting with the gorge line.

Extend to the overlapping area, crossing over the front centerline.

WL

Draw the lapel as sharply as a knife.

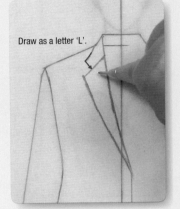

Draw as a letter 'L'.

Draw the collar. *13*

When lower than the WL of the body, the button is normally not closed.

Draw the button. Outerwear buttons are larger than those for innerwear (e.g. shirts), as the fabric is thicker. *14*

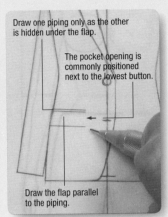

Draw one piping only as the other is hidden under the flap.

The pocket opening is commonly positioned next to the lowest button.

Draw the flap parallel to the piping.

Draw the side pocket. A double piping pocket with flap is selected. *15*

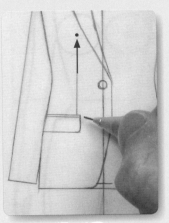

Draw the dart extending from the side pocket to the BP. *16*

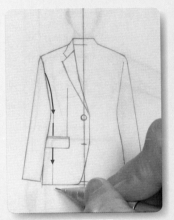

Draw the side seam (not visible depending on the design). *17*

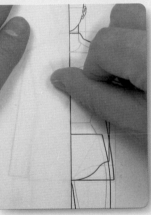

Fold the paper in half and transfer the drawn lines by strongly rubbing the reverse side with a fingernail or the like. *18*

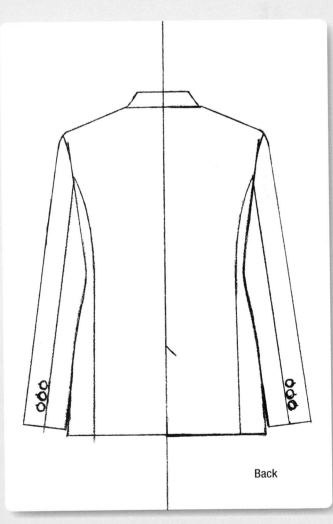

Back

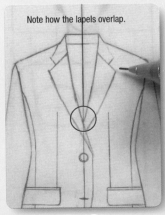

Note how the lapels overlap.

Strengthen the transferred thin lines. *19*

The left breast welt pocket is designed at an angle for easy use by the right hand.

Complete by drawing a nonsymmetrical part (breast pocket). *20*

Fold the paper vertically, aligning the fold line.

As the front and back share the same silhouette, transfer half of the front drawing by rubbing from the reverse side. Transfer also the parts sharing the same lines with the front, e.g. the armhole and side seam.

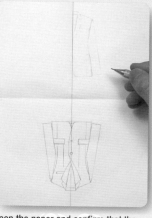
Open the paper and confirm that the drawing transferred. *02*

Strengthen the transferred thin lines. *03*

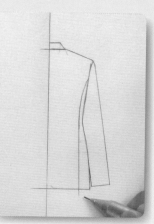
Draw the details, starting with the side seam. *04*

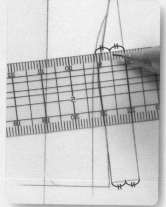
Add the sleeve seam by first marking two points at the center of the width. *05*

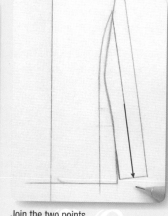
Join the two points. *06*

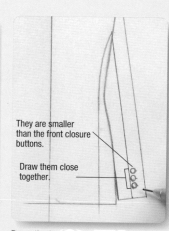
They are smaller than the front closure buttons.

Draw them close together.

Draw the buttons on the sleeve. *07*

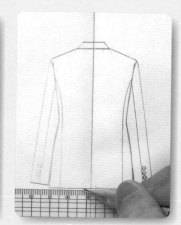
Fold the paper in half and transfer. *08*

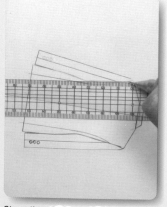
Strengthen the transferred thin lines. *09*

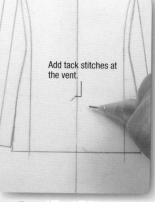
Add tack stitches at the vent.

Draw the center vent. *10*

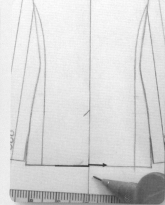
Complete by creating a step at the hem to show the raised right panel. *11*

## Phase 11 review

- Represent the subtle changes of length and volume, using the technical drawing guide as an underlay.
- Focus on the symmetrical elements.
- Confirm their structure, by carefully observing actual garments.

**Next, we will draw garments on the body!**

# Dressing

*All measurements in this phase are based on B4 size paper.

> Now we will draw garments on the body. The basic rules are the same as the technical drawing. Dress the body allowing extra room, while paying due consideration to the garment's length and volume. The following two points are different from the technical drawing.

1. Movements of the body e.g. directions and poses→Master the skill to cope with various movements using the median line of the body.

2. Creases→Creases on loosely fitting garments run vertically due to gravity, while those on closely fitting garments run sideways at the joint areas.

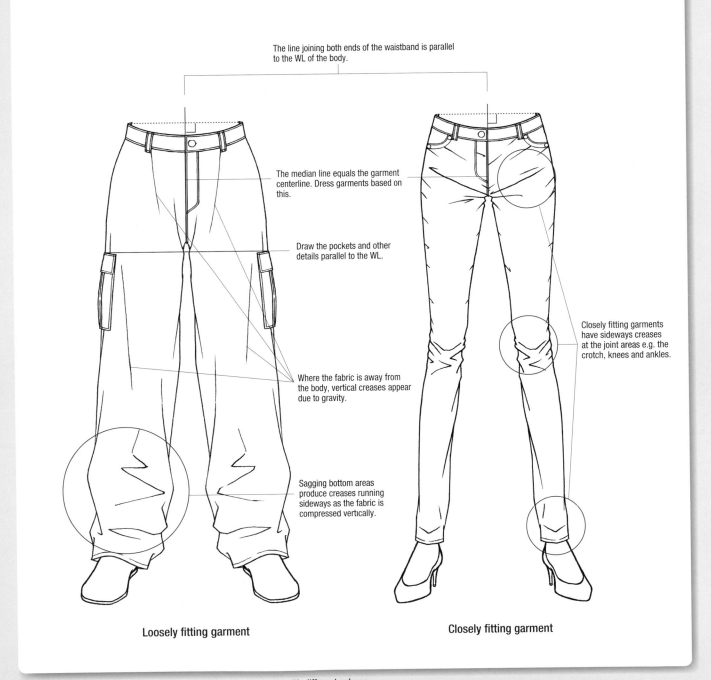

The line joining both ends of the waistband is parallel to the WL of the body.

The median line equals the garment centerline. Dress garments based on this.

Draw the pockets and other details parallel to the WL.

Where the fabric is away from the body, vertical creases appear due to gravity.

Sagging bottom areas produce creases running sideways as the fabric is compressed vertically.

Closely fitting garments have sideways creases at the joint areas e.g. the crotch, knees and ankles.

**Loosely fitting garment**

**Closely fitting garment**

Study the key points of dressing by comparing these two garments with different volume.

**Dressing (Skirt)**

The skirt is tilted towards the supporting leg in line with the movement of the WL. As it is loosely fitting, creases run vertically due to gravity.

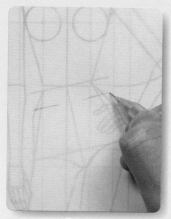

Draw the waistband guide line parallel to the WL. **01**

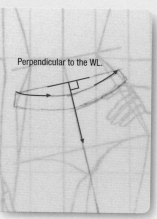

Perpendicular to the WL.

Draw the waistband and the centerline of the skirt. **02**

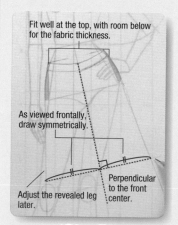

Fit well at the top, with room below for the fabric thickness.

As viewed frontally, draw symmetrically.

Perpendicular to the front center.

Adjust the revealed leg later.

Establish the hem position and draw the skirt outline. **03**

As it is flared, the skirt volume can be increased in line with the leg movement. Based on the idle leg, adjust the skirt outline. **04**

Draw the hem line as an arc, the bottom half of an oval, to give a 3-D effect. **05**

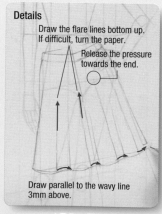

Draw the wavy line, typical of a flared hem. **06**

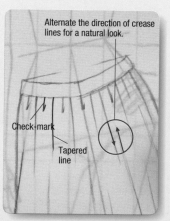

**Details**

Draw the flare lines bottom up. If difficult, turn the paper.

Release the pressure towards the end.

Draw parallel to the wavy line 3mm above.

Add depth to the wavy line to represent the flares. Draw as learned in the technical drawing. **07**

Alternate the direction of crease lines for a natural look.

Check-mark

Tapered line

Complete by adding the gather lines top-down. Alternating check marks and tapered lines, draw them to go well with the flares.

## Dressing (Pants)

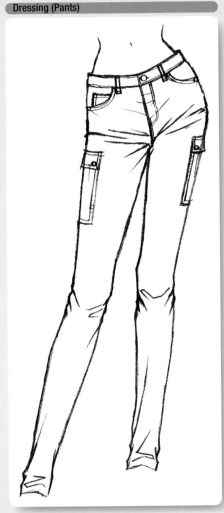

The pants are tilted towards the supporting leg in line with the movement of the WL. As they are closely fitting, creases appear around the joints.

**Outline**

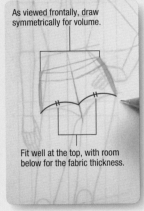

First draw the guide line parallel to the WL, and then the curved waistband.

Perpendicular to the WL.

Draw the waistband and the centerline of the pants. **01**

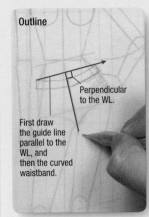

As viewed frontally, draw symmetrically for volume.

Fit well at the top, with room below for the fabric thickness.

Draw the hip part. **02**

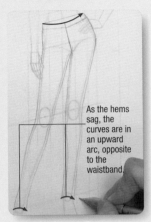

As the hems sag, the curves are in an upward arc, opposite to the waistband.

Draw the pants line with a little room along the leg lines. **03**

**Details**

Draw the details. Turn the paper to make the hip part vertical for easy drawing and to avoid distortion. **04**

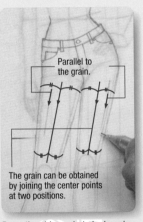

Parallel to the grain.

The grain can be obtained by joining the center points at two positions.

Draw the side pockets by keeping their vertical outline parallel to the fabric grain. **05**

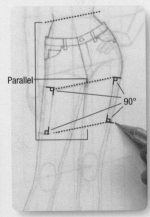

Parallel

90°

Draw the horizontal outline. **06**

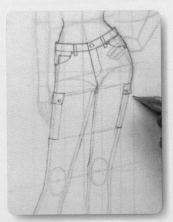

Draw the details. **07**

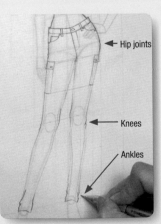

Hip joints

Knees

Ankles

As creases appear around the joints, reflect them in the outline. **08**

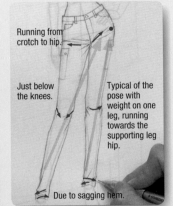

Running from crotch to hip.

Just below the knees.

Typical of the pose with weight on one leg, running towards the supporting leg hip.

Due to sagging hem.

Draw creases. As the pants are closely fitting, the creases run sideways. Draw as letters 'V' or 'Z'. **09**

Complete by adding the stitches and accompanying small creases. **10**

## Dressing (Shirt)

As the shirt covers both the upper body and hips, it is important to establish the front centerline in accordance with the movements of the median lines of both parts. This example has buttons on the front center.

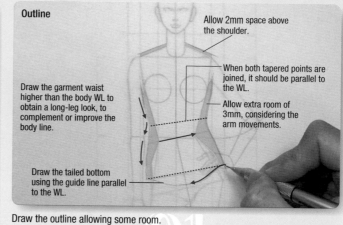

**Outline**

Allow 2mm space above the shoulder.

When both tapered points are joined, it should be parallel to the WL.

Allow extra room of 3mm, considering the arm movements.

Draw the garment waist higher than the body WL to obtain a long-leg look, to complement or improve the body line.

Draw the tailed bottom using the guide line parallel to the WL.

Draw the outline allowing some room. **01**

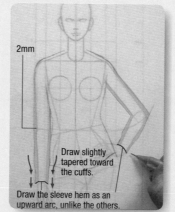

2mm

Draw slightly tapered toward the cuffs.

Draw the sleeve hem as an upward arc, unlike the others.

Draw the sleeves also allowing some room. **02**

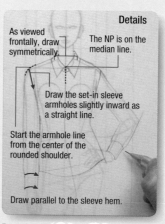

**Details**

As viewed frontally, draw symmetrically.

The NP is on the median line.

Draw the set-in sleeve armholes slightly inward as a straight line.

Start the armhole line from the center of the rounded shoulder.

Draw parallel to the sleeve hem.

Draw key detail elements e.g. sleeves, cuffs and armholes. **03**

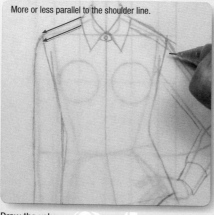

More or less parallel to the shoulder line.

Draw the yoke. **04**

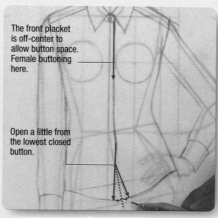

The front placket is off-center to allow button space. Female buttoning here.

Open a little from the lowest closed button.

Draw the front placket. **05**

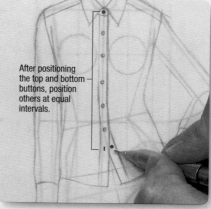

After positioning the top and bottom buttons, position others at equal intervals.

Draw the buttons on the front center. **06**

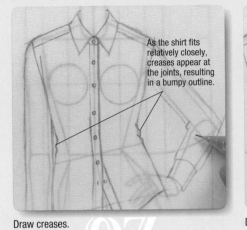

As the shirt fits relatively closely, creases appear at the joints, resulting in a bumpy outline.

Draw creases.

**07**

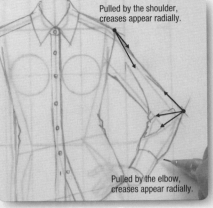

Pulled by the shoulder, creases appear radially.

Pulled by the elbow, creases appear radially.

Draw creases at the elbow.

**08**

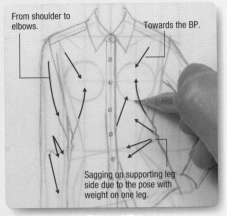

From shoulder to elbows.

Towards the BP.

Sagging on supporting leg side due to the pose with weight on one leg.

Complete by drawing other creases.

**09**

## Dressing (Jacket)

As the jacket also covers both the upper body and hips, it is important to establish the front centerline in accordance with the movements of the median lines of both parts. Despite the buttons on the front, it is often worn open. Thicker material has less creases than shirts.

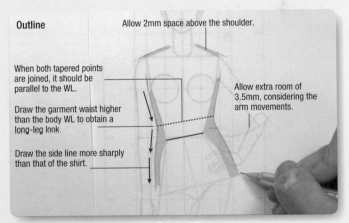

**Outline**

Allow 2mm space above the shoulder.

When both tapered points are joined, it should be parallel to the WL.

Draw the garment waist higher than the body WL to obtain a long-leg look.

Draw the side line more sharply than that of the shirt.

Allow extra room of 3.5mm, considering the arm movements.

Draw the outline allowing room. The jacket has more room as it is an outerwear.

**01**

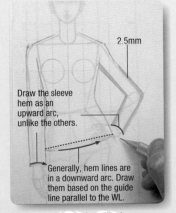

2.5mm

Draw the sleeve hem as an upward arc, unlike the others.

Generally, hem lines are in a downward arc. Draw them based on the guide line parallel to the WL.

Draw the sleeves also allowing some room.

**02**

**Details**

Collar line

Closure line

Front cut line

Keep the distance from the median line the same.

Draw the jacket front closure, in order of; collar, front closure and front cut.

**03**

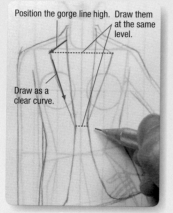

Position the gorge line high. Draw them at the same level.

Draw as a clear curve.

Draw the lapels. **04**

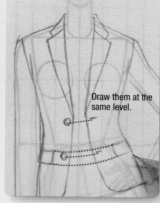

Draw them at the same level.

Draw the side pockets and buttons. **05**

Draw the darts and breast pocket. **06**

As the shirt fits relatively closely, creases appear at the joints, resulting in a bumpy outline.

Draw creases. **07**

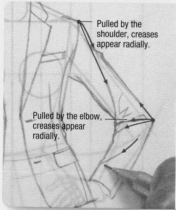

Pulled by the shoulder, creases appear radially.

Pulled by the elbow, creases appear radially.

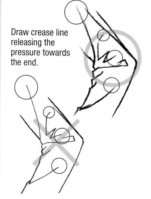

Draw crease line releasing the pressure towards the end.

Draw creases at the elbow. **08**

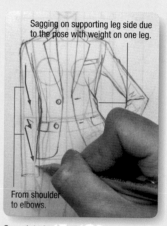

Towards the BP.

Draw creases at the waist. **09**

Sagging on supporting leg side due to the pose with weight on one leg.

From shoulder to elbows.

Complete by drawing other creases. **10**

---

**Dressing (Pumps)**

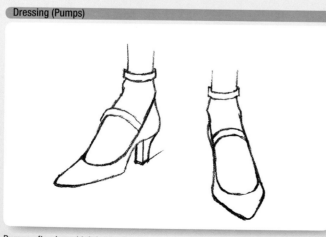

Pumps often have high heels. The key point is the lines from the heels to the arches of the feet.

**Outline**

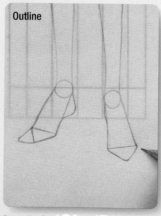

Draw the feet first using the grid as an underlay. A diagonal view is selected to draw the shoes pointing in different directions. (See p. 41) **01**

Draw the outline of the pumps using the feet drawing as an underlay. **02**

120

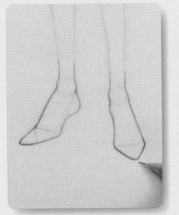

The 'pointed toe' was applied to the design of the shoe.
**03**

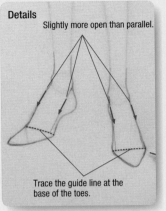

**Details**

Slightly more open than parallel.

Trace the guide line at the base of the toes.

Draw the guide lines for the top line of the shoes based on the lines of the underlay.
**04**

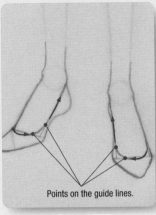

Points on the guide lines.

Draw the top line of the shoes as a smooth curve.
**05**

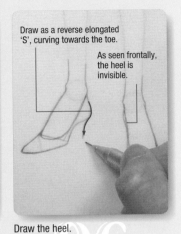

Draw as a reverse elongated 'S', curving towards the toe.

As seen frontally, the heel is invisible.

Draw the heel.
**06**

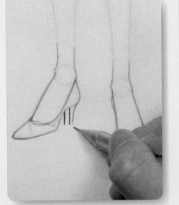

Continue the heel.
**07**

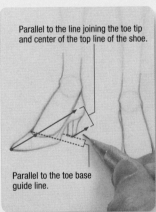

Parallel to the line joining the toe tip and center of the top line of the shoe.

Parallel to the toe base guide line.

Complete the heel.
**08**

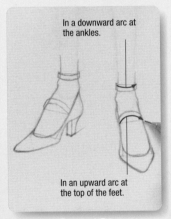

In a downward arc at the ankles.

In an upward arc at the top of the feet.

When adding straps, first draw the guide line and finish as an arc.
**09**

**Dressing (Sandals)**

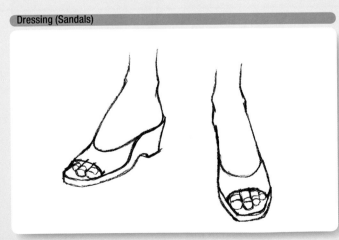

As sandals show the feet a great deal, draw the toes and tops of the feet well.

**Outline**

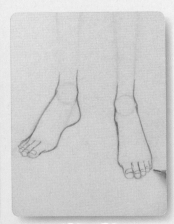

Draw the outline of the pumps using the feet drawing as an underlay.
**01**

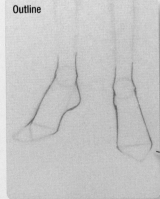

Draw the toes first as the sandals are open-toed.
**02**

**Details**

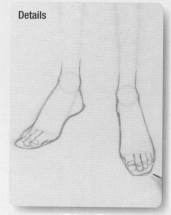

Draw the insole of the sandals.

**03**

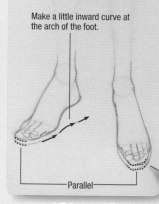

Make a little inward curve at the arch of the foot.

Parallel

Draw the outsole.

**04**

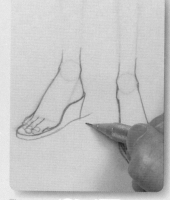

The wedge outsole is selected here.

**05**

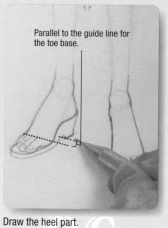

Parallel to the guide line for the toe base.

Draw the heel part.

**06**

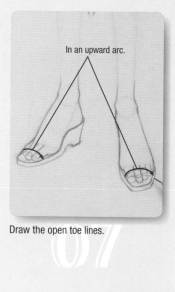

In an upward arc.

Draw the open toe lines.

**07**

**Dressing (Boots)**

The outline basically fits along the leg line.

Draw the top line in a downward arc.

Establish the length of the boots.

**01**

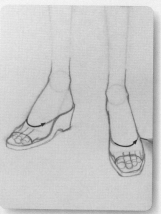

Complete by drawing the top line like those of the pumps.

**08**

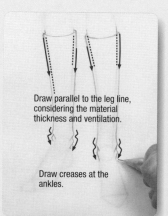

Draw parallel to the leg line, considering the material thickness and ventilation.

Draw creases at the ankles.

Draw the outline.

**02**

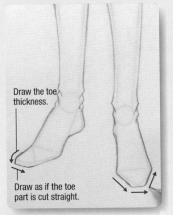

Draw the toe thickness.

Draw as if the toe part is cut straight.

The 'square toe' is used here.

**03**

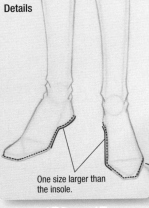

Details

One size larger than the insole.

Draw the edge of the sole.

**04**

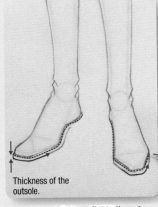

Thickness of the outsole.

Draw the outsole parallel to the edge of the sole.

**05**

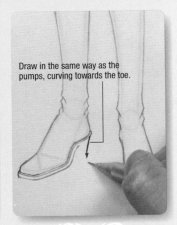

Draw in the same way as the pumps, curving towards the toe.

Draw the heel.

**06**

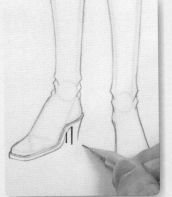

Continue the heel.

**07**

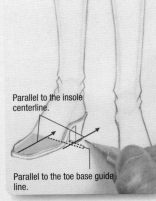

Parallel to the insole centerline.

Parallel to the toe base guide line.

Complete the heel.

**08**

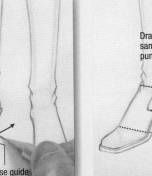

Draw these lines the same as the top line of the pumps.

Parallel

Draw the joint seam, separating the feet from the lower leg.

**09**

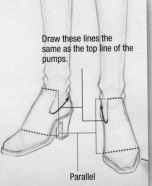

Draw the creases inward from the outline for a natural look.

Draw creases here.

Draw creases at the ankles.

**10**

**Dressing (Sneakers)**

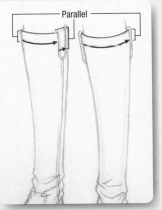

Parallel

Complete by drawing more details, e.g. straps at the top lines, vertical seam and stitches.

**11**

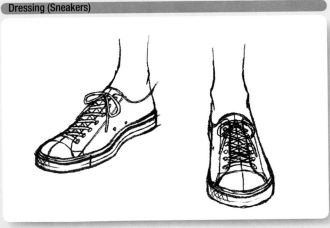

The key point is how carefully you represent the perspective of various detail elements e.g. shoelaces and shell toes.

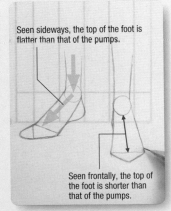

Seen sideways, the top of the foot is flatter than that of the pumps.

Seen frontally, the top of the foot is shorter than that of the pumps.

Draw the feet first using the grid as an underlay. The heels are not high. (See pp. 40 + 41)

**01**

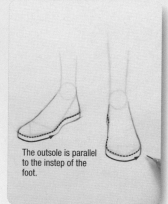

The outsole is parallel to the instep of the foot.

Draw the outline and outsole of the sneakers using the feet drawing as an underlay. 02

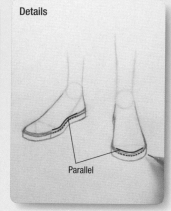

Details

Parallel

Add details to the outsole. 03

Unlike the pumps, they have tongues, making the tops of the feet higher.

Draw the top line. 04

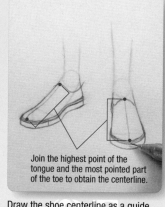

Join the highest point of the tongue and the most pointed part of the toe to obtain the centerline.

Draw the shoe centerline as a guide line for the drawing of details. 05

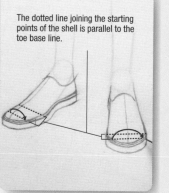

The dotted line joining the starting points of the shell is parallel to the toe base line.

Draw the toe shells. 06

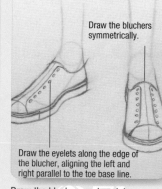

Draw the bluchers symmetrically.

Draw the eyelets along the edge of the blucher, aligning the left and right parallel to the toe base line.

Draw the bluchers and eyelets. 07

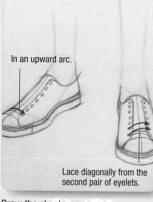

In an upward arc.

Lace diagonally from the second pair of eyelets.

Draw the shoelaces. 08

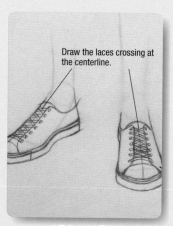

Draw the laces crossing at the centerline.

Draw the criss-cross lacing. 09

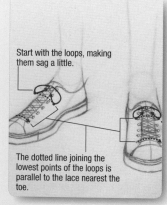

Start with the loops, making them sag a little.

The dotted line joining the lowest points of the loops is parallel to the lace nearest the toe.

Draw the bowknots. 10

Complete by drawing the details of the rest of the laces, stitches and toes. 11

## Phase 12 review

• The basis of the dressing lies in the body balance. Exercise drawing the body poses well.

• How you allow extra room for garments influences the dressing balance.

• The median lines are the most reliable guide line for detail drawing.

**Next, we will ink the pencil sketch!**

# 13 Inking

Pencil sketches often have many remaining unclear lines, which will dissolve when applying color, making them muddy. Inking solves such problems by transferring the sketch onto paper for coloring (Kent paper, art paper or watercolor paper), using bleed-free artist's materials; most commonly, drawing pens.

## Pen sizes for inking

There are many pen sizes available. For your reference, their standard applications are shown below.

**Drawing pens**
The following commonly available drawing pens, with sizes from 0.05 to extra bold and in multiple colors, can be used for a wide range of drawings from design to technical.

Nouvel Pigma Graphic
Pilot Drawing Pen
Copic Multiliner

| | | |
|---|---|---|
| 0.05 | (Super fine) | Eyes, nose, mouth, stitches |
| 0.1 | (Extra fine) | Hair lines, structural lines and other fine lines. |
| 0.3 | (Fine) | Skin, hair outline, illuminated lines |
| 0.5 | (Medium) | Outline (thin/soft materials) |
| 0.8 | (Bold) | Outline (thick/hard materials) |
| Brush | (Extra bold) | Outlines to be highlighted |

## Inking (Technical drawing)

### Transferring

Fill in strongly using a pencil with a B or softer lead.

Fill in the reverse side of the sketch. The denser the pencil, the better the transfer of the drawing. **01**

Secure the paper with mending tape.

Place it on the paper for inking. **02**

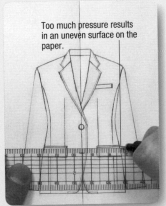

Too much pressure results in an uneven surface on the paper.

Transfer the sketch. If you carry out process 01 well, you will have no problem. **03**

Confirm that there are no missing lines. **04**

### Inking of the outline

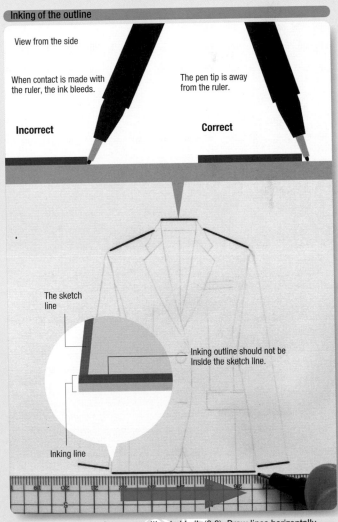

View from the side

When contact is made with the ruler, the ink bleeds.

The pen tip is away from the ruler.

**Incorrect**

**Correct**

The sketch line

Inking outline should not be inside the sketch line.

Inking line

Start with the outline using a pen with a bold nib (0.8). Draw lines horizontally, so that the pen tip has no contact with the ruler edge, to avoid bleeding. **05**

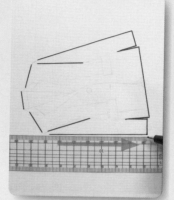

Draw the vertical lines horizontally by turning the paper sideways.
06

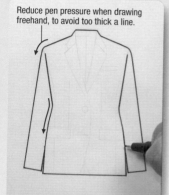

Reduce pen pressure when drawing freehand, to avoid too thick a line.

Draw the curve lines freehand. If difficult, use a curved template.
07


**Inking for details**

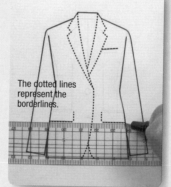

The dotted lines represent the borderlines.

Use a fine pen (0.3) for the borderlines e.g. where the fabric overlaps.
08

Use a curved template for the long curves of the lapel.

Draw vertical lines horizontally with a ruler by turning the paper and curved lines freehand.
09

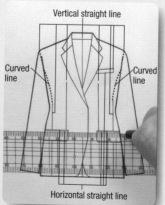

Vertical straight line

Curved line

Curved line

Horizontal straight line

Complete by drawing the details with an extra fine pen (0.1). Use a super fine pen (0.05) for stitches if any. Draw the horizontal, vertical and curved lines separately.

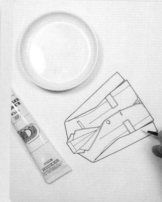

Use white opaque watercolor (e.g. poster paint) for correction. Be sure not to make it too thick when using correction fluid.

**Inking (Technical drawing)**

Front

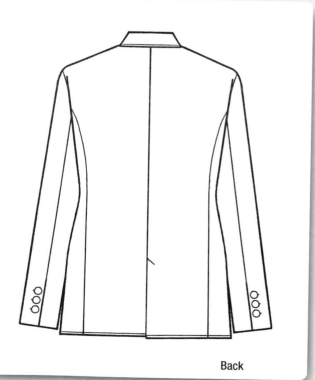

Back

Inking is done in the same way as the jacket.

Front

Front

Stitches can be in either solid or dotted line.
In the case of the latter, make the spaces very small.

Back

Back

Front

Front

Back

Back

## Inking (Dressed body drawing)

### Exercise 1 (Inking of the 'tubes')

Garments consist of various sizes of tube. In order to render the sense of volume and contrast with lines only, varying the pen pressure is the key.

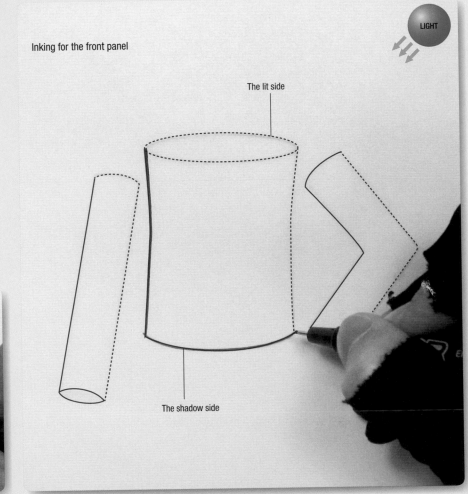

Inking for the front panel

LIGHT

The lit side

The shadow side

Light pressure produces a thin line.

Strong pressure produces a thick line.

Changes of thickness by the same pen. **01**

Setting the direction of the light source, draw as a bold line on the shadow side using a bold pen (0.8) with strong pen pressure. **02**

Inking for sleeves

### Exercise 2 (Inking of simple top)

Inking for outline

LIGHT

Draw as a thin line on the lit side with light pen pressure using the same bold pen (0.8). Using this method, contrast can be given to this simple tube. **03**

Apply inking to the tubes representing the sleeves in the same way. **04**

Setting the direction of the light source, draw as a bold line on the shadow side using a bold pen (0.8) with strong pen pressure. **01**

Draw as a thin line on the lit side with light pen pressure using the same bold pen (0.8). **02**

## Inking for details

Draw the armholes with an extra fine pen (0.1).

*03*

**Exercise 3 (Inking of layered tops)**

## Inking for outline

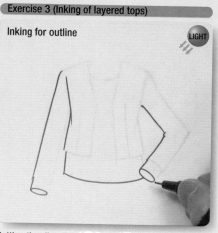

LIGHT

Setting the direction of the light source, draw as a bold line on the shadow side using a bold pen (0.8) with strong pen pressure.

*01*

## Inking for details

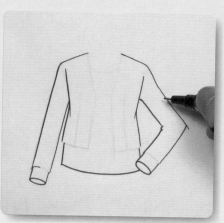

Draw as a thin line on the lit side with light pen pressure using a bold pen (0.8).

*02*

## Inking for the borderlines

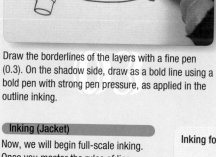

Draw the borderlines of the layers with a fine pen (0.3). On the shadow side, draw as a bold line using a bold pen with strong pen pressure, as applied in the outline inking.

*03*

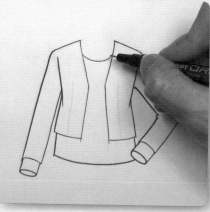

Draw as a thin line on the lit side with light pen pressure using a fine pen (0.3).

*04*

## Inking for details

Draw the armholes and darts with an extra fine pen (0.1).

*05*

### Inking (Jacket)

Now, we will begin full-scale inking. Once you master the rules of line thickness, begin applying the inking to dressed garments. Here we transfer the sketch using a light table. If a light table is not available, use the method of filling in the reverse side using pencil as shown on page 107.

## Inking for outline

LIGHT

Setting the direction of the light source, draw as a bold line on the shadow side using a bold pen (0.8) with strong pen pressure.

*01*

Draw as a thin line on the lit side with light pen pressure using a bold pen (0.8).

*02*

## Inking for the borderlines

Draw the borderlines of the layers with a fine pen (0.3). On the shadow side, draw as a bold line using a bold pen with strong pen pressure, as applied in the outline inking.

**Inking for creases**

Incorrect    Correct

Release the pen pressure towards the end. Do not press down.

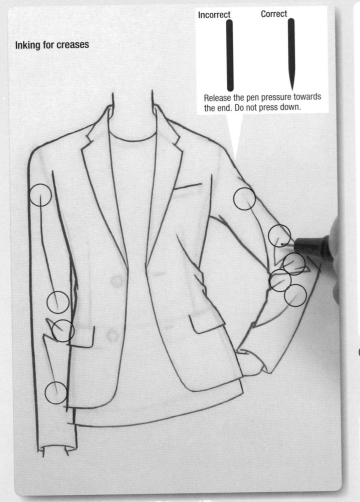

As the creases on jackets are deep, use a fine pen (0.3).

**04**

Completed.

**07**

**Inking for details**

Draw the armholes and darts with an extra fine pen (0.1).

**05**

Add stitches with a super fine pen (0.05). Stitches can be in either solid or dotted line. In the case of the latter, make the spaces very small.

The inking is applied based on each sketch in the same way as the jacket.

## Phase 13 review

- Apply the inking while considering the garment's sense of volume.
- Apply strong pen pressure (thick line) on the shadow side.
- Apply light pen pressure (thin line) on the lit side.
- Use a bold pen for the outline, and fine pen for the detail drawings.

**Next, we will prepare colors!**

# Coloring

**Artist's Materials for Coloring**

Now, we begin coloring using opaque watercolors (gouache) and color pencils. The combination of these two is most common for the basic coloring method. Opaque watercolors are a versatile painting material, as you can also use them to show through the base color when diluted with a lot of water, just like transparent watercolor. We use Holbein Artists' Gouache here. As some students may have difficulty with this material, I will proceed step-by-step with extra care. We use color pencils as auxiliary materials to render the texture of fabrics or materials and shading. We selected Sanford Prismacolors here for their good coloring property on watercolor.

**Water holder**
It comes in three convenient sections; for washing, rinsing, and holding water for diluting.

**Brushes**
We use two long-bristle brushes. Before using for the first time, it is recommended to remove starch from brushes by repeatedly washing them in cold or lukewarm water.

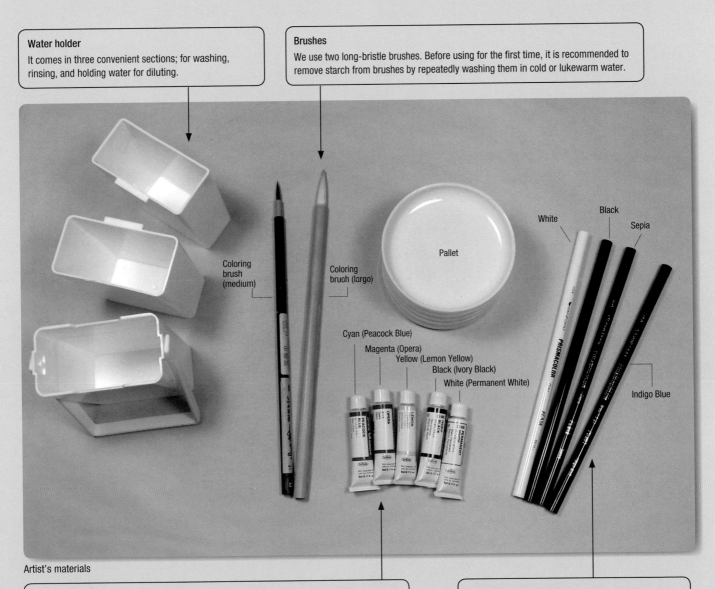

Coloring brush (medium)

Coloring brush (large)

Pallet

White

Black

Sepia

Indigo Blue

Cyan (Peacock Blue)
Magenta (Opera)
Yellow (Lemon Yellow)
Black (Ivory Black)
White (Permanent White)

Artist's materials

**Opaque watercolors**
All colors are created through the combination of four colors: cyan (C), magenta (M), and yellow (Y), plus black (K). Prepare, to start with, these four plus white; a total of five colors. This corresponds to the CMYK combination of inks in a standard inkjet color printer. Shown here are the opaque watercolors by Holbein.

**Color pencils**
We use color pencils on watercolors. Prepare white, black, dark brown (for red and yellow tone shadings) and navy (for blue and green tone shadings). Shown here are the Prismacolors by Sanford.

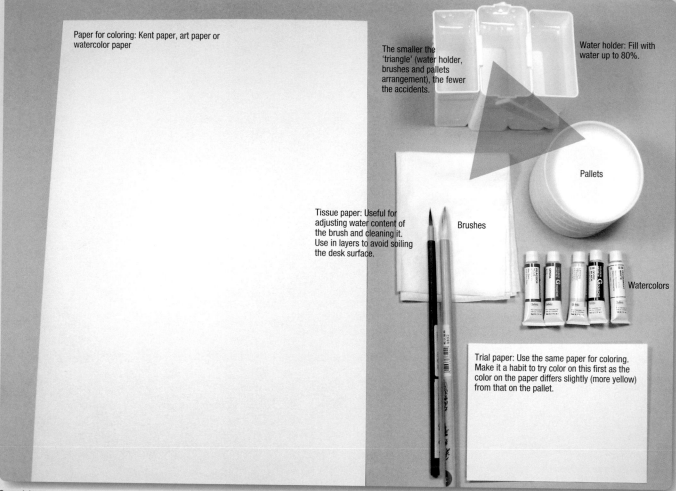

Paper for coloring: Kent paper, art paper or watercolor paper

The smaller the 'triangle' (water holder, brushes and pallets arrangement), the fewer the accidents.

Water holder: Fill with water up to 80%.

Pallets

Tissue paper: Useful for adjusting water content of the brush and cleaning it. Use in layers to avoid soiling the desk surface.

Brushes

Watercolors

Trial paper: Use the same paper for coloring. Make it a habit to try color on this first as the color on the paper differs slightly (more yellow) from that on the pallet.

Organizing:

Organize your desk for efficiency. If you are right-handed, place all tools e.g. water holder, pallets and brushes on the right side as shown above in a triangular arrangement. Place them so that you do not have to move a brush filled with paint over the paper, to avoid spoiling your drawing.

### Draw a color circle

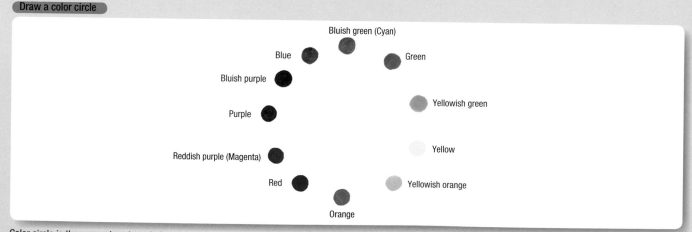

Bluish green (Cyan)

Blue

Green

Bluish purple

Yellowish green

Purple

Reddish purple (Magenta)

Yellow

Red

Yellowish orange

Orange

Color circle is the name given to a circle consisting of color hues (tone, shade and tint).

When coloring agent is applied to pure white paper, reflected color is produced. When the three primary colors CMY are all mixed in equal proportion, the result is black. The more color is mixed into the coloring agent the darker it becomes. This is known as subtractive color mixing.

Squeeze a small amount of paint onto the pallet.

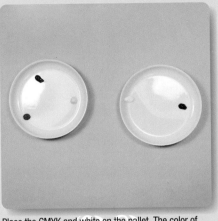

Place the CMYK and white on the pallet. The color of light is created through the combination of red (R), green (G), and blue (B). It involves adding color from a state of complete darkness, and is known as additive color mixing. Mixing all three of the RGB produces white.

Color shades change depending on the amount of water. Learn to adjust the amount by first painting the color on the trial paper.

First wet the brush with water and take some paint. Paint starting with cyan. **03**

Try to paint quickly and don't 'fuss', or the paint becomes uneven. If it does, wait until it dries, and apply another coat. Painting while the original is wet may damage the paper.

Once you obtain a desired color with the right amount of water, paint on the final paper. **04**

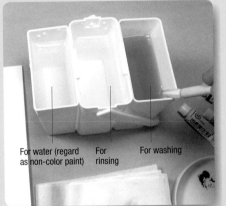

For water (regard as non-color paint)  For rinsing  For washing

Wash the brush when painting is finished. **05**

Remove the paint remaining in the brush thoroughly by pushing against the tissue paper. **06**

Repeat 03 to 06, with magenta. **07**

Try yellow next. **08**

Complete the colors in between. Create colors by adding cyan and magenta, increasing the amount of magenta little by little. Do the same to complete the gradation from magenta to yellow, and yellow to cyan.

## Now let's mix colors

Theoretically all colors can be made by mixing CMYK only, however we use the color of the paper also, which acts as white when no paint is applied.

### Skin color

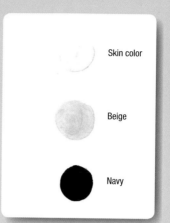

80% Magenta (representing the color of blood)

20% Yellow (representing the color of melanin pigment)

A small amount of water (just enough to mix paints)

Use the primary colors to start with. Create salmon pink by mixing magenta and yellow. Adding more magenta produces a healthy looking complexion, while more yellow produces a pale complexion.

*01*

Undiluted color

The color has been added to the water.

Mix the paint into water to make a light color e.g. the skin color selected here. Note that adding water to dilute the paint prepared in 01 (salmon pink) does not work easily.

*02*

The water/paint ratio is 95 to 20 (skin color).

The water/paint ratio is 80 to 20 (darker).

With different paint/water ratios, you can make so many different colors.

*03*

### Navy

Use the primaries also to produce dark colors. Create a bluish purple by adding a small amount of magenta to cyan.

*04*

Make it darker by adding black little by little.

*05*

### Beige

Using the primary colors, create orange by mixing magenta and yellow.

*06*

Dilute black in water to use for the dullness of beige.

*07*

Add orange to make beige.

*08*

Obtain the desired beige, by changing the water/paint ratio.

*09*

### Phase 14 review

- Paints and color pencils are the basic coloring tools.
- Create colors with CMYK.
- Adjust the water/paint ratio to obtain shades of color. Add more water for a lighter shade and less for a darker shade.

**Next, we will color!**

# The 3rd week

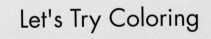

Let's Try Coloring

# Exercise 1 (Coloring of the 'tubes')

## Exercise 1 (Coloring of the 'tubes')

Three points for coloring:
1. Color evenly: Fill the brush tip with a good amount of water and apply color quickly.
2. Produce a good contrast: Setting a light source, apply color on the shadow side.
3. Shading in 3 places: Overall shadow on the tubes, overlapping parts/items and creases.

The basic method of coloring is "layering", which produces gradations i.e. different color shades created by many layers of the same color on the shadow areas. The ratio of water to paint is the key for this method.

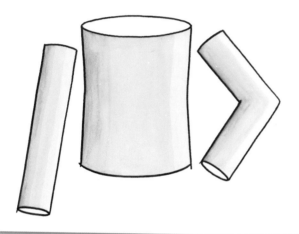

Garments consist of various tubes. By layering colors along either side of the tube outline, you can produce shading.

## Overall shadow on the tubes

First prepare the paint. Dilute it with water prepared in a separate dish. The key is to start with thin paint.

Paint dries from the outer edge. As the paint in this area produces a darker tone, use it for the second layer or thereafter for a contrasting effect.

Mix well to prevent paint separating from the water.

---

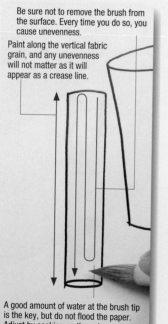

Be sure not to remove the brush from the surface. Every time you do so, you cause unevenness.

Paint along the vertical fabric grain, and any unevenness will not matter as it will appear as a crease line.

A good amount of water at the brush tip is the key, but do not flood the paper. Adjust by soaking up the extra water with a tissue paper.

First coating (solid painting): Paint as if filling with water throughout the subject area, so that the paint particles will be evenly spread with the moisture, to avoid unevenness. Be sure to use enough water to avoid a dry brush look.

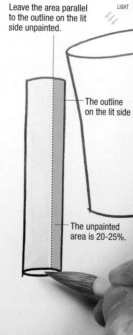

Leave the area parallel to the outline on the lit side unpainted.

LIGHT

The outline on the lit side

The unpainted area is 20-25%.

Second coating (omitted painting method): Apply an additional layer to produce a gradation towards the shadow to render shading.

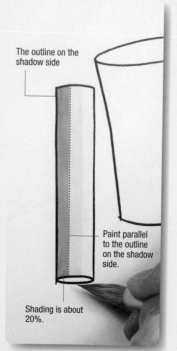

The outline on the shadow side

Paint parallel to the outline on the shadow side.

Shading is about 20%.

Third coating (shadow painting): Paint in more layers on the shadow areas. Ideally the color obtained here should be your final desired color.

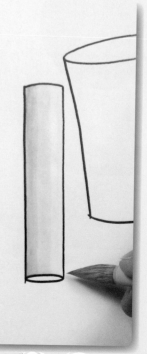

Fourth coating (blurring): After producing 3 gradations, apply blurring by quick strokes at the noticeable edges of the paint with a brush soaked in clean water.

Apply the process 03 to 05 to the rest of the tubes. In reality, follow the process per color at one time, not tube by tube. 07

**Correction of paint run over**

If the paint runs over the edge...... 08

Immediately dissolve the paint using a brush that contains clean water only...... 09

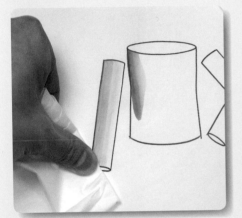

Press strongly with a tissue to soak up the paint. 10

**Correction of dry brush look**

If the paint becomes dry brush-like...... 11

Dissolve the paint using a brush that contains clean water only...... 12

Press strongly with a tissue to soak up the paint. 13

Confirm that the color is removed. 14

Repaint evenly. This time use more water. 15

Color a T-shirt, as if it consists of 1 tube (body) and 2 tubes (sleeves).

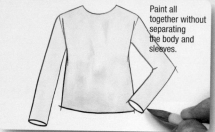

Paint all together without separating the body and sleeves.

First coating (solid painting): Paint as if filling with water throughout the subject area.

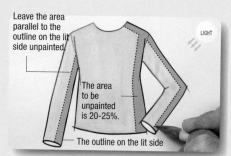

Leave the area parallel to the outline on the lit side unpainted.

LIGHT

The area to be unpainted is 20-25%.

The outline on the lit side

Second coating (omitted painting method): Apply an additional layer to produce a gradation towards the shadow to render shading.

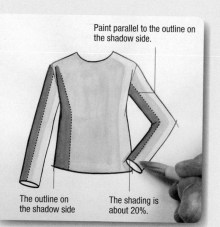

Paint parallel to the outline on the shadow side.

The outline on the shadow side

The shading is about 20%.

Third coating (shadow painting)/Fourth coating (blurring): Paint in more layers on the shadow areas. Ideally the color obtained here should be your final desired color. After producing 3 gradations, apply blurring by quick strokes over the entire area, with a brush soaked in clean water.

Regardless of the number of layers, apply shading based on the idea of 1 body tube.

### Overall shadow on the tubes

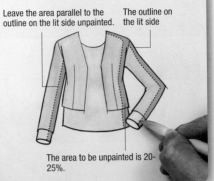

Leave the area parallel to the outline on the lit side unpainted.

The outline on the lit side

The area to be unpainted is 20-25%.

First coating (solid painting)/Second coating (omitted painting method: Following the solid painting, apply an additional layer to produce a gradation towards the shadow to render shading.

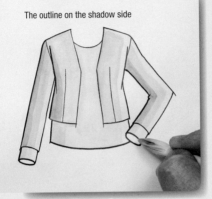

The outline on the shadow side

Third coating (shadow painting)/Fourth coating (blurring): Paint in more layers on the shadow areas. Ideally the color obtained here should be your final desired color. After producing 3 gradations, apply blurring by quick strokes over the entire area, with a brush soaked in clean water.

### Shadows along the borderlines

LIGHT

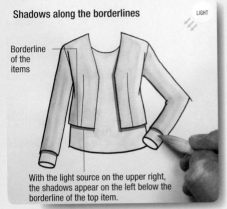

Borderline of the items

With the light source on the upper right, the shadows appear on the left below the borderline of the top item.

When garment items are layered, the shadows appear on the inside item.

### Coloring of a jacket

Now, we will begin full-scale coloring. Once you have acquired the rules of shading, try to color real garment items. Despite the various detailed elements of a jacket, the concept is that it is a collection of different size tubes. Be sure to add shading on 3 places; overall shadow on the tubes, overlapping parts/items and creases.

### Overall shadow on the tubes

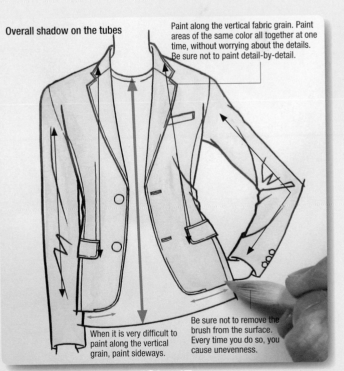

Paint along the vertical fabric grain. Paint areas of the same color all together at one time, without worrying about the details. Be sure not to paint detail-by-detail.

When it is very difficult to paint along the vertical grain, paint sideways.

Be sure not to remove the brush from the surface. Every time you do so, you cause unevenness.

First coating (solid painting): Paint as if filling with water throughout the subject area, so that the paint particles will be evenly spread with the moisture, to avoid unevenness.

The outline on the lit side

The area to be unpainted is 20-25%.

Leave the area parallel to the outline on the lit side unpainted.

Second coating (omitted painting method): Apply an additional layer to produce a gradation towards the shadow to render shading.

Paint parallel to the outline on the shadow side.

The shading is about 20% of the tubes.

The outline on the shadow side

Third coating (shadow painting): Paint in more layers on the shadow areas. Ideally the color obtained here should be your final desired color.

## Shadows along the borderlines

LIGHT

Borderline of the parts

With the light source on the upper right, the shadows appear on the left below the borderline of the parts.

When garment items are layered, the shadows appear on the inside item.

## Shadows of creases

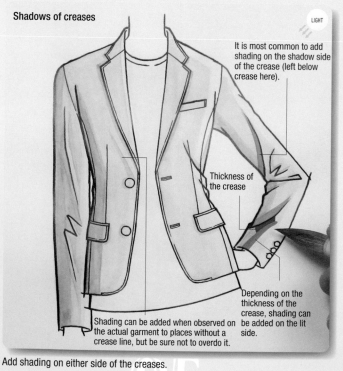

It is most common to add shading on the shadow side of the crease (left below crease here).

Thickness of the crease

Depending on the thickness of the crease, shading can be added on the lit side.

Shading can be added when observed on the actual garment to places without a crease line, but be sure not to overdo it.

Add shading on either side of the creases.

LIGHT

Borderline of the items: It is most common to add shading on the shadow side of the crease (left below crease here).

After producing 3 gradations, apply blurring by quick strokes at the noticeable edges of the paint with a brush soaked in clean water.

Add shading on the innerwear as on the Jacket.

## Coloring of a shirt

As shirts are often white, you can simply add shading, while using the base color of white.

## Overall shadow on the tubes

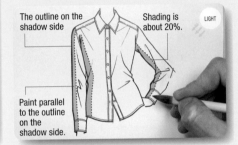

Dilute black paint in water as much as possible with a ratio of 5% black to 95% water. 01

The outline on the shadow side

Shading is about 20%.

LIGHT

Paint parallel to the outline on the shadow side.

Shadow painting: Apply the black to the shadow areas. 02

## Shadows along the borderlines

Borderline of the parts. With the light source on the upper right, the shadows appear on the left below the borderline of the parts.

LIGHT

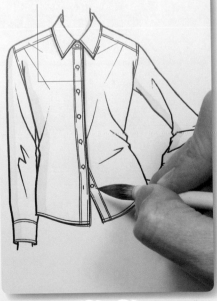

When the parts overlap, the shadows appear on the parts underneath. 03

## Shadows of creases

It is most common to add shading on the shadow side of the crease (left below crease here).

In some cases, shading can be added on the lit side.

Add shading on either side of the creases. 04

## Blurring

Apply blurring by quick strokes at the edges of the paint with a brush soaked in clean water to give an overall soft impression. 05

Pants consist of 1 tube (lower torso) and 2 tubes (legs). Be aware that both legs have shading.

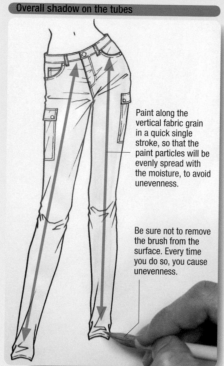

Paint along the vertical fabric grain in a quick single stroke, so that the paint particles will be evenly spread with the moisture, to avoid unevenness.

Be sure not to remove the brush from the surface. Every time you do so, you cause unevenness.

First coating (solid painting): Paint as if filling with water throughout the subject area.

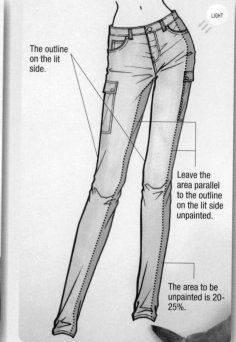

LIGHT

The outline on the lit side.

Leave the area parallel to the outline on the lit side unpainted.

The area to be unpainted is 20-25%.

Second coating (omitted painting method): Apply an additional layer to produce a gradation towards the shadow to render shading.

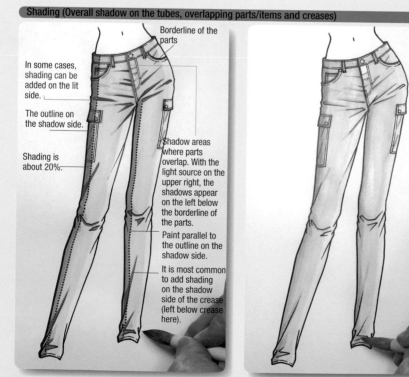

Borderline of the parts

In some cases, shading can be added on the lit side.

The outline on the shadow side.

Shading is about 20%.

Shadow areas where parts overlap. With the light source on the upper right, the shadows appear on the left below the borderline of the parts.

Paint parallel to the outline on the shadow side.

It is most common to add shading on the shadow side of the crease (left below crease here).

Third coating (shadow painting): Paint in more layers on the shadow areas. Ideally the color obtained here should be your final desired color.

Fourth coating (blurring): Apply blurring by quick strokes at the edges of the paint with a brush soaked in clean water to give an overall soft impression.

## Phase 15 review

- The principle is to dilute color significantly, and make it darker by layering.
- Apply shading to 3 places; overall shadow on the tubes, overlapping parts/ items and creases.
- If the base is white, use it as a color and apply only shading.

**Next, we will try various coloring methods!**

# How to Color (Applications)

The coloring method learned in the previous phase is for creating shading by applying multiple thin layers. However, in real practice, more sophisticated coloration may be required. In this phase, we will focus on denser and better coloration for shading.

**Densely layered painting**

Apply solid painting twice to make the base color dense.

**Overall shadow on the tubes**

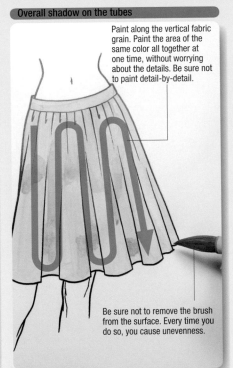

Paint along the vertical fabric grain. Paint the area of the same color all together at one time, without worrying about the details. Be sure not to paint detail-by-detail.

Be sure not to remove the brush from the surface. Every time you do so, you cause unevenness.

First coating (solid painting): Paint as if filling with water throughout the subject area, so that the paint particles will be evenly spread with the moisture, to avoid unevenness.

Second coating (solid painting): Another solid painting makes the base color denser, which contributes to better coloration, but do not make it too dense at this point, as it hinders you achieving denser color. Be sure to apply 2 layers, but thinly.

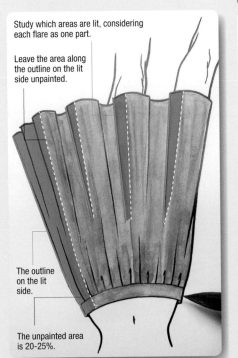

Study which areas are lit, considering each flare as one part.

Leave the area along the outline on the lit side unpainted.

The outline on the lit side.

The unpainted area is 20-25%.

Third coating (omitted painting method): Apply an additional layer to produce a gradation towards the shadow to render shading.

**Shading**

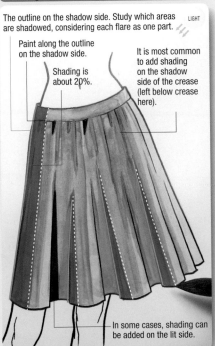

The outline on the shadow side. Study which areas are shadowed, considering each flare as one part. LIGHT

Paint along the outline on the shadow side.

Shading is about 20%.

It is most common to add shading on the shadow side of the crease (left below crease here).

In some cases, shading can be added on the lit side.

Fourth coating (shadow painting): Paint in more layers on the shadow areas (overall shadow on the tube together with shadows of creases). Ideally the color obtained here should be your final desired color.

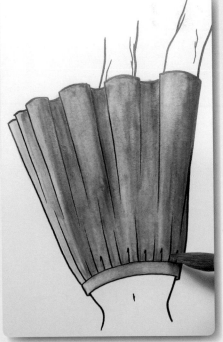

Fifth coating (blurring): Apply blurring by quick strokes at the edges of the paint with a brush soaked in clean water to give an overall soft impression.

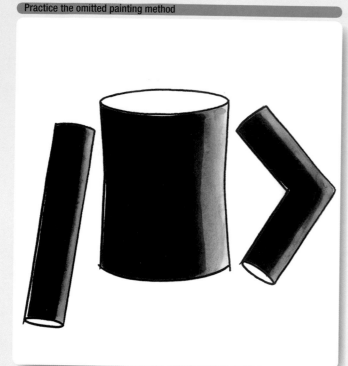

It is impossible to achieve a dark color such as black, no matter how many thin layers you apply. Thinking conversely, instead of trying to make it darker, start with a dark color and make it lighter. This is the principle of the omitted painting method.

Use less water than for layered painting, with a paint to water ratio of 1 to 2. Be sure to avoid a dry brush look.

**01**

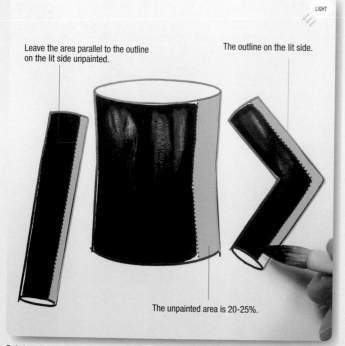

LIGHT

Leave the area parallel to the outline on the lit side unpainted.

The outline on the lit side.

The unpainted area is 20-25%.

Paint well to avoid the paper showing through, leaving the lit areas unpainted.

**02**

While dissolving the color on the border, blend and spread to the unpainted area.

Apply blurring to the borderline at the edges of the paint with a brush soaked in clean water.

**03**

**Omitted painting method**

Let us try this on a jacket. Although it has many detailed elements, the coloring process is the same as that for tubes.

Use less water than for layered painting, with a paint to water ratio of 1 to 2. Be sure to avoid a dry brush look.

**01**

Leave unpainted here when the jacket is open.

Leave the area parallel to the outline on the lit side unpainted.

The outline on the lit side

The unpainted area is 20-25%.

Paint well to avoid the paper showing through, leaving the lit areas unpainted.

**02**

While dissolving the color on the border, blend and spread to the unpainted area.

Apply blurring to the borderline at the edges of the paint with a brush soaked in clean water.

**03**

Redraw lost lines with a white color pencil.

**04**

Apply greater color contrast to garment items with luster. Make the luster areas white, and the dull areas black. The key is to render such color differences in gradations.

**Luster areas**

Peak of creases

Raised area of parts

Luster on tube

First coating (omitted painting method): Apply paint thinly, leaving the luster areas unpainted. **01**

Second coating (layered painting): Paint in layers, leaving the pale color areas unpainted. **02**

Apply blurring by quick strokes at the edges of the paint with a brush soaked in clean water to give an overall soft impression. **03**

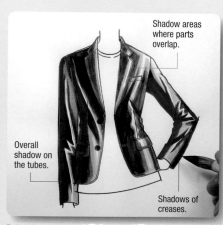

Shadow areas where parts overlap.

Overall shadow on the tubes.

Shadows of creases.

Paint the shadow area black to produce contrast. **04**

## Phase 16 review

• Make the base color dark, if you seek good coloration of the layered painting.

• The omitted painting method is based on the reverse of layered painting. First apply dark paint and then make it thin and blur.

• For luster painting, clearly render contrasting light and shadow; the light is in white, and shadow in black.

**Next, we will render patterns!**

# Textile Rendition 1: Focused on the fabric grain

In this phase, we begin by learning how to render the fabric texture. Textiles can be largely divided into those that are woven and those that are knitted, and both consist broadly of two kinds; one has its own unique texture and the other various patterns. In this phase, we will practice drawing patterns based on the grain of the fabric. The fabric grain means the crosswise and lengthwise directions of woven fibers. A fabric becomes distorted, unless cut correctly along a straight grain. Therefore the bottom hems of garments are usually perpendicular or parallel to the fabric grains. This means that patterns based on such grains appear perpendicular or parallel to the hems.

The fabric texture will be rendered by applying patterns on the base paint. When drawing on size B4, which will be approx. 20% of the actual size, it is recommended to draw from a distance of about two meters away from the subject fabric, without getting too close, while grasping the overall impression of the garment.

### Stripes

A stripe pattern consists of continuous parallel lines, usually vertical. When vertical and horizontal stripes cross, it is called check pattern.

## How to draw vertical stripes

Exercise 1 (Stripes on tubes)

Garments consist of various tubes. Draw vertical stripes on them.

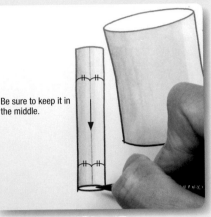

Be sure to keep it in the middle.

First draw the centerline of the tube. 01

Alignment line

Draw more lines on both sides at constant intervals parallel to the center alignment line. 02

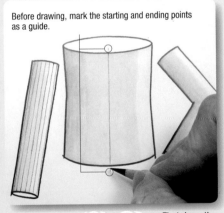

Before drawing, mark the starting and ending points as a guide.

Draw the center tube in the same way. First draw the centerline. 03

Alignment line

Draw more lines on both sides at constant intervals parallel to the center alignment line. 04

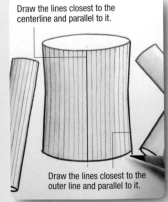

Draw the lines closest to the centerline and parallel to it.

Draw the lines closest to the outer line and parallel to it.

When the sides of the tube are curved, draw carefully, adjusting to the outer lines as they get closer. 05

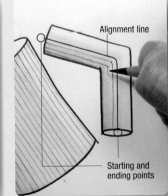

Alignment line

Starting and ending points

Start with the centerline also for the bent tube. 06

Complete by drawing the lines at constant intervals. 07

**Exercise 2 (Stripes on a simple top)**

The key point is to draw the lines right in the center.

The top consists of one body tube and two sleeve tubes. First draw a line in the center.

As the side line is shaped by the cut of the fabric, do not draw stripes parallel to it as in the case of tubes.

Alignment line

Sewing pattern of the back panel.

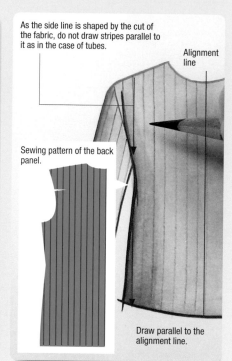

Draw parallel to the alignment line.

Draw more lines on both sides at constant intervals parallel to the center alignment line.

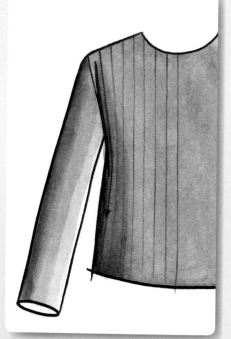

Do not draw parallel to the side line.

**Exercise 3 (Stripes on a layered top)**

In the case of tops open at the front, use the front vertical opening edge as the alignment line.

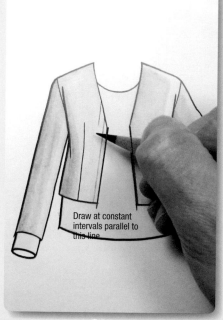

Draw at constant intervals parallel to this line.

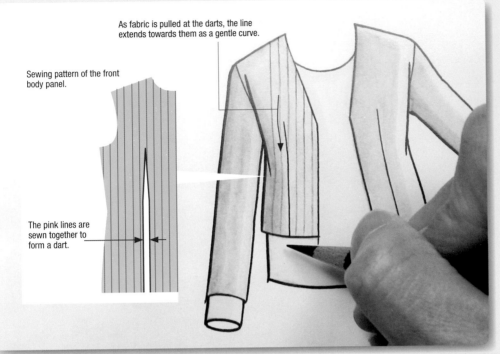

Sewing pattern of the front body panel.

As fabric is pulled at the darts, the line extends towards them as a gentle curve.

The pink lines are sewn together to form a dart.

Draw thinner lines for the lit area.

Draw the left side in the same way. **03**

Fabric grains at darts: Darts are added so that the fabric which is otherwise flat, fits the body well. Here darts are applied to give volume to the breast. **02**

**Stripes on a jacket**

Now, we will begin to draw on a more realistic garment. Add stripes carefully based on the method applied to the tubes, and a curving line due to the darts.

Ignore the creases. Design drawings place priority on the regularity of pattern, rather than precise volume by showing fabric distortion.

Draw stripes starting from the center of the sleeve. **01**

The front edges are more open at the bottom.

Draw at constant intervals parallel to this line.

In the case of tops open at the front, use the front vertical opening edge as the alignment line. **02**

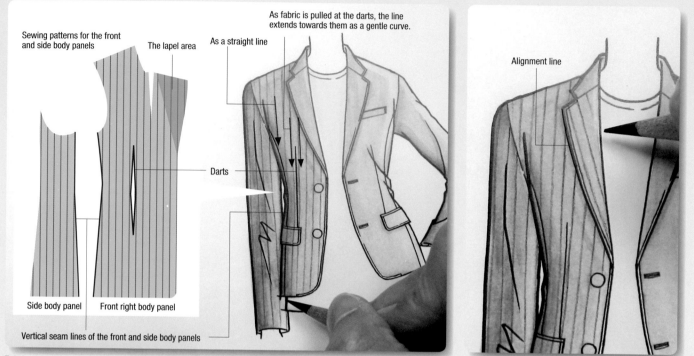

Sewing patterns for the front and side body panels

The lapel area

As a straight line

As fabric is pulled at the darts, the line extends towards them as a gentle curve.

Darts

Side body panel

Front right body panel

Vertical seam lines of the front and side body panels

Fabric grains at darts

*03*

Draw stripes on the lapel parallel to its outer edge.

Alignment line

*04*

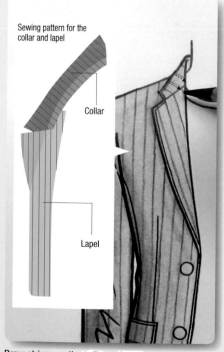

Sewing pattern for the collar and lapel

Collar

Lapel

Draw stripes on the collar perpendicular to its outer edge.

*05*

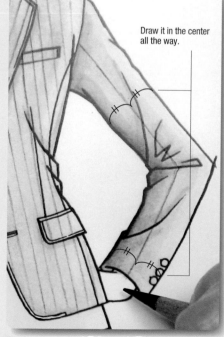

Draw it in the center all the way.

For the bent sleeve also, start with the center alignment line.

*06*

Complete by drawing more lines on both sides at constant intervals parallel to the center alignment line.

*07*

**Stripes on pants**

The key point is to be aware of the fabric grain based on the movements of each leg.

Ignore the creases. Design drawings place priority on the regularity of pattern, rather than precise volume by showing fabric distortion.

Draw stripes starting with the centerline i.e. center crease, in accordance with the leg movements.

Waistband: As the grain is horizontal, add stripes parallel to the band line.

Sewing pattern for the pants (front)

The stripes extend diagonally from the fly line, forming an inverted 'V' when left and right are combined.

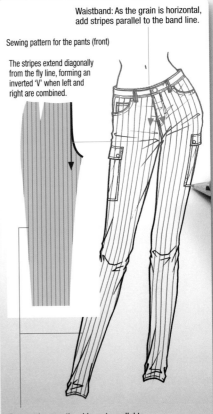

Draw stripes on the side, not parallel to the outline but to the center alignment line.

Draw stripes at constant intervals based on the alignment line.

Stripes on a gathered skirt

The key point is the rendition of gather and flare lines at the waistband.

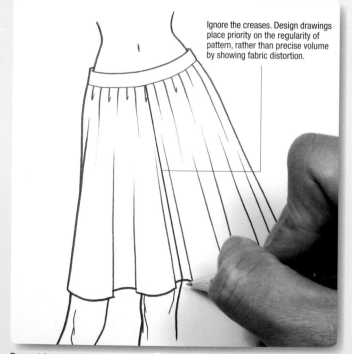

Ignore the creases. Design drawings place priority on the regularity of pattern, rather than precise volume by showing fabric distortion.

Draw stripes starting with the front centerline.

01

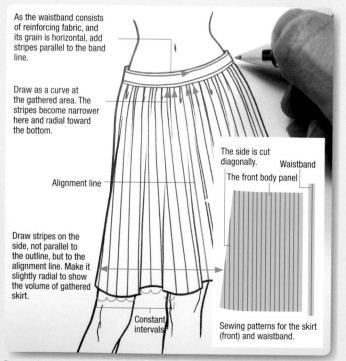

As the waistband consists of reinforcing fabric, and its grain is horizontal, add stripes parallel to the band line.

Draw as a curve at the gathered area. The stripes become narrower here and radial toward the bottom.

Alignment line

Draw stripes on the side, not parallel to the outline, but to the alignment line. Make it slightly radial to show the volume of gathered skirt.

Constant intervals

The side is cut diagonally.

Waistband

The front body panel

Sewing patterns for the skirt (front) and waistband.

Draw stripes at constant intervals based on the center alignment line. Note that stripes at the gathered area curve due to volume.

02

## How to draw horizontal stripes

**Exercise 1 (Horizontal stripes on tubes)**

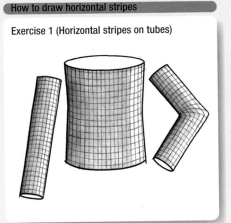

Garments consist of various tubes. Draw horizontal stripes on them. Note that they are often curved, representing the roundness of the body. When added to the vertical stripes, a check pattern results.

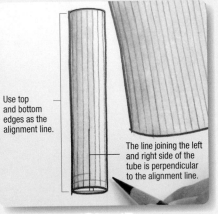

Use top and bottom edges as the alignment line.

The line joining the left and right side of the tube is perpendicular to the alignment line.

Draw lines parallel to the bottom of the tube.

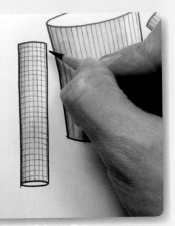

Repeat at constant intervals upward.

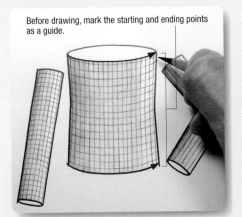

Before drawing, mark the starting and ending points as a guide.

Draw stripes on the center tube in the same way, starting with the first line parallel to the bottom, repeat at constant intervals upward.

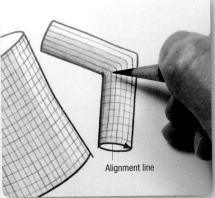

Alignment line

Follow the same basic rules for the bent tube, starting with the first line parallel to the bottom, repeat at constant intervals upward.

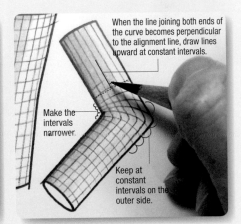

When the line joining both ends of the curve becomes perpendicular to the alignment line, draw lines upward at constant intervals.

Make the intervals narrower.

Keep at constant intervals on the outer side.

Adjust the bent corner by making the intervals narrower.

**Exercise 2 (Horizontal stripes on a simple top)**

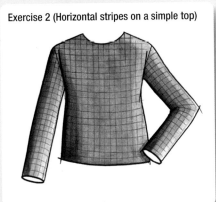

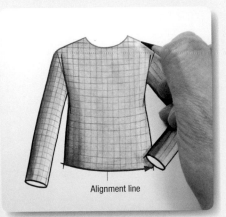

Sewing pattern for the sleeve.

Sleeve cap: The sleeve is sewn to the body panels here i.e. the armhole.

The top consists of one body tube and two sleeve tubes. Draw the first line parallel to the bottom, and repeat at constant intervals upward.

Alignment line

Draw the front in the same way, starting with the first line parallel to the bottom, repeat at constant intervals upward.

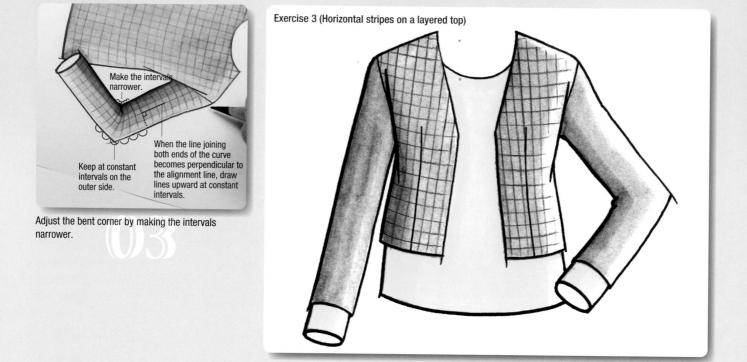

Make the intervals narrower.

When the line joining both ends of the curve becomes perpendicular to the alignment line, draw lines upward at constant intervals.

Keep at constant intervals on the outer side.

Adjust the bent corner by making the intervals narrower.

03

Exercise 3 (Horizontal stripes on a layered top)

Alignment line

Draw as if the lines are joined.

When the front is open, draw as if the lines are joined.

01

Draw parallel to the hem, even when it is apart.

Repeat at constant intervals upward.

02

**Horizontal stripes on a jacket**

Now, we will begin to draw on a more realistic garment. Apply the rules learned in the exercise for the tubes.

**01**

Alignment line

The top consists of one body tube and two sleeve tubes. Draw the first line parallel to the bottom, and repeat at constant intervals upward.

**02**

Draw as if the lines are joined.

Alignment line

When the front is open, draw as if the lines are joined.

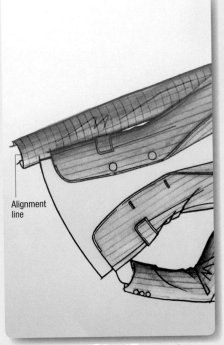

Collar

Parallel

90°

Lapel

Draw lines on the lapel perpendicular to its outer edge, and parallel to the collar.

**03**

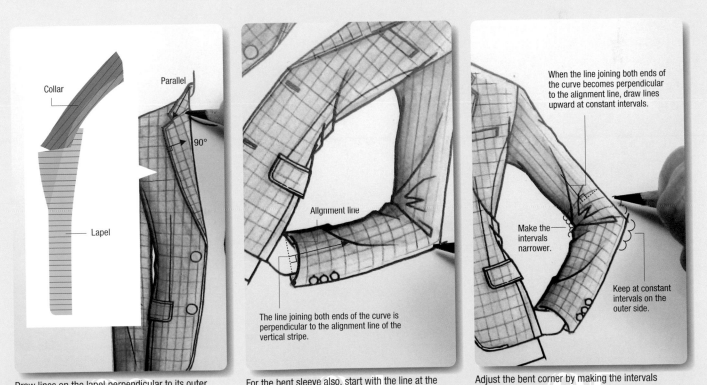

Alignment line

The line joining both ends of the curve is perpendicular to the alignment line of the vertical stripe.

For the bent sleeve also, start with the line at the cuff.

**04**

When the line joining both ends of the curve becomes perpendicular to the alignment line, draw lines upward at constant intervals.

Make the intervals narrower.

Keep at constant intervals on the outer side.

Adjust the bent corner by making the intervals narrower.

**05**

**Horizontal stripes on pants**

The key point is to be aware of the fabric grain based on the movements of each leg.

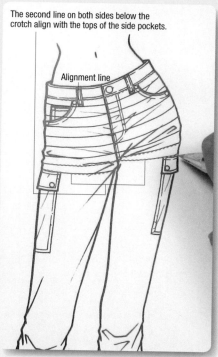

The second line on both sides below the crotch align with the tops of the side pockets.

Alignment line

Draw lines by dividing the pants into two: the lower torso and legs. Start with the torso part by adding lines parallel to the waistband at constant intervals.

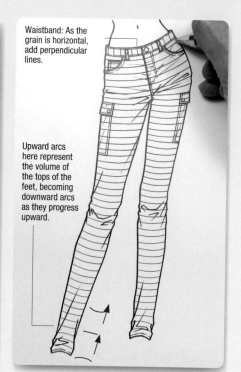

Waistband: As the grain is horizontal, add perpendicular lines.

Upward arcs here represent the volume of the tops of the feet, becoming downward arcs as they progress upward.

Draw lines at constant intervals.

**Horizontal stripes on a gathered skirt**

The key point is the rendition of gather and flare lines at the waistband.

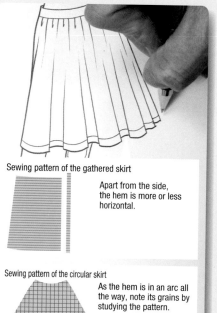

Sewing pattern of the gathered skirt

Apart from the side, the hem is more or less horizontal.

Sewing pattern of the circular skirt

As the hem is in an arc all the way, note its grains by studying the pattern.

Draw lines parallel to the skirt hem.

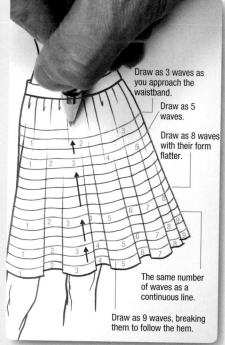

Draw as 3 waves as you approach the waistband.

Draw as 5 waves.

Draw as 8 waves with their form flatter.

The same number of waves as a continuous line.

Draw as 9 waves, breaking them to follow the hem.

Draw lines upward to the waistband, gradually decreasing the number of waves.

## Various grain patterns

### Tartan

Among check patterns, a tartan is most complex as it consists of many colors and stripe sizes, but can be drawn successfully when the correct steps are followed.

First draw a swatch sample. Draw a square frame with drawing pen. **01**

Evenly paint the base in red. No shading is required for a swatch. **02**

Use a density that allows the base red to be seen through.

When many colored stripes are involved, start with the widest color band, i.e. the dark green one here. Note that it comes as a set of two. Use a fine brush. **03**

Add extra dark green to the parts where the two bands meet. **04**

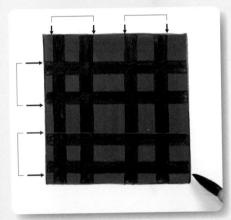

Add dark blue lines to the outer edges of each set of two bands. **05**

Add two black lines to the red areas between the two bands, using a drawing pen with a 0.05 nib. **06**

Add two lines to the dark green bands; a yellow one on the outer side and white one on the inner side of the set. **07**

Add another white line to the center of the red areas between the two bands. **08**

**Tartan on a gathered skirt**

Once you have mastered the composition of a tartan, try it on a skirt.

At constant intervals.

LIGHT

The bands become slightly radial toward the sides.

First paint the base in red, and then dark green along the lengthwise grain. With the light source on the upper right, apply good shading considering the volume of the skirt.

01

The same thickness as the vertical one.

Add horizontal bands from the bottom.

02

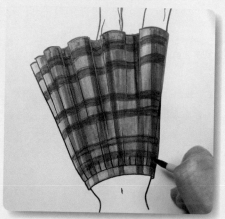

As they get closer to the waistband, the bands become flatter.

03

Add extra dark green to the parts where the two bands meet.

04

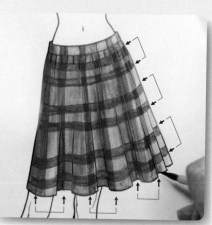

Add dark blue lines to the outer edges of each set of two bands.

05

Add two black lines to the red areas between the two bands, and yellow and white on the outer and inner sides of the set respectively.

Add another white line to the center of the red areas between the two bands.

07

Complete by emphasizing the shadow areas to give contrast using a color pencil.

08

**Woolen knitwear**

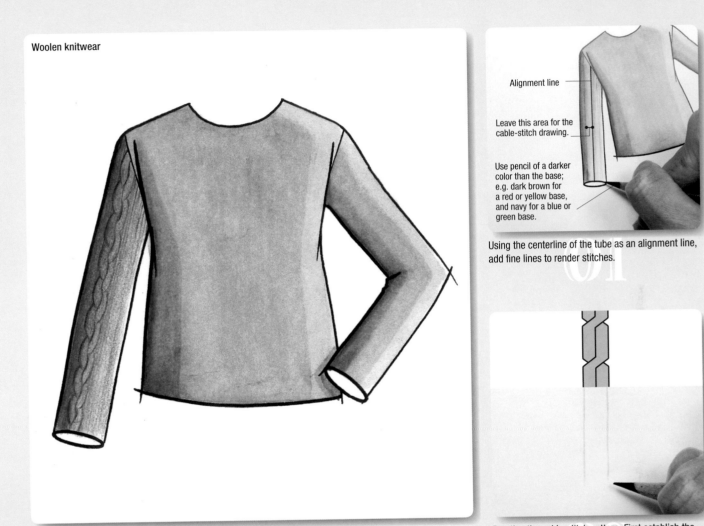

Render the softness of woolen fabric with color pencils, by creating a rough texture for a napped appearance. The knit stitches appear to be a stripe when seen from a distance. Here the cable-stitch is selected out of various sophisticated stitches.

Alignment line

Leave this area for the cable-stitch drawing.

Use pencil of a darker color than the base; e.g. dark brown for a red or yellow base, and navy for a blue or green base.

Using the centerline of the tube as an alignment line, add fine lines to render stitches. 01

Practice the cable-stitch pattern. First establish the size. 02

As it is complex, we simplify the pattern here. First draw two reverse 'J'-like parallel lines as shown above. 03

Draw two more 'J'-like lines a little lower. Repeat this. 04

Be sure to keep each stitch the same size. 05

Add to the actual drawing. 06

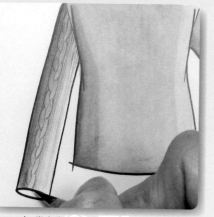

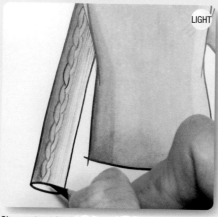

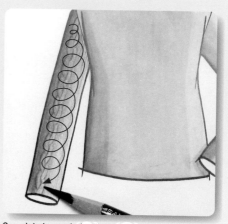

Keep each stitch the same size.

Give contrast by drawing over the shadowed lines.

Complete by rendering the rough napped texture of wool using the side of the lead of a color pencil, darker than the base color (navy here). Apply softly in circular strokes to avoid producing pencil lines.

**Corduroy**

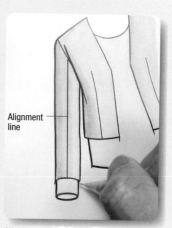

Using a mechanical pencil without exposing the lead, scribe the surface, starting with the alignment line.

Add fine lines at constant intervals parallel to the alignment line.

Fine vertical ribs with about 3mm intervals are the distinctive feature here. Render the uneven surface by adding actual grooves.

Complete by rendering the rough napped texture of wool using the side of the lead of a color pencil, darker than the base color (navy here). Apply softly in circular strokes to avoid producing pencil lines.

**Polka-dots**

The key point is to add polka-dots at every second crossing point of the gridlines.

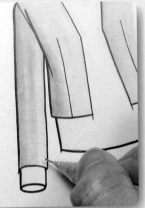

Draw the grid. *01*

Prepare the color for the dot. Use a small amount of water to avoid the base showing through. *02*

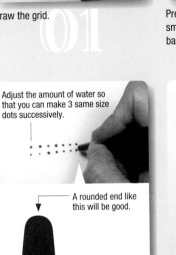

Adjust the amount of water so that you can make 3 same size dots successively.

A rounded end like this will be good.

Stamping easily produces nice dots. Find and use a semispherical cross-section surface. *03*

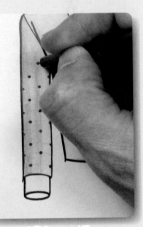

Make dots on every other crossing point of the gridlines. *04*

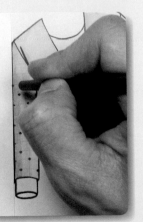

When making half a dot, mask the background with another piece of paper. *05*

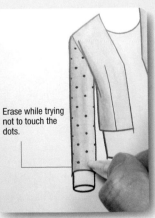

Erase while trying not to touch the dots.

Wait until dots are completely dry, and erase the grid lines to complete. *06*

## Phase 17 review

- To render stripes, first draw an alignment line on the center of each part of the garment and add lines at constant intervals parallel to it on both sides.
- Horizontal stripes are usually parallel to the hem.
- A complex check pattern actually consists of simple checks. Use the thick bands as a guide.
- Try to understand the fabric grain through observation of actual garments or sewing patterns.

**Next, we will continue to render patterns!**

# Textile Rendition 2: Various materials/patterns

In this phase, we will practice to render a textile's own unique texture and various other patterns. The fabric texture will be rendered by applying patterns on the base paint. When drawing on size B4, which will be approx. 20% of the actual size, it is recommended to draw from a distance of about two meters away from the subject textile, without getting too close, while grasping the overall impression of the garment.

**Denim**

The name is derived from the French 'serge de Nimes'. Serge is a type of twill fabric with diagonal ridges, and Nimes is the name of a region in France. Denim therefore means the serge woven in Nimes.

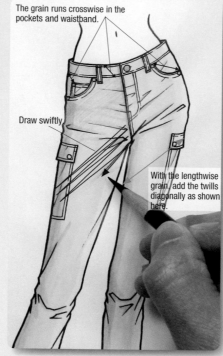

The grain runs crosswise in the pockets and waistband.

Draw swiftly

With the lengthwise grain, add the twills diagonally as shown here.

After applying layered painting to the base drawing, add twills at 45° angles using a darker color pencil (navy here) than the color of the base.

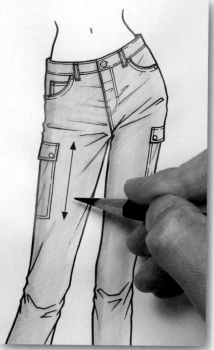

To render a faded indigo-look, apply vertical strokes with a color pencil. Denim consists of warp in indigo blue and weft of bleached or unbleached cotton fiber. It acquires a well-worn quality as the color fades.

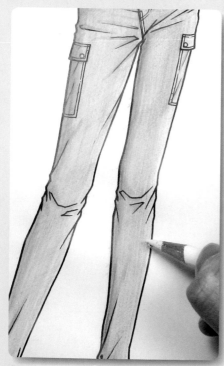

If required use a white color pencil for places lighter in color.
**03**

Give depth to the creases to highlight the sense of faded indigo.

Give the entire garment good contrast by applying shading using a darker color pencil (navy here) than the color of the base.
**04**

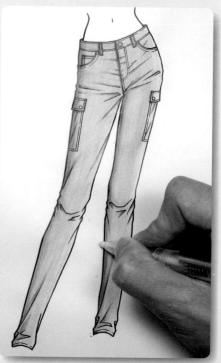

Complete by erasing unwanted lines.
**05**

## Nubby tweed

Tweed is a rough-surfaced carded woolen fabric, featuring various color nubs on its surface.

Push the brush down on the palette to separate and open the bristles. **01**

When separated, you can paint many dots at one time.

Adjust the bristles when they are too open. **02**

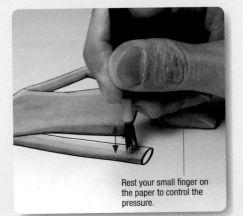

Rest your small finger on the paper to control the pressure.

Apply dots by gently tapping on the paper. **03**

Create depth by applying various colors. **04**

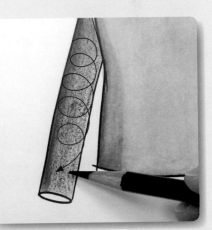

Complete by rendering the rough napped texture of wool using the side of the lead of a color pencil, darker than the base color (navy here). Apply softly in circular strokes to avoid producing pencil lines.

## Furby tanning

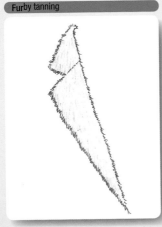

animal skin while keeping its fur. One of the first garment materials human beings used.

Make a simple draft, using a pencil. **01**

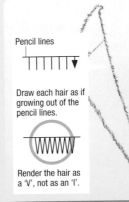

Pencil lines

Draw each hair as if growing out of the pencil lines.

Render the hair as a 'V', not as an 'I'.

Render a fur-look at the pen and ink stage. **02**

After the ink is dry (wait about 2 mins), erase the pencil lines. **03**

Paint the base color thinly, using a sufficient amount of water. Note that the hair will not show well if the paint is too thick.

Paint the hair on the base in the same color diluted with less water.

Color the fur with a color pencil darker than the base (brown here).

LIGHT

Make the shadowed area darker with more pressure to show the volume of fur.

Complete by rendering the rough napped texture of wool using the side of the lead of a color pencil, darker than the base color (brown here). Apply softly in circular strokes to avoid producing pencil lines.

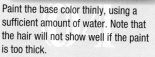

Fur patterns vary depending on the animal. Leopard fur is most well known with its black ring-like spots.

Draw half dots also for better and more realistic rendition.

First paint the base fur in light beige, and black spots in an 'O' or 'C' shape.

Complete by painting the center of the spots in brown.

**Floral pattern**

Floral patterns have various variations, from realistic to abstract.

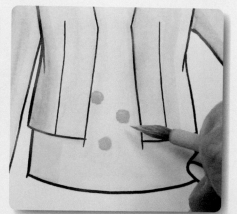

Paint slightly distorted solid circles to render the base of a flower. Use less water to avoid the base showing through.

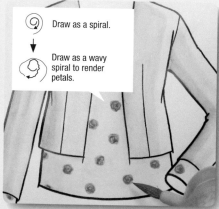

Draw as a spiral.

Draw as a wavy spiral to render petals.

Render each petal by using a darker color than the flower base.

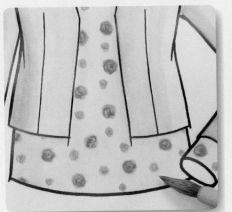
Add more in different sizes and color.

**03**

Draw leaves.

**04**

Complete by adding luster with white paint.

**05**

## Sheer fabrics

### Chiffon

Chiffon is a light and sheer flat weave fabric, usually of silk, but some come in rayon and other synthetic materials.

Paint the base color. When completely dry, apply inking to the sheer fabric part.

**01**

Prepare the color for the chiffon. Add white when the top color is light.

**02**

Use a good amount of water and apply quickly. Do not take too long, or the base paint will dissolve.

**03**

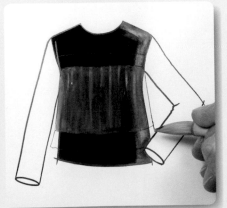
Apply another coat to the shadow area.

**04**

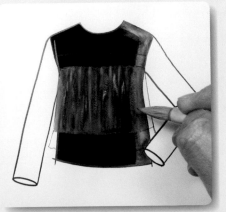
Finish the surface using a brush that contains clean water only. Again do this quickly to prevent the base paint dissolving.

**05**

Complete by redrawing the disappearing outline with a white pencil. Adjust the color of the outline when the fabric underneath is very dark.

Lace

Lace is a fine open fabric with woven patterns. Paint the lace outline. If the desired color drawing pen is available, it is more preferable to achieve a finer and better rendition of lace.

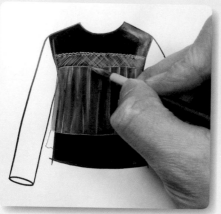

Draw woven threads. The finer, the better.

Practice drawing a rose. The basic form is a spiral.

Make the spiral wavy to represent a rose. The red dots are places where the lines make contact.

Complete by adding the leaves.

Apply the rose pattern using watercolor.

Completed.

**Knitted-lace**

Knitted fabric with many lace-like openings. Draw each stitch one by one in a rounded square.

*01*

Add more rows, keeping the stitches in the same size.

*02*

Complete by rendering the rough napped texture of wool using the side of the lead of a color pencil, darker than the base color (navy here). Apply softly in circular strokes to avoid producing pencil lines.

*03*

## Phase 18 review

- To render fabric texture, use mainly color pencils.
- When applying watercolor on top of the base color, use less water to prevent the base showing through.
- When applying watercolor on top of the base color, and the color is light, add white.

**Next, we will draw fashion drawings based on photographs!**

# Design Drawing from a Photograph: 1

We will now practice the eight-head proportion design drawing based on poses and styling of sample photographic images. If you select such an image from magazines or other available materials, please be aware that it is important to assess whether it is suitable for design drawings. Keep in mind that you should choose one which matches the principles of the poses you have learned so far in this book.

The process of design drawing is as follows:

### Drafting

- Body: Draw it in good balance with the eight-head proportion, selecting a suitable pose based on what he or she is wearing.

- Dressing: Apply dressing based on the garment length, volume and structure. Draw the details carefully also.

Use a pencil until this stage.

### Coloring

- Inking: Transfer the draft to the paper for coloring. Use various drawing tools based on the image.

- Coloring: Color carefully from the base to the texture and patterns.

### Finishing

Hair and make-up: Try various hairstyles and make-up based on the garment.
- Redrawing: Do not forget to redraw the lines nearly erased during drawing.

- Giving contrast to outlines: It may be effective in some cases to accentuate the outlines as a final touch.

Now let's try while confirming these key points at each step.

### Photo analysis

To analyze the pose of the photo image, observe three points; the feet position, the WL angle and the median line.

Front neck point (FNP)

Mark the shoulder points. **01**

Join the two points. **02**

A little longer   A little shorter

Establish and mark the FNP. As the pose is angled, it is a little off-center. **03**

Standing pose

Central axis

The axis is perpendicular when standing normally.

Extend a line straight down from the FNP to represent the central axis. **04**

Mark the supporting leg with a double circle.

Mark the ankles. The one closer to the central axis is of the supporting leg. Now you know this is the pose with weight on the left leg. **05**

WL angle
The WL is parallel to the waistband and the line joining the knees. The latter is used here. First identify the knee center.

Take the most concave point.

Divide thigh and lower leg at the knee center.

To find the WL angle hidden here, use other indicators influenced by it. **06**

Draw the kneecaps half the size of the face. **07**

Draw a line joining the centers of the knees. **08**

Check the angle of the dress hem. Mark both its edges. **09**

Join them and you will find it is not angled as much as the WL, as the dress is free around the waist. **10**

Join the ankles also, and you will find all lines angle in the same direction. **11**

The WL aligns with the elbow of the arm that hangs straight down.

Parallel

Establish the WL parallel to the line joining the knees. **12**

**Median line**

The median line (center of garment) meets the bottom of the 'V' opening.

Draw the body line over the garment.

Longer at the closer side.

Shorter at the further side.

Find the WP and join it with the FNP.

13

When the pose is diagonal, the median line curves a little.

14

As seen diagonally, the median line curves slightly toward the crotch.

W. L

90°

The line extending from the WP perpendicular to the WL represents the median line of the lower torso.

15

To find the correct angle towards the face, draw the actual neck line.

Draw the median line of the neck.

16

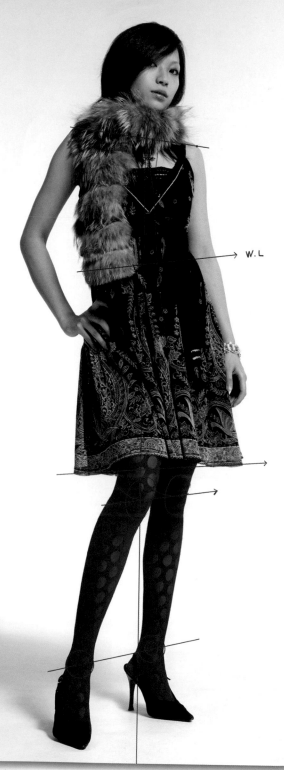

W. L

The analysis is completed.

17

**Pose analysis: Skirt**

Front neck point (FNP)

Mark the shoulder points, and join them. *01*

Mark the FNP. As the pose is frontal, it is at the center. *02*

Standing pose

Central axis

The axis is perpendicular when standing normally.

Extend a line straight down from the FNP to represent the central axis. *03*

Mark the supporting leg with a double circle.

Mark the ankles. The one closer to the central axis is of the supporting leg. Now you know this is the pose with weight on the right leg. *04*

WL angle

The WL is parallel to the waistband and the line joining the knees, and perpendicular to the centerline of the bottom wear. Here, the WL angle is based on the waistband as it is exposed. *05*

The WL aligns with the elbow of the arm that hangs straight down.

W.

Parallel

Establish the WL parallel to the line joining the knees. *06*

173

w.L. ←

90°

The median line is at the front center of the skirt and perpendicular to the WL.
When frontal, it is straight.

07

FNP

WP

Join the WP and FNP to establish the median line of the upper torso. When frontal, it is straight.

08

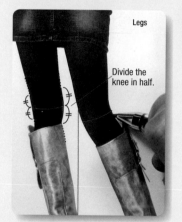

Legs

Divide the knee in half.

Divide the legs at the knees.

09

Draw the kneecaps half the size of the face.

10

Join the centers of the knees and ankles, and you will find both lines are angled in the same direction.

11

To find the correct angle towards the face, draw the actual neck line.

Draw the median line of the neck.

12

W.L. ←

The analysis is completed.

13

**Pose analysis: Pants**

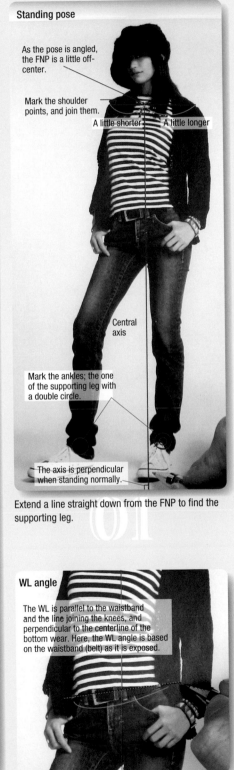

**Standing pose**

As the pose is angled, the FNP is a little off-center.

Mark the shoulder points, and join them.

A little shorter     A little longer

Central axis

Mark the ankles; the one of the supporting leg with a double circle.

The axis is perpendicular when standing normally.

Extend a line straight down from the FNP to find the supporting leg.

01

**WL angle**

The WL is parallel to the waistband and the line joining the knees, and perpendicular to the centerline of the bottom wear. Here, the WL angle is based on the waistband (belt) as it is exposed.

Join both side points of the belt to represent the WL angle.

02

The WL aligns with the elbow of the arm that hangs straight down.

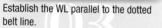

Parallel

Establish the WL parallel to the dotted belt line.

*03*

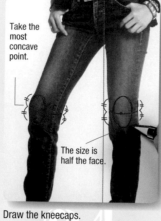

Take the most concave point.

The size is half the face.

Draw the kneecaps.

*04*

Horizontal

Join the centers of the knees and ankles. When the supporting leg is forward, the idle leg is placed sideways. (See p. 60)

Median line

90

w.

The median line is at the front center of the pants and perpendicular to the WL. As seen diagonally, it curves slightly toward the crotch.

FNP

WP

Join the WP and FNP to establish the median line of the upper torso. When frontal, it is straight. As seen diagonally, the median line curves with the bust as its peak.

To find the correct angle towards the face, draw the actual neck line.

w. L

Draw the median line of the neck.

*08*

The analysis is completed.

*09*

### Phase 19 review

• For the pose analysis based on photo images, observe three points; the feet position, the WL angle and the median line.

• Make good use of exposed places e.g. the hem and front center to analyze the hidden areas.

• Note the front centerline of the garment, as it represents the median line.

• The median line is straight only when seen from the front.

**Next, we will draw poses based on these analyses!**

176

# Design Drawing from a Photograph: 2

We will now draw the body based on the pose analysis we made in phase 19. Be aware that it is not our aim to copy photo images, but to draw the eight-head proportion body in the same pose as the photo image.

*All sizes shown in this phase are based on the paper size B4.

## The body in a dress

**Balance check**

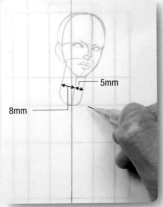

Using the attached grid as an underlay, transfer the central axis and balance points of the body.

Establish the neck position before drawing the head.

Marking the FNP as a dot, draw the median line of the neck at the same angle with that of the photo.

Adjust the height to this grid.

The vertical to horizontal ratio is 3 to 2.

Draw the outline of the head.

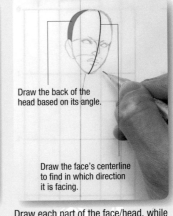

Draw the back of the head based on its angle.

Draw the face's centerline to find in which direction it is facing.

Draw each part of the face/head, while considering the balance.

5mm

8mm

Draw the neck to 1/2 head-width (13mm). As it is angled, the forward side appears wider due to perspective.

**Slightly angled upper torso**

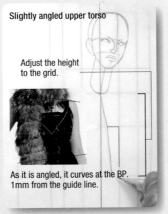

Adjust the height to the grid.

As it is angled, it curves at the BP. 1mm from the guide line.

Draw the median line of the upper torso at the same angle as that of the photo.

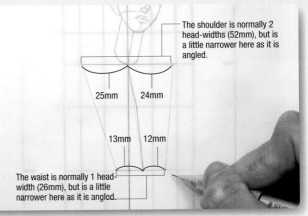

The shoulder is normally 2 head-widths (52mm), but is a little narrower here as it is angled.

25mm    24mm

13mm    12mm

The waist is normally 1 head-width (26mm), but is a little narrower here as it is angled.

Draw the upper torso. As it is angled, the forward side appears wider due to perspective.

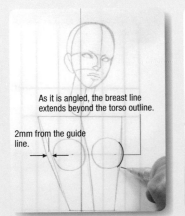

As it is angled, the breast line extends beyond the torso outline.

2mm from the guide line.

Give some roundness to the upper torso, and draw the breasts.

**Slightly angled lower torso**

The WL meets here at the WP.

Draw the WL at the same angle as that of the photo.

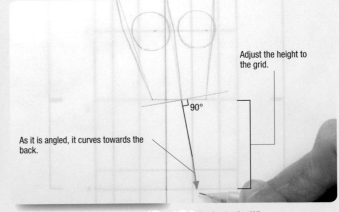

Adjust the height to the grid.

90°

As it is angled, it curves towards the back.

Draw the median line of the lower torso perpendicular to the WL.

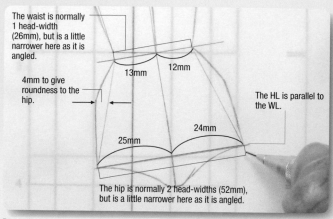

The waist is normally 1 head-width (26mm), but is a little narrower here as it is angled.

4mm to give roundness to the hip.

13mm 12mm

The HL is parallel to the WL.

25mm 24mm

The hip is normally 2 head-widths (52mm), but is a little narrower here as it is angled.

Draw the lower torso details.

**11**

Draw the supporting leg first.

Close to the central axis.

Central axis

Draw the ankle of the supporting leg.

**12**

Draw the line joining the hip joint to the ankle.

**13**

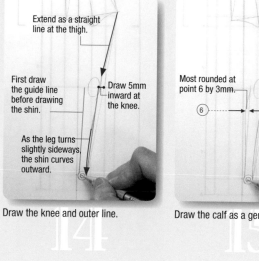

Extend as a straight line at the thigh.

First draw the guide line before drawing the shin.

Draw 5mm inward at the knee.

As the leg turns slightly sideways, the shin curves outward.

Draw the knee and outer line.

**14**

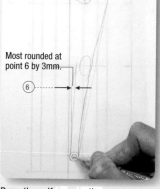

Most rounded at point 6 by 3mm.

6

Draw the calf as a gentle curve.

**15**

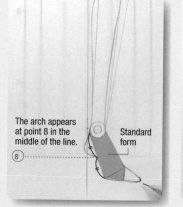

The arch appears at point 8 in the middle of the line.

Standard form

8

Draw the foot.

**16**

The right ankle aligns vertically with the shoulder joint based on the photo.

Draw the lines joining the knees and ankles respectively to establish their positions.

**17**

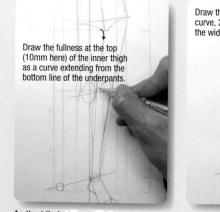

Draw the fullness at the top (10mm here) of the inner thigh as a curve extending from the bottom line of the underpants.

As the idle leg can be moved freely, it can be drawn per part like the arms, divided into the thigh and shin.

**18**

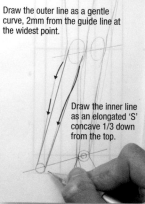

Draw the outer line as a gentle curve, 2mm from the guide line at the widest point.

Draw the inner line as an elongated 'S' concave 1/3 down from the top.

Draw straight lines from the knee to ankle and use as guide lines.

**19**

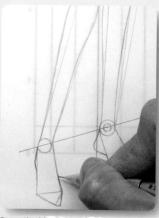

Draw the idle leg a little larger due to perspective, as it is more forward than the supporting leg.

**20**

**The shoulder moves independently.**

Be sure to go over the FNP.

Add the shoulder movement.

**21**

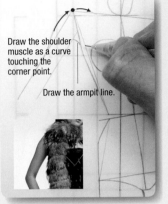

Draw the shoulder muscle as a curve touching the corner point.

Draw the armpit line.

Draw the upper arm.

**22**

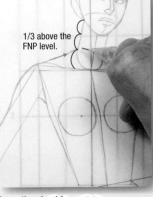

1/3 above the FNP level.

Draw the shoulder.

**23**

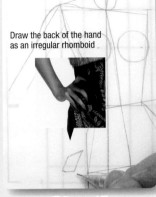

Draw the back of the hand as an irregular rhomboid.

The forearm length often changes subject to perspective. Draw the hand first to secure a good balance.

**24**

Draw the fingers, by dividing into the index finger and other three.

**25**

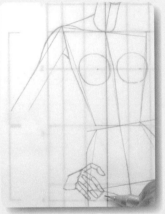

Draw as three fingers. The middle finger is the longest.

**26**

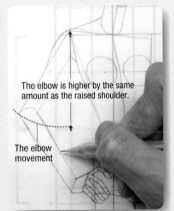

The elbow is higher by the same amount as the raised shoulder.

The elbow movement

Join the elbow and wrist, adding some roundness to the forearm.

**27**

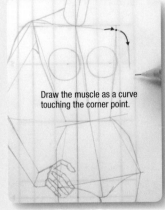

Draw the muscle as a curve touching the corner point.

Draw the upper arm.

**28**

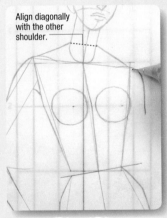

Align diagonally with the other shoulder.

Draw the shoulder.

**29**

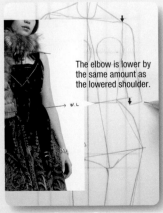

The elbow is lower by the same amount as the lowered shoulder.

W.L

Draw the upper arm.

**30**

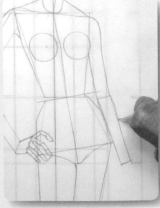

Draw the forearm.

**31**

Draw the back of the hand.

**32**

Draw the thumb as if it is growing out of the wrist.

Draw the fingers.

**33**

Completed.

34

Establish the neck position before drawing the head.

Using the attached grid as an underlay, transfer the central axis and balance points of the body.

Marking the FNP as a dot, draw the median line of the neck at the same angle as that of the photo. 01

Draw the face's centerline to find in which direction it is facing.

Adjust the height to this grid.

Draw the back of the head based on its angle.

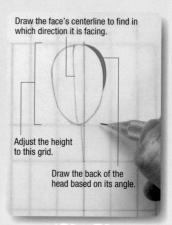

Draw the outline of the head, while considering the balance. 02

Draw the neck to 1/2 head-width (13mm). As it is frontal, the bottom line is symmetrical. 03

### Slightly angled upper torso

As it is frontal, the median line is straight.

Adjust the height to the grid.

Draw the median line of the upper torso at the same angle as that of the photo. 04

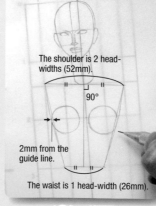

The shoulder is 2 head-widths (52mm).

90°

2mm from the guide line.

The waist is 1 head-width (26mm).

Draw the upper torso. 05

### Slightly angled lower torso

The WL meets here at the WP.

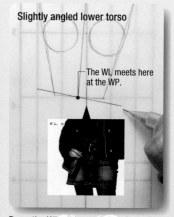

Draw the WL at the same angle as that of the photo. 06

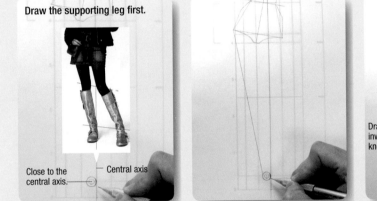

The HL is parallel to the WL.

90°

Median line

Adjust the height to this grid.

HL

Draw the median line of the lower torso and the HL. 07

The waist is 1 head-width (26mm).

Give roundness (4mm).

The hip is 2 head-widths (52mm).

Draw the lower torso details. 08

**Draw the supporting leg first.**

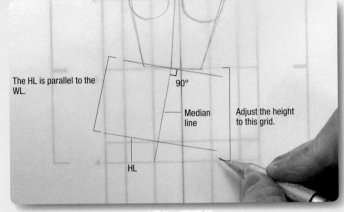

Close to the central axis.

Central axis

Draw the ankle of the supporting leg. 09

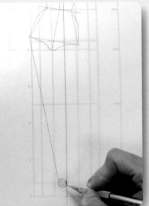

Draw the line joining the hip joint to the ankle. 10

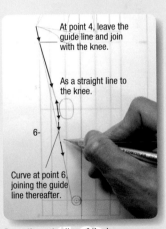

The size is half the face.

Draw 5mm inward at the knee.

Draw the knee. 11

At point 4, leave the guide line and join with the knee.

As a straight line to the knee.

6-

Curve at point 6, joining the guide line thereafter.

Draw the outer line of the leg. 12

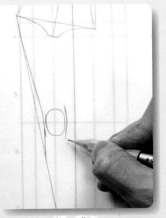

Draw the inner knee line as a curve along it. 13

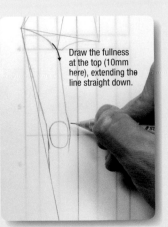

Draw the fullness at the top (10mm here), extending the line straight down.

Draw the inner thigh by smoothly joining the crotch and knee. 14

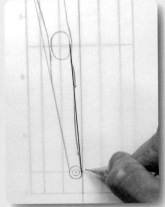

Draw the inner shin line as an elongated 'S' based on the guide line. 15

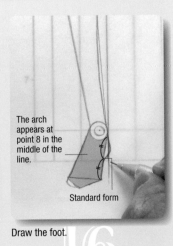

The arch appears at point 8 in the middle of the line.

Standard form

Draw the foot. 16

The left ankle aligns vertically with the outer line of the elbow based on the photo.

Draw the lines joining the knees and ankles respectively to establish their positions.

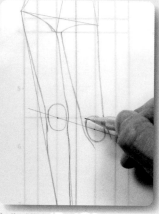

As the idle leg can be freely moved, you can draw its parts, i.e. the thigh and lower leg separately as in the case of the arm.

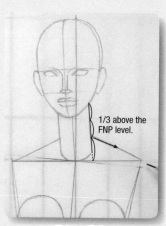

Draw the outer line as a gentle curve, 2mm from the guide line at the widest point.

Draw the inner line as an elongated 'S' concave 1/3 down from the top.

Draw straight lines from the knee to ankle and use as guide lines.

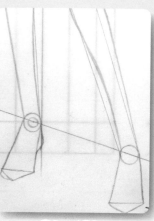

Draw the idle leg a little larger due to perspective, as it is more forward than the supporting leg.

**The shoulder moves independently.**

Be sure to go over the FNP.

Add the shoulder movement.

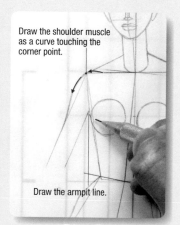

1/3 above the FNP level.

Draw the shoulder.

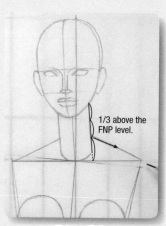

Draw the shoulder muscle as a curve touching the corner point.

Draw the armpit line.

Draw the upper arm.

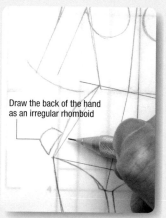

Draw the back of the hand as an irregular rhomboid

The forearm length often changes subject to perspective. Draw the hand first to secure a good balance.

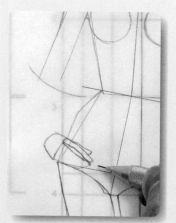

Draw the fingers, by dividing into the index finger and other three.

Draw as three fingers. The middle finger is the longest.

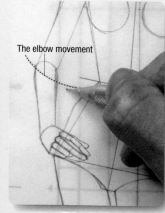

The elbow movement

Join the elbow and wrist, adding some roundness to the forearm.

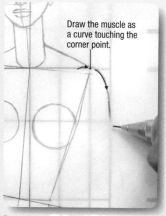

Draw the muscle as a curve touching the corner point.

Draw the upper arm.

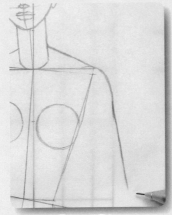

Draw the outer line of the upper arm.

*29*

Draw the back of the hand.

When the arm has movement, draw the hand first to secure a good balance.

*30*

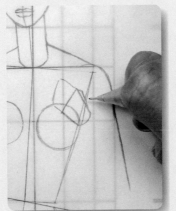

Draw the outline of fingers.

*31*

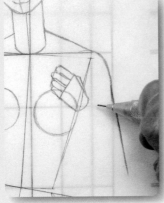

Draw as four fingers.

*32*

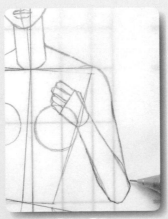

Join the elbow and wrist, adding some roundness to the forearm.

*33*

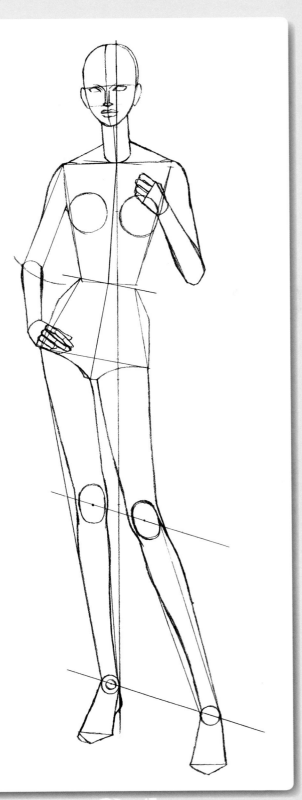

Completed.

*34*

**Establish the neck position before drawing the head.**

Using the attached grid as an underlay, transfer the central axis and balance points of the body.

Marking the FNP as a dot, draw the median line of the neck at the same angle as that of the photo. 01

Draw the face's centerline to find in which direction it is facing.

Adjust the height to this grid.

Draw the back of the head based on its angle.

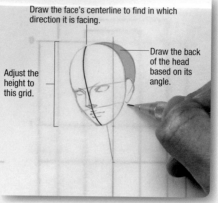

Draw the outline of the head, while considering the balance. 02

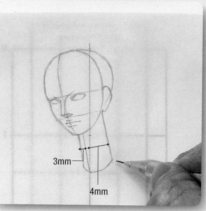

3mm

4mm

Draw the neck to 1/2 head-width (13mm). As it is angled, the forward side appears wider due to perspective. 03

**Angled upper torso**

As it is angled, it curves at the BP, 3mm from the guide line.

Adjust the height to the grid.

Draw the median line of the upper torso at the same angle as that of the photo. 04

The shoulder is normally 2 head-widths, but is a little narrower here as it is angled.

18mm    30mm

Give roundness of 6mm.

As it is angled, the breast sticks out.

10mm    15mm

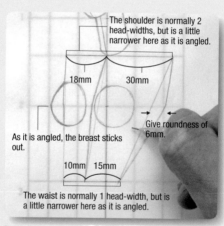

The waist is normally 1 head-width, but is a little narrower here as it is angled.

Draw the upper torso. As it is angled, the forward side appears wider due to perspective. 05

**Angled lower torso**

The WL meets here at the WP.

Draw the WL at the same angle as that of the photo. 06

90°

As it is angled, it curves towards the back.

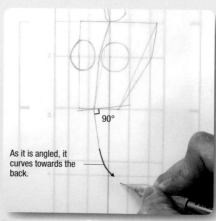

Draw the median line of the lower torso perpendicular to the WL. 07

The waist is normally 1 head-width, but is a little narrower here as it is angled.

10mm

Give roundness of 6mm.

15mm

Give roundness of 3mm.

30mm    18mm

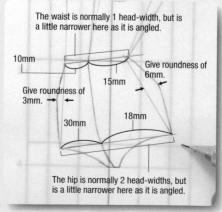

The hip is normally 2 head-widths, but is a little narrower here as it is angled.

Draw the lower torso details. 08

**Draw the supporting leg first.**

Close to the central axis.

Central axis

Draw the ankle of the supporting leg. 09

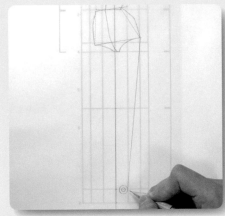

Draw the line joining the hip joint to the ankle. **10**

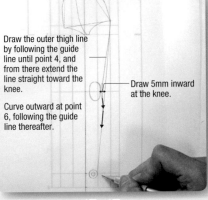

Draw the outer thigh line by following the guide line until point 4, and from there extend the line straight toward the knee.

Curve outward at point 6, following the guide line thereafter.

Draw 5mm inward at the knee.

Draw the knee and outer line of the leg. **11**

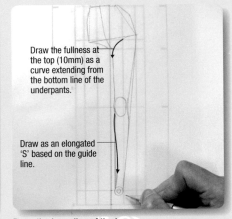

Draw the fullness at the top (10mm) as a curve extending from the bottom line of the underpants.

Draw as an elongated 'S' based on the guide line.

Draw the inner line of the leg. **12**

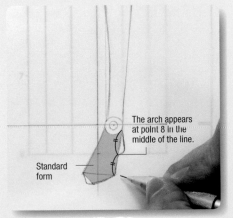

The arch appears at point 8 in the middle of the line.

Standard form

Draw the foot. **13**

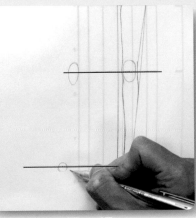

Draw the lines joining the knees and ankles respectively to establish their positions. **14**

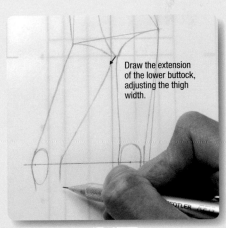

Draw the extension of the lower buttock, adjusting the thigh width.

As the idle leg can be moved freely, it can be drawn per part like the arms, divided into the thigh and lower leg. **15**

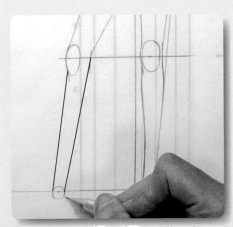

Draw straight lines from the knee to ankle and use as guide lines. **16**

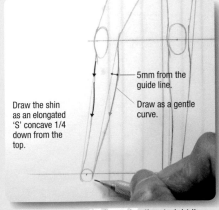

Draw the shin as an elongated 'S' concave 1/4 down from the top.

5mm from the guide line.

Draw as a gentle curve.

Render the concave shin line using the straight line as a guide. **17**

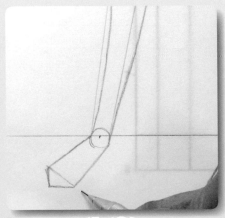

The foot is horizontal as the idle leg is sideways. **18**

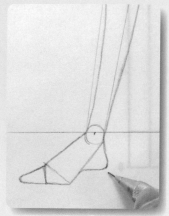

Draw the heel and tips of the toes. *19*

**The shoulder moves independently.**

Be sure to go over the FNP.

Add the shoulder movement. *20*

Draw the shoulder. *21*

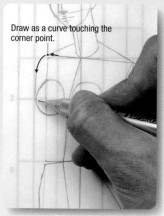

Draw as a curve touching the corner point.

Draw the shoulder muscle. *22*

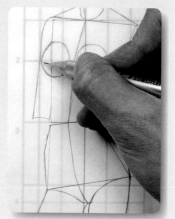

Draw the upper arm. *23*

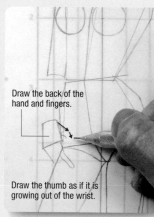

Draw the back of the hand and fingers.

Draw the thumb as if it is growing out of the wrist.

The forearm length often changes subject to perspective. Draw the hand first to secure a good balance. *24*

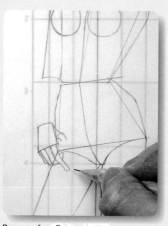

Draw as four fingers. *25*

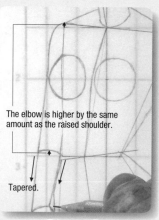

The elbow is higher by the same amount as the raised shoulder.

Tapered.

Draw the forearm by joining the elbow and wrist. *26*

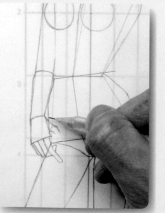

Add some roundness to the forearm. *27*

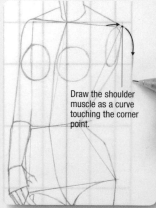

Draw the shoulder muscle as a curve touching the corner point.

Draw the upper arm. *28*

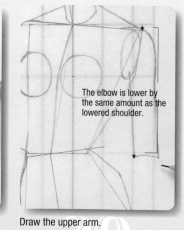

The elbow is lower by the same amount as the lowered shoulder.

Draw the upper arm. *29*

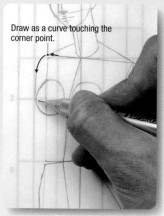

Draw the back of the hand.

As the left forearm is also subject to perspective, draw the hand first. *30*

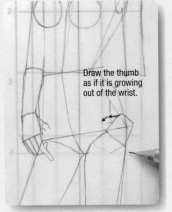

Draw the thumb as if it is growing out of the wrist.

Draw the fingers.

31

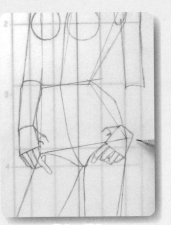

Draw as four fingers.

32

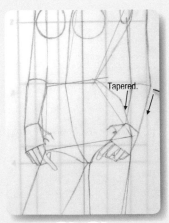

Tapered.

Draw the forearm by joining the elbow and wrist.

33

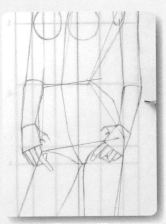

Add some roundness to the forearm.

34

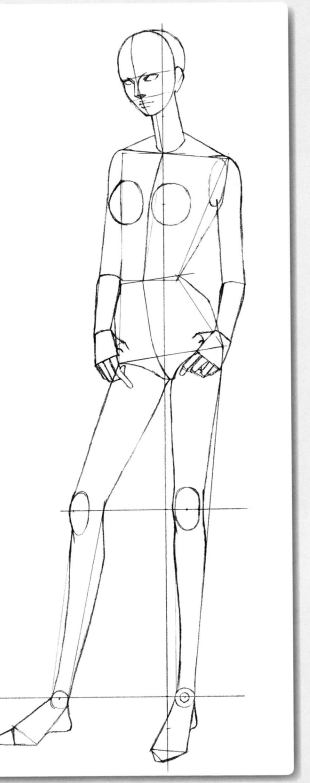

Completed.

35

## Phase 20 review

- Draw by carefully observing the analyzed photo image, and you will surely be successful.

- Use the grid as an underlay to draw in the eight-head proportion.

- Try to draw poses viewed from various directions based on wide ranging photo images.

**Next, we will complete drawings by dressing!**

# Design Drawing from a Photograph: 3

Now we will dress garments on the bodies we drew in phase 20. The key point is not to forget to allow extra room.

**Dress**

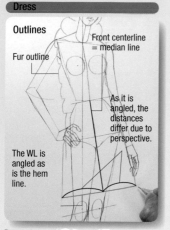

**Outlines**

Fur outline

Front centerline = median line

As it is angled, the distances differ due to perspective.

The WL is angled as is the hem line.

Draw the outlines of garments. Render in simple lines here, as detail lines are added later. *01*

**Division**

Observe the volume of each item.

Give volume to the skirt hem.

First roughly divide garments per item, and add details. *02*

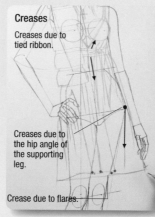

**Creases**

Creases due to tied ribbon.

Creases due to the hip angle of the supporting leg.

Crease due to flares.

As the dress is loosely fitting, many vertical creases result due to gravity. *03*

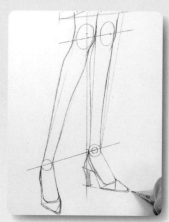

Draw shoes in the same way. *04*

The dressed body drawing is completed. *05*

**Dressed body drawing**

Place a paper on the draft and trace. *06*

Carefully draw the details. *07*

Draw the creases in swift strokes. *08*

Trace and join smoothly the lines of the joints e.g. the knees and ankles. *09*

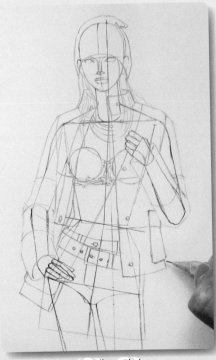

Completed.

**10**

**Skirt**

**Outlines**

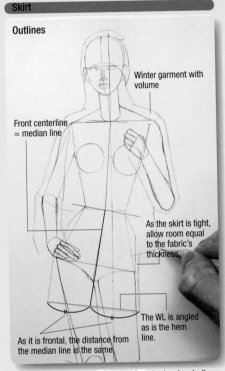

Winter garment with volume

Front centerline = median line

As the skirt is tight, allow room equal to the fabric's thickness.

The WL is angled as is the hem line.

As it is frontal, the distance from the median line is the same.

Draw the outlines of garments. Render in simple lines here, as detail lines are added later.

**01**

**Division**

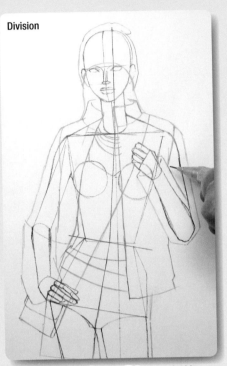

First roughly divide garments per item, and add details.

**02**

Add small elements e.g. the pocket.

**03**

**Creases**

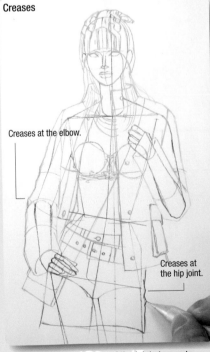

Creases at the elbow.

Creases at the hip joint.

Add bumps at the outlines of the joints to create creases.

**04**

Draw the outline at the ankle bumpy to render creases.

Add creases on the garments.

**05**

The dressed body drawing is completed.

**06**

Place a paper on the draft and trace necessary lines.

**07**

Trace and join smoothly the lines of the joints e.g. the knees and ankles.

**08**

Completed.

**10**

Carefully draw the boots with various detail elements.

**09**

**Pants**

Outlines

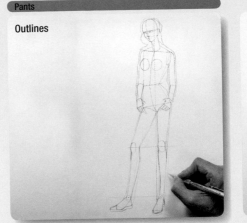

Draw the outlines of garments. Render in simple lines here, as detail lines are added later.

*01*

Division

First roughly divide garments per item, and add details.

*02*

Creases

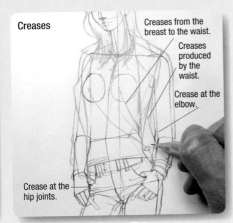

Creases from the breast to the waist.

Creases produced by the waist.

Crease at the elbow.

Crease at the hip joints.

Add bumps at the outlines of the joints to create creases.

*03*

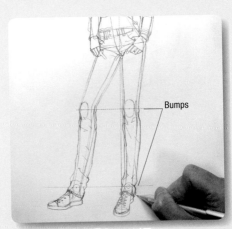

Bumps

The creases at the crotch, knees and ankles are typical for the pants.

*04*

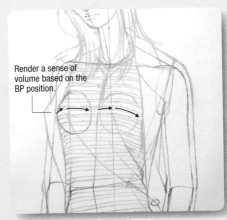

Render a sense of volume based on the BP position.

Draw horizontal stripes considering the body form.

*05*

The dressed body drawing is completed.

*06*

**Dressed body drawing**

Place a paper on the draft and trace necessary lines.

*07*

First draw three or more key stripes where they change form, and fill in the rest.

*08*

Fill in some parts of the black stripes to make them clear.

*09*

Completed.

*10*

### Phase 21 review

- Make dressed body drawings in order of the outline, garment details, outline bumps and creases.
- Try to allow room in garments while considering ventilation and warmth insulation.
- Draw the face also at this stage.

**Next, we will color a dress!**

# The 4th week

Master Design Drawing and Make
Your Own Design

# Design Drawing from a Photograph: 4

Now we will apply color to complete the drawing. The process is as follows: the inking of the dressed body drawing on the coloring paper (Kent paper or other thick drawing paper) after transferring →Base painting → Fabric pattern painting → Hair and Make-up → Finish painting. In this phase the focus is on the patterns of the dress and fur. First, make some copies of the inked drawing and practice on them to gain confidence before the final try, you will be more relaxed and can enjoy it.

**Inking**

Transfer lightly.

It is recommended to practice the dressed body drawing and inking using separate papers, as it is easier to cope with mistakes, and thus less stressful. First, fill in the reverse side of the dressed body drawing in black, using a pencil with B or softer lead. The blacker you make it, the clearer the lines will be when transferred.

Add any details you may have missed.

Simply draw lightly over the lines to successfully transfer. Be careful not to apply too much pressure, or you will mark the paper.

Using a color ball-point pen helps show the lines you have finished. You can avoid missing any.

Place a paper for coloring (Kent paper is used here) underneath the drawing and fix it with clips or mending tape. Transfer the lines by drawing over it with a fine ball-point pen such as size 0.3mm.

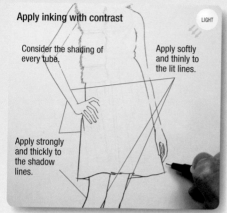

Apply inking with contrast

Consider the shading of every tube.

Apply softly and thinly to the lit lines.

Apply strongly and thickly to the shadow lines.

LIGHT

Apply the ink. See p. 125 for the nib size of the drawing pen, and p. 129 for more detail concerning inking of the dressed body drawing. Render contrast using a drawing pen with thick nib (0.8mm) by varying the pressure.

Draw each part separately with a fine pen (0.3mm).

04

Add creases with a fine pen (0.3mm).

05

The inking is completed.

Add details with an extra fine pen (0.1mm).

06

Wait 2 to 3 minutes until the ink dries, and erase the pencil lines. Do not rub too strongly, or you will erase some ink.

07

08

## Coloring

We use opaque watercolors as the main painting material, and color pencils as supplements. We can create all colors using the opaque watercolors consisting of five colors:

C (cyan) → Peacock Blue
M (magenta) → Opera
Y (yellow) → Lemon Yellow
K (black) → Ivory Black
W (white) → Permanent White

By creating all colors with CMYK mixture, you can study color formulations and develop your sensibility for coloration. We use color pencils for white, black, brown and navy.

**Paint the skin color**

Dilute with plenty of water for coloring. Layer this many times to create desired color.

Undiluted watercolor

Less water

More water

The color appears a little yellowish on the paint dish. Be sure to try it on the paper.

Create the skin color with watercolors (60% magenta, 40% yellow and a good amount of water).

**Paint the stocking base color**

First coating (solid painting): Paint as if filling with water throughout the subject area, so that the paint particles will be evenly spread with the moisture, to avoid unevenness.

LIGHT

Second coating (omitted painting method): Paint in layers on the shadow areas. Ideally the color obtained here should be your final desired color. The shadow is about 20%.

Third coating (blurring): Apply blurring by quick strokes over the noticeable edges of the paint with a brush soaked in clean water.

As it is a strong color, use the omitted painting method (based on 80% magenta, 15% yellow, 5% black), and paint well so that the paper does not show through. Leave 20% of the lit area unpainted.

Apply blurring to the borderline at the edges of the paint with a brush soaked in clean water.

Dress

Lightly draw with a pencil the color borderline as a position guide.

Apply the omitted painting method for dark colors (100% black). Be sure to paint well to avoid the paper showing through.

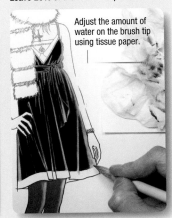

Adjust the amount of water on the brush tip using tissue paper.

Apply blurring to the borderline at the edges of the paint with a brush soaked in clean water.

Using a fine brush, first position the larger patterns (based on 50% magenta, 40% yellow, 10% black). As this is a top layer, use less water to avoid showing the layer beneath.

Finish the difficult patterns of the dress first, and you will not be too upset even if you fail. On the other hand, if you fail with them after perfectly finishing the rest of the easier parts, you will be greatly disappointed.

Based on the position of the largest patterns, paint the next largest ones (based on 60% magenta, 30% yellow and 10% black).

Paint the green patterns (based on 45% cyan, 35% yellow and 20% white). Now you can see the bird pattern repeated.

Paint the smaller green patterns.

Paint the small beige patterns (based on 15% magenta, 20% yellow and 65% white).

Draw the small black patterns with a drawing pen (0.05mm).

Paint the innerwear (100% black).

Fill in the lace with a drawing pen (0.05mm), and then the floral pattern with a drawing pen (0.1mm).

Fur

The more layers you give to fur, the more it becomes thick and attractive. First apply the base paint.

Protect the dress part you have completed.

Draw each hair. At this stage it does not have to be fine.

A hair at the first stage.

A hair for the top layers, made gradually finer.

Add hairs by making them gradually finer in various colors.

Draw darker fur to produce a 3-D effect.

Draw brown fur.

Add white and grey fur.

31

Using the side of the lead of a color pencil darker (brown here) than the base color, go over the fur to give a rough texture to produce a napped appearance.

Add fine hairs with color pencils for the final touch.

33

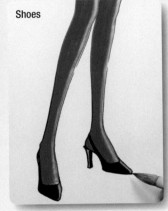

**Shoes**

Apply the omitted painting method to the shoes (100% black). Leave the lit area unpainted, and then blur the borderline with a brush soaked in clean water to blend.

**Patterns on the stockings**

Fabric grains

Draw the polka dots on the stockings with a white color pencil.

35

**Details**

Draw other small items e.g. accessories.

36

Add the shading on the dress with a black color pencil.

37

Redraw lost lines with a drawing pen.

38

**Hair and Make-up**

Paint the hair by densely layered painting (70% magenta, 20% yellow and 10% black).

39

Apply a second layer with solid painting.

40

Leave the area unpainted as if bandaged.

Apply a third layer to produce gradations with bands of highlight in mind.

41

Cheeks

Paint the upper lip darker for a 3-D effect.

Paint the lips and cheeks.

**42**

Add shading to the eyeballs, eyelashes, eyebrows and hair with a dark brown color pencil. Then apply eye makeup by adding eyeliner and eyeshadow.

43

## Phase 22 review

- For inking, you can produce contrast by adjusting the pen pressure, even when using the same size nib.

- For coloring, do not paint immediately. Be sure to first test the color.

- It is better to finish complicated patterns first in order to ease your mind.

Next, we will try coloring for the skirt style!

Completed.

**44**

# Design Drawing from a Photograph: 5

## Inking

First, fill in the reverse side of the dressed body drawing in black, using a pencil with B or softer lead. The blacker you make it, the clearer the lines will be when transferred.

Using a color ball-point pen helps show the lines you have finished. You can avoid missing any.

Simply draw lightly over the lines to successfully transfer. Be careful not to apply too much pressure, or you will mark the paper.

Place a paper for coloring (Kent paper is used here) underneath the drawing and fix it with clips or mending tape. Transfer the lines by drawing over it with a fine ball-point pen such as size 0.3mm.

It is fun to use different colors based on the image. Here a Copic Multi Liner 'Sepia' is selected for a soft finish.

Third coating (blurring): Apply blurring by quick strokes over the noticeable edges of the paint with a brush soaked in clean water.

## Coloring

### Paint the skin color

First coating (solid painting): Create the skin color (70% magenta, 30% yellow and a good amount of water). Paint as if filling with water throughout the subject area, so that the paint particles will be evenly spread with the moisture, to avoid unevenness.

Second coating (shading): Paint in layers on the shadow areas. Ideally the color obtained here should be your final desired color. The shadow is about 20%.

### Paint the base

As the blouson is in thick fabric and has patterns, apply solid painting (based on 60% cyan, 30% magenta and 10% black). Be sure to paint well to avoid the paper showing through.

As the innerwear is a dark color, apply the omitted painting method (100% black). Leave 20% of the lit area unpainted. Be sure to paint well to avoid the paper showing through.

Denim requires good contrast. Apply layered painting and well contrasting shading (based on 70% cyan, 20% magenta and 10% black).

Stockings also require good contrast. Apply layered painting and well contrasting shading (100% black).

Apply blurring by quick strokes over the edges of the paint with a brush soaked in clean water.

As boots require luster, apply the 'luster painting' method by first leaving the luster areas unpainted while layering the color on the remainder (based on 50% yellow, 40% magenta and 10% black).

Apply shading strongly to gain a good contrasting density.

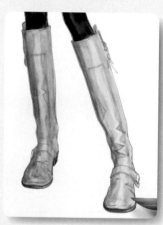

Apply blurring to the borderline by quick strokes at the edges of the paint with a brush soaked in clean water.

Paint accessories densely to avoid the skin color showing through. Prepare silver based on 30% black and 70% white, and gold based on 50% yellow, 30% magenta, 10% white and 10% black.

Paint the knitted cap (based on 80% yellow and 20% black). By making it ultra-thin with water, you can obtain off-white.

Apply shading with ultra-thin black.

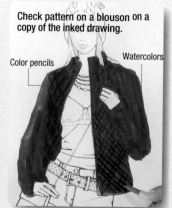

**Check pattern on a blouson on a copy of the inked drawing.**

Color pencils · Watercolors

Test the patterns using watercolors and color pencils. Watercolors produce an obvious print-like pattern, but color pencils produce the wooly woven texture. We use the latter here.

The bias runs oblique to the fabric grains. · Fabric grain

Draw the thick brown check lines with a brown color pencil. Note that they are in bias.

Draw more lines crossing the others at right angles.

Draw along the edge of the brown pattern with a black color pencil.

Add shading with a black color pencil.

To complete, give a rough texture to produce a napped appearance using a navy color pencil.

**Knitted wooly texture**

Add the knitted pattern with a color pencil darker (brown here) than the base color.

Add shading with a color pencil to produce contrast.

To complete, give a rough texture to produce a napped appearance using a color pencil.

**Faded denim**

Render the twill weave of denim by lightly and finely drawing with a color pencil darker (navy here) than the base color, as diagonal strokes from right to left.

Apply vertical strokes with a color pencil to render the faded denim-look.

Emphasize shading

Apply horizontal strokes also with a color pencil to enhance the faded look.

Use a white color pencil to further enhance the faded look.

**Luster of boots**

Emphasize shading with a color pencil darker (brown here) than the base color.

Emphasize the luster with a white color pencil.

Scatter the white watercolor as dots to create luster. 33

Spangles on the pochette

Add regularly spaced dots densely in a color prepared by adding white to the base color (based on 60% magenta, 10% yellow and 10% black).

Add finer dots in a thinner color with more white than 34. 35

Add white dots on the lit side to create luster. 36

Add shading with a black color pencil. 37

Finishing

Redraw lost lines with a drawing pen. 38

Hair and Make-up

Paint the hair lightly (70% magenta, 20% yellow and 10% black). 39

Leave the area unpainted as if bandaged.

Apply a second layer by leaving bands of highlight unpainted. 40

Apply blurring by quick strokes at the noticeable edges of the paint with a brush soaked in clean water.

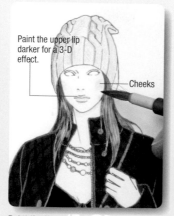

Paint the upper lip darker for a 3-D effect.

Cheeks

Paint the lips and cheeks. 42

Add a star mark to create luster.

Add shading to the eyeballs, eyelashes and eyebrows with a dark brown color pencil. Then apply eye makeup by adding eyeliner and eyeshadow. Make the accessories appear shiny with white watercolor.

Draw the patterns of the camisole with a white color pencil. 44

Completed.

45

Next, we will try coloring for the pants style!

**Transferring**

Fill in the reverse side of the dressed body drawing in black, using a pencil with B or softer lead. The blacker you make it, the clearer the lines will be when transferred.

Using a color ball-point pen helps show the lines you have finished. You can avoid missing any.

Place a paper for coloring (Kent paper is used here) underneath the drawing and fix it with clips or mending tape. Transfer the lines by drawing over it with a fine ball-point pen.

Simply draw lightly over the lines to successfully transfer. Be careful not to apply too much pressure, or you will mark the paper.

The transfer is completed.

**Coloring**

Make corrections to undesired lines if any before coloring.

**Paint the skin color**

As the inking is applied later in this case, first create the skin color with watercolors (70% magenta, 30% yellow and a good amount of water), and paint as if filling with water throughout the subject area.

Second coating (shading): Paint in layers on the shadow areas. Ideally the color obtained here should be your final desired color. The shadow is about 20%.

Third coating (blurring): Apply blurring by quick strokes over the noticeable edges of the paint with a brush soaked in clean water.

**Paint the base**

As the T-shirt base is white, apply shading with gray made by diluting black with plenty of water.

Apply black in the layered painting to the casquette and cardigan. Paint as if filling with water throughout the subject area, so that the paint particles will be evenly spread with the moisture, to avoid unevenness.

Paint in layers on the shadow areas. Ideally the color obtained here should be your final desired color. The shadow is about 20%.

Apply blurring by quick strokes over the noticeable edges of the paint with a brush soaked in clean water.

Create the color for denim (40% cyan, 10% magenta and 50% black). Note that the denim contains magenta.

*Try colors on another paper to confirm.*

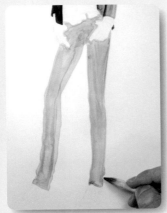

Paint the color as if filling with water throughout the subject area, so that the paint particles will be evenly spread with the moisture, to avoid unevenness.

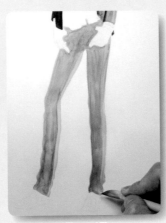

Paint in layers leaving the lit areas (25%).

Paint in layers on the shadow areas. Ideally the color obtained here should be your final desired color. The shadow is about 20%.

Apply blurring over the edges of the paint with a brush soaked in clean water.

As the sneakers are white, apply shading with gray made by diluting black with plenty of water.

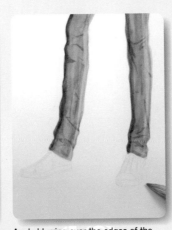

Apply blurring over the edges of the paint with a brush soaked in clean water.

**Casquette material texture**

Apply the method used for painting the nubby tweed. First, push the brush down to open the bristles.

Apply dots by gently tapping on the paper.

*Rest your small finger on the paper to control the pressure.*

Mix a few gray shades in black to give depth to the material.

Complete by rendering the rough napped texture of wool using the side of the lead of a color pencil, darker than the base color (black here). Apply softly in circular strokes to avoid producing pencil lines.

**Knitted jacket texture**

Draw the details with a color darker than the base (black here) before adding patterns.

Draw them as fine wavy lines for a natural look.

The knit stitches appear as a biased pattern from a distance. Draw diagonal lines using a color pencil.

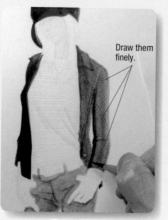

Draw them finely.

Draw the hem as a rib knit.

Complete by rendering the rough napped texture of wool using the side of the lead of a color pencil, darker than the base color (black here). Apply softly in circular strokes to avoid producing pencil lines.

Cover with paper to avoid spoiling the pencil drawing.

**Details**

Apply the omitted painting method to the horizontal stripes (70% cyan, 20% magenta and 10% black).

Apply blurring by quick strokes over the edges of the paint with a brush soaked in clean water.

Apply the omitted painting method to the belt.

**Vertical fade of denim**

Add twills lightly and finely diagonal to the fabric grain from top right to bottom left, using a color pencil darker (black here) than the base.

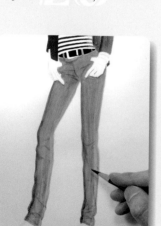

Apply fine vertical strokes with a color pencil to render the vertical fade of denim.

Use a white color pencil to further enhance the faded look.

Emphasize contrast by applying shading with a color pencil darker (black here) than the base.

**Hair and Make-up**

Leave the area unpainted as if bandaged.

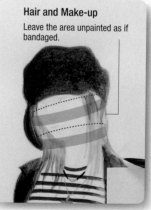

Draw the necklaces clearly in black and silver (60% black and 40% white) as they are on a strong pattern. Draw the hair in layered painting (70% magenta, 20% yellow and 10% black).

Apply the second coat. **36**

Apply blurring by quick strokes over the edges of the paint with a brush soaked in clean water. **37**

Paint the upper lip darker for a 3-D effect.

Cheeks

Paint the lips and cheeks. **38**

Paint the eyeballs with brown (70% magenta, 20% yellow and 10% black). **39**

### Inking

Apply eye makeup; eyelashes, eyebrows, eyeliner and eyeshadow.

Apply the inking with a brown color pencil here to create a very soft impression. Draw fine details while the lead is sharp, and the outline when it becomes dull. **40**

Give metallic shading to the necklaces with a drawing pen. **41**

Redraw the lost detail lines. Use a white color pencil on the black garment for visibility. **42**

Apply inking to the other garment items with black to separate them from the color of the skin. **43**

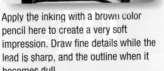

Draw the stitches on the denim with brown. **44**

Draw all the details on the sneakers carefully. **45**

Completed.

### Phase 20 review

• By using color pencils for the inking, you can obtain a soft impression.

• Apply the inking with color pencils at the end to avoid smudging.

• Black can have a different appearance depending on how you apply the sense of fabric texture and depth.

Next, we will draw our original designs!

# Sketch Ideas for Original Design

What are the focal points for fashion designers when they design garments?

They do not simply put down ideas as they come to mind. In reality, they represent their ideas in garments based on the background and fashion of the times, while taking into consideration the planning concept (including the target, design theme, garment configuration, color, material, pattern and price range) of the brand they are responsible for.

There are often cases that what satisfies their esthetics is not necessarily what sells. Despite the conflict with such discrepancy, designers constantly pursue their own creation on a high spiritual level.

What do young students need in order to steadily produce fine design work under such an environment following graduation?

First of all, they have to know themselves; what they like and what they want to do. In order to communicate these by means of garments, it is essential for them to practice drawing and presentation. In other words, only when they know themselves are they able to see their environment, and to understand what they should do or what is needed.

Above all, it is necessary that you create fashion drawings that are readily understandable, not for you alone, but more importantly for the people involved such as merchandisers and patterners.

---

**Sketching ideas: Pay attention to the following.**

---

### Let's set a theme.
It is recommended that you train yourself to always set the objective of creating original designs, rather than starting with a vague idea.

For example;
1. Take a new look at old styles such as "Mod" and "Punk" and modify them to meet today's fashion.
2. Focusing on an individual garment item such as jacket or skirt, dismantle it and reconstruct it in a new style that complies with the present.
3. Design based on images e.g. something airy, sparkling etc.
4. Setting a target group such as elegant women in their 20s or fashion-oriented schoolgirls in their late teens (based on race, age, career, etc.), design for them.
5. Selecting a specific performance, film or occupation e.g. Les Miserables on stage, the Rolling Stones concert in Japan, Romeo and Juliet in the film, or even an Air France flight attendant, design suitable costumes and uniforms.

Based on such themes, you can enhance your image and come up with your own concept, so that you will be able to answer questions like;
Why did you select the design?
Why is the design needed today?
How does a new design inspire?

The concept or keyword will initiate your design.

### Key design points
These are the focal points for your design.

#### Silhouette
The silhouette represented by the length and sense of volume of garments determines its overall balance, the most important factor.

Consider and apply various silhouettes while adjusting the length of the sleeves and total garment. When designing a skirt for example, we tend to select the length and style we are used to drawing or are familiar with e.g the knee-length flared skirt, resulting in a fixed and boring design. The garment length is such an important element as it may determine the name of the garment. A difference of 5cm can be crucial. For example, the knee-length skirt becomes a mini-skirt when it is 5cm shorter.

Let's study this so that you will improve your skill to incorporate a difference of one centimeter into your design.

When the length and volume are different, the dresses have a different impression despite the same A-line design.

## Styling

Styling is how you coordinate garment items. It makes a big difference to the total impression whether you dress the body with an outerwear opened at the front or closed, or position a hat at an angle or straight. So, outfits which at first glance appear to have the same silhouette can be quite different in balance depending on the coordination of each item.

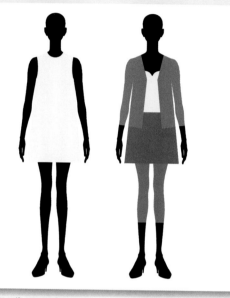

Both are based on the same A-line silhouette. One is simply a dress, while the other is coordinated with a camisole, cardigan, skirt and leggings. Exercise to coordinate ten different styles using the one silhouette.

## Details

Garments with the same silhouette look very different with different details.

Jackets with the same silhouette can look very different depending on the design detailes; one with a single closure and the other with double.

## Materials and patterns

Garments with the same design/silhouette can look very different with different materials and patterns.

One is tweed and the other a lighter material with floral pattern. Despite their same color and design, they look totally different, as they differ in texture, suppleness and thickness.

## Color

Garments with the same design and pattern can look very different in a different color.

These white-collar shirts, although having the same stripes, look different when the color is different. The black one gives a sharper impression with a strong contrast with the white collar and cuffs.

If you keep these points in mind when designing, the possibilities expand endlessly. All you have to do is to eliminate what you do not need and complete your design with the essentials only.

## Theme

Here we selected "Bikers" as the theme. Biker fashion, the origin of today's Street Style, was born in California soon after World War II during the period 1947 to 1950.

Biker gangs consisted mainly of returned military men, and were introduced in the film "The Wild One (1953)" starring Marlon Brando, who rode a Harley-Davidson instead of flying a bomber aircraft, wearing a leather jacket, jeans, boots and T-shirt. This created a stir and initiated the immortal Street Style which spread throughout the world. Combined with rock 'n' roll in the UK later, the style evolved into the Rocker and then Punk-rocker fashion in the 70s, establishing itself as the mainstream street fashion.

The male-oriented Street Style has since been highly diversified, and includes young women today. The theme "Bikers" was selected here in the hope that it may provide an opportunity for us to question anew "what fashion is and how and why we select what we wear", by returning to the origin of style.

In terms of the actual garment design, the focus is placed on the creation of a new Street Style in the unisex fashion, by combining fashionable color and material coordination with the masculine quality of the Biker style.

## Material

Selecting relatively soft sheep skin for the leather jacket, combine silk chiffon and lace.

## Color

Try chic and modern color coordination with white, black and beige, with the intention of eliminating the monotone image of the Biker style.

## Items and key points of the design

Rider's jacket, studs, dress, tiered skirt, ribbons and floral pattern.

## Target

Women in their early 20s who are full of curiosity, wishing to be highly fashionable while having the powerful spirit of rock 'n' roll.

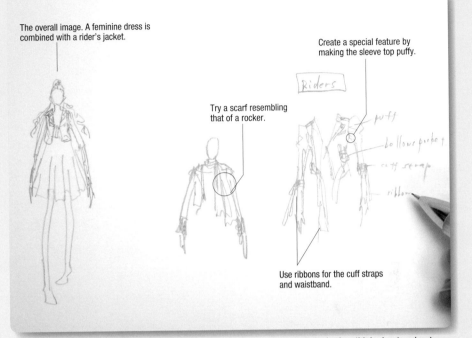

The overall image. A feminine dress is combined with a rider's jacket.

Create a special feature by making the sleeve top puffy.

Try a scarf resembling that of a rocker.

Use ribbons for the cuff straps and waistband.

Sketching ideas: Without being bothered by the body balance and other technical rules, think about and put down various new ideas on paper. In rough sketches, you often find the jewel of an idea.

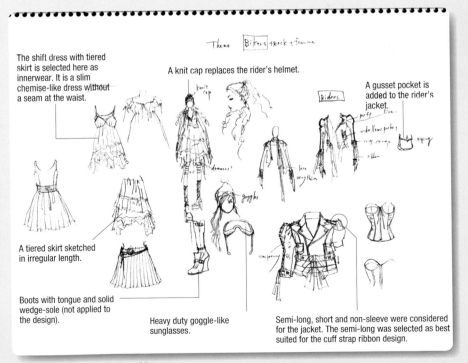

The shift dress with tiered skirt is selected here as innerwear. It is a slim chemise-like dress without a seam at the waist.

A knit cap replaces the rider's helmet.

A gusset pocket is added to the rider's jacket.

A tiered skirt sketched in irregular length.

Boots with tongue and solid wedge-sole (not applied to the design).

Heavy duty goggle-like sunglasses.

Semi-long, short and non-sleeve were considered for the jacket. The semi-long was selected as best suited for the cuff strap ribbon design.

Once established, organize your ideas.

# Technical Drawing Draft

Once the design is established, make technical drawings to grasp the garment's configuration.

**Rider's jacket**

### Outline

Leg of mutton sleeve. Note the puffed top part.

Slim silhouette with high waist.

Relatively short length.

Semi-long sleeve.

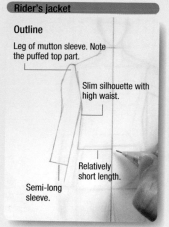

Place paper over the technical drawing guide (p. 99), aligning the front centerline, and fix the side subject to drawing only with mending tape. Note the jacket volume, length and sleeve length.

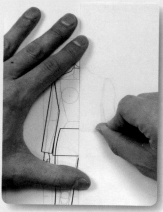

Fold the paper in half and transfer the drawn lines by strongly rubbing their reverse side with a fingernail or the like.

### Details

Collar stand

As a gentle curve.

The zipper closure is diagonal.

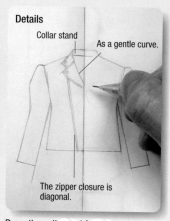

Draw the collar and front closure. *03*

Transfer and check the collar balance. *04*

Add studs.

Add studs to the epaulet.

Panel line with piping.

Pocket flap with piping.

Ribbon is used for the wasitband.

Ribbon is used for the cuff strap.

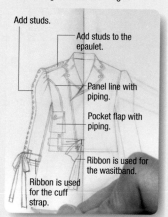

Draw the details. *05*

Transfer and check the balance. *06*

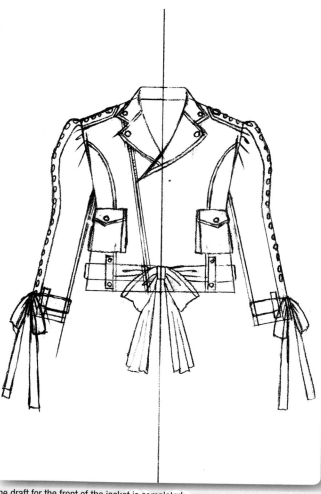

Adjust the pocket by moving towards the center.

Adjust the front closure by moving towards the center.

Adjust the unbalanced parts. *07*

Go over the transferred lines. *08*

The draft for the front of the jacket is completed. *09*

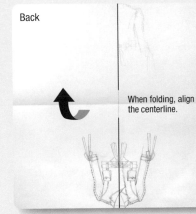

As the front and back share the same silhouette, transfer half of the front drawing by rubbing from the reverse side, including the armhole which remains the same.

Add the details. 11

Complete further details. 12

Fold the paper in half and transfer by rubbing. Check the overall balance. 13

Adjust the yoke line.

Adjust the details. 14

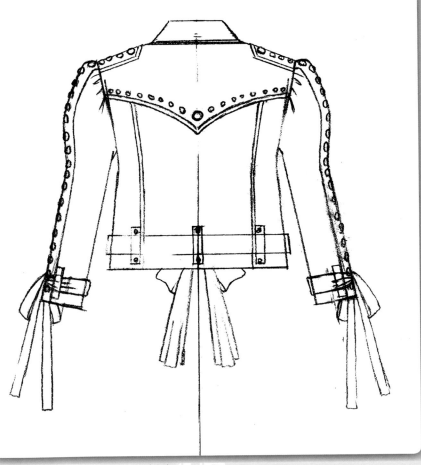

The draft for the back of the jacket is completed. 15

## Shift dress

### Outline

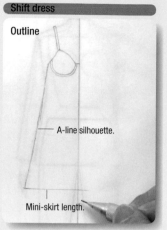

A-line silhouette.

Mini-skirt length.

Place paper over the technical drawing guide (p. 99), aligning the front centerline, and fix the side subject to drawing only with mending tape. Note the jacket volume, length and sleeve length.

Draw the tiered skirt. *02*

Fold the paper in half and transfer the drawn lines. *03*

### Details

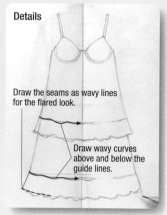

Draw the seams as wavy lines for the flared look.

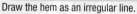

Draw wavy curves above and below the guide lines.

Draw the hem as an irregular line. *04*

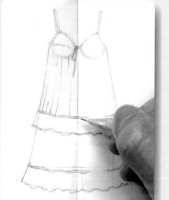

Add the details; gathers, frills and ribbons. *05*

Draw the flare lines radially. *06*

Transfer and go over the transferred lines. *07*

Back opening line

As the front and back share basically the same design, use this for both by adding the back opening line here. *08*

The draft for the dress is completed. *09*

# Fashion Design Drawing Draft

Once the design is established, draw the poses. Select a pose that enhances the key design points. Here, as the garment includes the tiered skirt, the pose with weight on one leg is selected to highlight its flare.

**The nine-head proportion body**

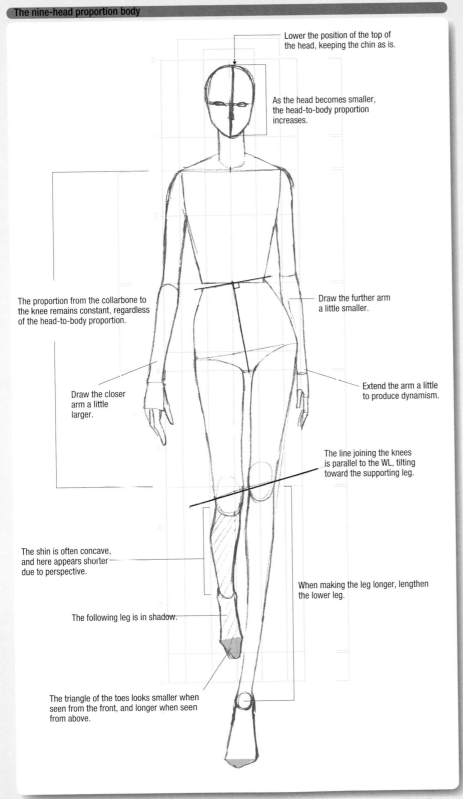

Lower the position of the top of the head, keeping the chin as is.

As the head becomes smaller, the head-to-body proportion increases.

The proportion from the collarbone to the knee remains constant, regardless of the head-to-body proportion.

Draw the further arm a little smaller.

Draw the closer arm a little larger.

Extend the arm a little to produce dynamism.

The line joining the knees is parallel to the WL, tilting toward the supporting leg.

The shin is often concave, and here appears shorter due to perspective.

When making the leg longer, lengthen the lower leg.

The following leg is in shadow.

The triangle of the toes looks smaller when seen from the front, and longer when seen from above.

**Dressing**

Place paper over the body drawing to see the garment design more clearly as you draw. First draw the overall outline, paying attention to the length and volume.

Dress the cap and goggles. The volume of the hair is very important as it influences the overall silhouette. At this stage, draw the face for positioning only.

You can change the head-to-body proportion depending on your drawing. Here, as we want to highlight the garment, the nine-head proportion is selected. In this case, the balance of the body from the upper/lower torso to the knees should remain unchanged, in order not to disturb the overall body balance.

Make sure that the positions are aligned.

A long scarf is dressed to create movement. Draw the items arranged outside the garment last, to make it easier to draw the garment beneath.

Once the outline is established, start adding the details.

04

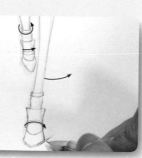

Be aware of the direction of the curves of the shoe straps.

05

Draw the flare lines and tiered part of the skirt. Draw the creases by tapering the lines.

The dressed body drawing is completed.

07

## Inking

Transfer the dressed body drawing to paper for coloring. If available, using a light table is the best method. Lay the paper over the drawing on the light table, and you can easily trace the drawing even on thicker paper e.g. Kent paper.

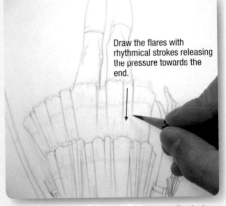

Draw the flares with rhythmical strokes releasing the pressure towards the end.

When applying the inking with a color pencil, start with fine lines. Draw fine details while the lead is sharp, and the outline when it becomes dull.

LIGHT

The inking is completed: Setting the light source on the top right, draw the lines on the shadow side (left) of each part as bold lines using strong pen pressure.

When you have finished the inking, apply various color coordinations. As the target core users are women in their early 20s, the colors (achromatic colors, beige, brown and navy) that look good against the skin were mainly used to produce an adult look.

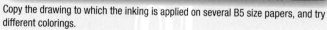
### Color coordination

**Test coloring**

Copy the drawing to which the inking is applied on several B5 size papers, and try different colorings. 01

Try to draw various materials and patterns. 02

Selecting the color for the scarf and ribbon.

When you cannot decide the color of a part, cut it out from the copies and lay over the original to compare color alternatives. 03

You can also place a cutout next to the drawing to compare. 04

**Color variations**

Totally black with a contemporary appeal.

*01*

White rider's jacket with piping seam.

*02*

A totally white fairy-like look

*03*

Street style with a pink floral pattern and leggings..

*04*

Black gloves and white leggings for good contrast.

*05*

Coordinated with subtle differences of beige, and with piping seams on the rider's jacket. This is the final choice.

*06*

We use markers in this phase. They are one of the indispensable artist's tools to be found in the design/planning room of apparel makers for their easy-to-use and rich coloring property. However, as it is rather expensive to have a good assortment in order to make full use of them, it is recommended that beginners first purchase the colors they often use, such as skin color and gray, and to gradually increase them by adding gradation colors of the three primaries. Here we use Copic Sketch Markers.

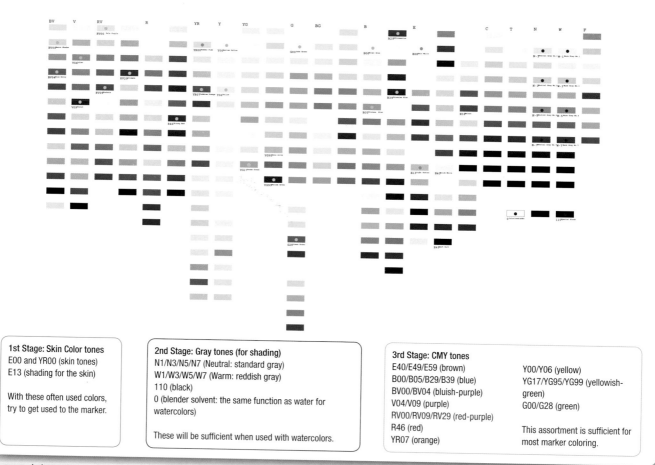

### 1st Stage: Skin Color tones
E00 and YR00 (skin tones)
E13 (shading for the skin)

With these often used colors, try to get used to the marker.

### 2nd Stage: Gray tones (for shading)
N1/N3/N5/N7 (Neutral: standard gray)
W1/W3/W5/W7 (Warm: reddish gray)
110 (black)
0 (blender solvent: the same function as water for watercolors)

These will be sufficient when used with watercolors.

### 3rd Stage: CMY tones
E40/E49/E59 (brown)
B00/B05/B29/B39 (blue)
BV00/BV04 (bluish-purple)
V04/V09 (purple)
RV00/RV09/RV29 (red-purple)
R46 (red)
YR07 (orange)

Y00/Y06 (yellow)
YG17/YG95/YG99 (yellowish-green)
G00/G28 (green)

This assortment is sufficient for most marker coloring.

Recommended assortment of Copic Sketch Markers

Copic Sketch Markers

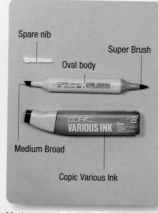

Marker set: Double-nibbed marker

Spare nib
Oval body
Super Brush
Medium Broad
Copic Various Ink

Exchanging the nib: Remove the old nib with the Copic Tweezers, which have tooth edges for a good grip.

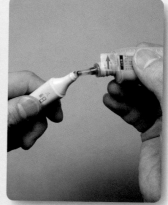

Refilling the ink: Remove the nib and pour in Copic Various Ink. If necessary, attach the Copic Booster to the tip of the ink container.

It is very easy to exchange the nib. Simply insert the new one.

**Layered painting with markers**

Layered painting is the basic method as markers are highly transparent. For the first coat, use E00 for the skin, leaving the right side white as the light source is at the top right.

Apply shading as the second coat, using YR00, one shade darker than E00. Use shades of a color as the marker cannot be made thinner. Paint the sleeves in skin color as they are see through.

Go over with E00 to blend the entire painted area in the same way you do with watercolors.

The skin color is seen under the beige.

Paint the jacket evenly for the first coat, leaving the right side white as the light source is at the top right.

Apply shading as the second coat using the Super Brush, as the areas are small.

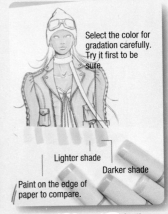

Select the color for gradation carefully. Try it first to be sure.

Lighter shade

Darker shade

Paint on the edge of paper to compare.

Go over with the beige used for the first coat to blend the entire painted area. Be sure to use the same kind of paper for the color trial.

Paint the shift dress in a little redder beige than the jacket. Having different shades of beige is useful.

Paint the knit cap in a grayish beige.

Paint the goggles as a gradation using black and shades of gray.

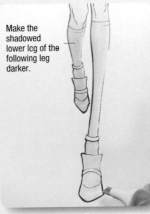

Make the shadowed lower leg of the following leg darker.

The same color is selected for the leggings and dress, and another for the shoes and cap.

**Material texture/ pattern**

Draw the knit stitches and floral patterns on the lace sleeves with a color pencil.

Draw the floral pattern in mixed sizes to give contrast.

With small intervals as if drawing stripes.

Draw the typical knit stitches on the cap.

Draw the knit stitches on the leggings.

Color the studs with silver ball-point pen. Make the piping one shade darker.

Leave the area unpainted as if bandaged.

Leave the bands of highlight on the hair unpainted to create luster.

Blend with a color one shade lighter. Leave the white area as is for luster.

Draw the small areas e.g. eyebrows and eyeballs with color pencils. Instead of buying a set which consists mainly of solid colors, buy individually and increase your selection gradually.

Use color pencils also for the eyeliner, mascara and eyeshadow.

Use a color pencil also for the lips. Draw the lit lower lip lighter.

Use a color pencil also for the cheeks. Draw in gentle strokes.

Blend the color on the face. Enjoy make-up of your own choice.

Seen from the reverse side of the paper. The ink of the markers is soaked into the paper in some areas.

Complete by applying inking to the technical drawings.

## Postscript

So how did you get on?
This book set out to explain the process to beginners by taking them through it in as much detail as possible. Now you should practice repeatedly until you have mastered the techniques.

Once you have made ten design drawings, and if you have taken care over them, you will definitely notice signs of improvement. On the other hand, even if you make one hundred drawings, if you do them without enthusiasm, you will not advance at all. That is how important it is to work with care.

For those who already have many years of experience, I hope this provides a good opportunity to assess your work so far, for example, thinking as you read, 'yes, that's quite right' or 'ah, that's what it meant', etc. By reaffirming the ideas behind things you do unconsciously every day in your work, those of you who have progressed imperceptibly in the course of your career should be able to see how far you have come. Where you have developed, what hasn't changed, and where you have gone a little astray...

The fashion world appears glamorous at first sight, but sometimes the work is anything but exciting. However this unglamorous work is where you will discover true creativity, design, skill and a sense of achievement, so you should not look down on it. People who only want to experience the surface glitter of the industry and cherry-pick the best aspects without putting in personal effort are the kind who miss out on opportunities. If you look at those to who opportunities come, they often seem to be positive characters who make you think "I'd like to work with that person" and who at the same time have a serious and committed approach to their work.

When an opportunity goes to someone else, we may feel envious or grudging and deprecate ourselves as having no talent, but that is a defensive instinct and we can do little about it. Everyone has this reaction as a way of protecting their ego and staying mentally calm. But we should not dwell on these feelings for too long. To keep moving forward, we should remain curious, taking an interest in a variety of things and relating to them emotionally. Without a high level of mental strength we will not retain the sensitivity we need to do this. Being talented means having a non-biased attitude to things.

People who create good things often say that we should enjoy work, but being able to enjoy work is also a talent. Enjoying something doesn't just mean having an easy time and smiling. I think it means being passionate enough about your work to take time over it no matter how busy you are. A piece of work that you have spent time over is one that is invested with feeling and that will move people. Even if it doesn't move them, there will definitely be a lesson you can learn for next time. So you should make sure to find an enjoyable aspect in the work or task that you are doing now that will allow you to spend your time in a fulfilling way. If we have to do it anyway, we may as well enjoy it.

Finally, I would like to offer my sincere thanks to Masaki Okuda who watched over the project sympathetically during the three years from the planning of the book till its completion, to Yoshihiro Suzuki of BBI Studio who designed this book, Yasuo Imai, photographer, and to the many people whom I have met through this work.

Zeshu Takamura

May 2007

## Author's Biography

**Zeshu Takamura**
Graduated from the Faculty of Education, Tokyo Gakugei University, and the Department of Dress Design, Kuwasawa Design School.

While studying at Kuwasawa Design School, worked as assistant for the fashion illustrator Reiko Saito. Following graduation, established atelier cubis, and engaged in mainly fashion illustration and design works for publishers, advertising agencies and apparel makers.

Taught at Bunka Design College, Vantan Visual Institute, and Tokyo Mode Gakuen as instructor, and since 2007 has been Professor at Bunka Women's University.

Publications include; The Use of Markers in Fashion Illustration, Fashion With Style: Ladies Fashion Items, Roots of Street Style and Fashion Design Techniques, Fashion Design Drawing: A Super Reference Book for Beginners (Graphic-sha Publishing Co. Ltd.).